Russia between East and West

International Studies
in Sociology
and Social Anthropology

Series Editors

Tukumbi Lumumba-Kasongo
Rubin Patterson
Masamichi Sasaki

VOLUME 102

Russia between East and West

Scholarly Debates on Eurasianism

Edited by

Dmitry Shlapentokh

BRILL

LEIDEN · BOSTON
2007

This book is printed on acid-free paper.

Library of Congress Cataloging-in-Publication Data

Russia between East and West : scholarly debates on Eurasianism / edited by Dmitry Shlapentokh.
  p. cm. — (International studies in sociology and social anthropology, ISSN 0074-8684 ; v. 102)
  Includes bibliographical references and index.
  ISBN-13: 978-90-04-15415-5 (alk. paper)
  ISBN-10: 90-04-15415-9 (pbk. : alk. paper)
  1. Russia (Federation)—Civilization. 2. Eurasian school. I. Shlapentokh, Dmitry.

DK32.7.R875 2006
303.48'24705—dc22

                                                                    2006049207

ISSN 0074-8684
ISBN 90 04 15415 9

PRINTED IN THE NETHERLANDS

CONTENTS

Acknowledgments

This book, as well as my other works could not have emerged without the inspiration and help of many people. I certainly owe a lot to Professor Jeffrey Brooks, Richard Hellie and Gary Hamburg. I have benefited from the expertise of many others, such as Alexander Motyl, Roman Sporluk, Nicholas and Alexander Riasanovsky, John Bushnell, and Andrzej Walicki, to name a few. I would like to thank Mehdi Parvizi Amineh for reviewing this book and for his invaluable advice on earlier drafts of the manuscript. I also could not have produced this book without the patience of my wife Natalia, my mother-in-law Liudmila Mogileva, and, of course, my parents Vladimir and Liuba. I am also grateful for the inspiration and prayers of my late grandmother, Raisa Alievskaia, who taught me never to give up. Finally, this book is dedicated to my children, whom I wish, as do all parents, to be healthy and happy.

January 19, 2006

Introduction:
Eurasianism and Soviet/
Post-Soviet Studies

Dmitry Shlapentokh

Eurasianism became increasingly popular in the USSR and then in post-Soviet Russia in the 1990s, but it took almost a generation before the importance of Eurasianism, or at least the term "Eurasian," was acknowledged by Western scholars as an important framework for the study of the former USSR.

American scholars have accepted the idea of Eurasianism and domesticated it as an intellectual import from Europe. The very fact that Eurasianism in various forms has been recognized in the USA after such a delay—in fact, no book is published on it in English despite a proliferation of publications on all aspects of Russian intellectual history—is not accidental. Eurasianism is deeply "politically incorrect." It does not fit well in any of the paradigms espoused by the political and intellectual elite prevailing in the USA. And this usually does not bode well for a theme/subject. Manuel Sarkisyanz, an elderly specialist in Russian studies (she received her Ph.D. from the University of Chicago in 1952), elaborating on intellectual life in the USA, wrote in her recent Russian *Russian Ideologies and the Messianism of the Orient,* "The freedom of print protects [in America] only what has been printed [over there], and it is not advised to write what is not commonly accepted for it would not be printed and is thus protected from censorship." This means, of course, that those manuscripts that openly challenge the accepted paradigms would never be published, at least not by a major publisher (Sarkisyanz 2005: 227). And this explains why her book has never been published in the USA. The book is based on her 1952 University of Chicago Ph.D. dissertation. It sees the Russian revolutionary movement deeply soaked not in Western Marxism, but in Russian religious thinking. The book glorifies those Russian revolutionaries who, inspired by the notion of suffering stemming from Russian Orthodox tradition, wanted to build the ideal society, the kingdom of God on earth. And, in this emotional drive for universal brotherhood, these Russian revolutionaries were actually much more noble and superior, at least from a moral point of view, than those espousing Western liberal capitalism with its emphasis on individualism and crass materialism.

The dissertation and the book were hardly a success. Upon reading her manuscript, one of her peers at the University of Chicago informed the author in a friendly way that if she wished to work in the USA, she should change her outlook and write what is "acceptable by society" (227). This individual added that because of her views, not only would her manuscript not be published in America but she would not be able to get a permanent position. And this proved to be correct. Sarkisyanz was able to obtain a job only for a few years at Bishop College, a black school in the South at the bottom of the pecking order in black college ranking. This position made her even less acceptable to American academia. Elaborating on this, Sarkisyanz stated that the American academic community is extremely hierarchical and ranking depends exclusively on geographical location. All colleges/universities in the Deep South fall in the category of institutions with extremely low prestige. And, therefore, those who work in these institutions, especially if it were a small college for predominately black students, are automatically transformed into a sort of *untermensch*, or, in Sarkisyanz's case, *unterfrau*. This, as Sarkisyanz said, made the dissemination of her ideas even harder, for no one seriously accepted the views of those who took teaching positions in institutions of such low status. This also, of course, made the publication of her manuscript even more difficult. And it was not surprising, she added, with an air of sarcasm, that her Chicago friends regarded her teaching position at Bishop College as being "worse than death" (227).

One, of course, could respond that Sarkisyanz certainly missed the intellectual and political trends that followed her departure from the USA in the 1950s. If she had endured at Bishop College or in a similar institution for a few years, she would have seen an abrupt reversal in the political and intellectual climate in America. In the 1960s, socialism was praised and the spirituality, morality, and implicit wisdom of non-Western people were applauded. Their "discourse" was seen as definitely superior to the "hegemonistic ideology" of the white middle class. And, finally, there was critical "deconstruction" of the entire system of Western capitalism. Her views would not have been cause for damnation but on the contrary would be a magic key that would open doors to the dream job. In fact, this ideological key—French postmodernism/post-structuralism in its Leftist interpretation, for a long time passé in its place of origin, continued to be extremely popular in the USA. And if Sarkisyanz had stayed longer at Bishop, she might have been invited to work with such academic luminaries as Stanley Fish, the postmodernist leftist guru, who wielded great influence at Duke University, hardly a backwater in American academia despite its location in the Deep South.

One, of course, could also ignore Sarkisyanz's diatribes and see them just as an obsessive fixation on American political/intellectual life during the McCarthy era and the bitterness of an émigré academic who was not able to find a job. Still, taking all these caveats into consideration, one should not discard Sarkisyanz's assessment of American academic life as absolutely irrelevant. It is not just that her statement that the extreme stratification of American academia, where respect and acceptance of one's views often depend on formal placing inside the academic hierarchy, is basically correct. There is another reason not to dismiss her assessments. Respectable publishing houses publish accepted views. And it is the types of books that do not go against the prevailing views in the scholarly community and society in general that are usually bought by libraries, read, and quoted. Conformity with the prevailing mood can sometimes be even more important than position in the scholarly hierarchy. Consider the case of the individual who wrote the foreword to Sarkisyanz's manuscript in 1955, none other than Pitirim Sorokin.

Sorokin, a fellow émigré from Russia, had enjoyed an academic career that could hardly be compared with that of Sarkisyanz. Soon after his arrival in the USA, he not only became employed in one of the leading research universities but soon landed a tenured job at Harvard. And, as he informed his acquaintance, the other émigré, he immediately became a member of the academic aristocracy. Still, despite his formidable academic position, Sorokin soon was plainly ignored by his fellow sociologists. During his academic career he elaborated several ideas, one of them, which he stuck to for his entire life, the assumption that human civilization would not survive if it could not be instilled with the feeling of brotherly love.

It was spiritual religiosity that made Sarkisyanz's book so attractive to him. But the very idea evoked nothing but scorn among his colleagues, who practically ostracized him. His other works, for example, the books on totalitarian regimes, which he saw as the only way to keep some societies together, were also totally ignored, plainly because they exposed political philosophy quite different from what was advocated by the majority (Sorokin 1925, 1942). Indeed, the assumption that mass use of violence is needed to keep some societies from falling apart would lead to nothing but disgust among the majority in academia as well as the general public.

All this explains why Eurasianism made a slow entrance to the field of post-Soviet studies. Indeed, the major ideas of Eurasianism are in sharp contrast to the basic paradigm shared by most American specialists in Russian studies, regardless of their political affiliation. This ideology, deeply imbedded in the tradition of Anglo-Saxon enlightenment and usually universalizing human history, for example, prevails, despite the bitterness of conflict between Left and Right, practically all of whom believe that political democracy is the destiny of humanity.

It is true that the idea of "cultural diversity" is constantly reinforced in American academia; in fact, this maxim is repeated with the same frequency as references to Marxism-Leninism the USSR in Soviet times. Still, the American notion of multiculturalism is rarely acknowledged as a fundamental civilizational difference; it is usually assumed that with all the cultural/regional differences, humanity is striving for "government for the people and by the people." The success of Francis Fukuyama's famous essay "The End of History" (1992), i.e., the triumph of American liberal capitalism as the omega of world history—and here American liberalism/capitalism is seen almost like communism in official Soviet philosophy—could not be explained just by the collapse of the USSR. The end of the Soviet empire and the regime just reinforces the principles of Anglo-Saxon enlightenment, which has been the guiding principle of America throughout its entire history.

In fact, different from Europe, America not only had no Middle Ages but also no romantic reaction in which the principles of enlightenment were challenged. The end of the USSR and the spreading of American geopolitical influence in East Europe, the imperial domain of the previous competitor, led to the belief that American political culture would spread globally. Recently, as global tensions have increased and it has become clear that American liberal capitalism, in fact, political democracy in its Anglo-Saxon manifestation, is not universally applicable, one can see the growing popularity of Samuel Huntington's "Clash of Civilizations." Yet, despite Huntington's reputation and his formidable position at Harvard, his theory has not been universally embraced, at least to the degree that Fukuyama's ideas were. The reason is transparent: Huntington's theory actually discards globalization, the universalism of American liberal capitalism, and American civilization in general. Indeed, instead of the internal peace of societies of liberal capitalism, which, in general should follow the American model, Huntington professes civilizations not just basically different from each other but engaged in bitter war. Here, one can easily find similarities between his philosophy and that of Oswald Spengler and Arnold Toynbee. In his idea of the conflict of civilizations, Huntington is similar not to Spengler or Toynbee— he is apparently influenced by them to this or that degree—but to the Russian Nikolai Danilevskii, of whom he most likely was not aware.

Danilevskii promulgated not only that Russia and the West were absolutely different from each other but that they could not coexist with each other: they would engage in war. As the chaos and tension in the world has intensified, the Huntingtonian approach to the past and the present has become more acceptable. The reason is not just that political/international reality continues to prove that the world has not developed according to the Fukuyamaian model. but also that Huntingtonism and Fukuyamaism are not as far apart as one would assume, at least at first glance.

Huntington completely discards Fukuyama's notion of the final triumph of liberal capitalism. He clearly assumes that the spread of the liberal American type of capitalism would not be peaceful or, at least, not be a result of an internal process in each non-Western civilization. He predicts that the people of these civilizations would not transform their countries according to the American model by their own will but that it would be the result of a long struggle in which Western pressure would play the paramount role. It is clear that Huntington does not believe that this struggle would be endless; sooner or later one of the warring sides would be vanquished. And it is also clear that Huntington does not doubt who would be the victorious civilization; of course, it would be the West, led by the USA. Fukuyamaism would finally triumph, but with the help of American military might.

Huntington's view could also be well connected with "neo-conservatism." In fact, he can be seen as sort of an intellectual "missing link" between Fukuyama and the neo-conservatives. Indeed, similar to Fukyama, neo-conservatives strongly assert the inevitable triumph of liberal American capitalism. On the other hand, similar to Huntington, neo-conservatives trust American military might as the major force of the transformation of global polity. The "end of history," thus, should not be entrusted to history itself but to the volition of the American elite.

In a curious way, neo-conservatives' views on promoting American capitalism as the omega of world history, with the help of the bayonets of the American army, are similar to Trotsky's idea of promoting world-wide revolution and the Soviet brand of socialism. This was also seen, if not as the omega of world history, at least as the sure path to the "end of history"—communism by the bayonets of the Red Army. It also had some structural resemblance to the idea of global jihad, which also shall ultimately lead to global salvation.

All the above-mentioned thinkers or groups of thinkers assumed that history will follow, in general, the same road to the ultimate end; that the American brand of capitalism will finally triumph through American-led globalization. Yet, as time progresses, it has become clear that real history is pervasively "politically incorrect"; it does not fit any available models that imply a unified and mostly homogeneous and democratic global community. A considerable part of the world are not going to accept "the end of history" of their own volition. Nor are they willing to bend under pressure; in fact, these countries/civilizations have become profoundly unchangeable, retaining as a part of their national fabric a sort of immutable core that is preserved regardless of external modifications. Russia, for example, remains in many ways autocratic, regardless of the change of systems. The same can be said about most of the Central Asian countries of the former Soviet Union. And on this point, an increasing number of American academics have slowly begun to understand that in the case of many societies, "transition" has become actually meaningless and civilizational differences will persist for a long time. And it is at this point that the idea of Eurasianism—in this or that form—started to be slowly incorporated in cultural discourse, albeit still [few] fully understand the political implications of the new term. It is not accidental that a contributor to the new journal *Kritika* made the following comments in the introduction to the first issue: "In North America, at least, foundations, academic programs, and even job searches have begun to use the term 'Eurasian,' thus effectively reinventing it in a scholarly and, one hopes, neutral incarnation" (*Kritika* 2000: 2). Thus "Eurasia" and "Eurasianism" have been finally introduced to the North American, and in general, Western, intellectual community. And it has become of paramount importance to provide some general brief outlines of the history of Eurasianism and—this is especially important in our view—to place Eurasianism in the broad intellectual context of Eurasian space.

What is Eurasianism? How was the movement and ideology born? Eurasianism as an intellectual and political trend emerged in 1921 when a group of Russian émigrés published the brochure, "Turn to the East." The movement attracted attention among members of the Russian Diaspora and increased in size. By 1929, the movement experienced splits with the emergence of the left Eurasianists. By the end of World War II, Eurasianism had become known in the USSR, with Lev Gumilev as one of the major representatives. Upon the collapse of the USSR, it became one of the major ideological tenets of what was called "Red to Brown" opposition to the Yeltsin regime. In 2002, under Vladimir Putin, two Eurasian parties were launched. In the process of its political/ideological development, Eurasianism changed and diversified. At the same time, however, all representatives of the movement shared a common ideological base. All of them assumed that Russia-Eurasia is a separate civilizational unit, different from both Asia and Europe. In some of the Eurasianists' doctrines, Eurasia included Europe and a good part of Asia proper. In recent years, Eurasianism has been discussed, at least briefly, in many articles and books. Still, there is much to be done for a comprehensive study of the movement. To our knowledge there are actually only three book-length monographs that treat Eurasianism at length (Boss

1961; Laruelle 1999; Kaiser 2004). Russian works on the subject often are polemical writings. Their authors' major goals are not so much the elaboration of Eurasianism as the promotion of this or that political creed. Even less is done to discuss Eurasianism in historical context. This work could well be regarded as the first step in showing how Eurasianism emerged and developed over the course of time.

This book is divided into six chapters. These chapters—either separately or *en paire*—address several important themes. Marlène Laruelle's "The Orient in Russian Thought at the Turn of the Century" addresses the present intellectual milieu that has made the rise of Eurasianism possible. Stephan Wiederkehr's "Eurasianism as a Reaction to Pan-Turkism" dwells on pan-Turkism as the alternative to Eurasianism or actually the alternative model of constructing identity, identity not based on the commonality of culture/space but on the ties of blood.

Françoise Lesourd's "Karsavin and the Eurasian Movement" and Ryszard Paradowski's "Absolutism and Authority in Eurasian Ideology: Karsavin and Alekseev" address the problem of the relationship between Eurasianism and the Soviet regime. Both of these essays show that Eurasianism was sort of a "Freudian slip" of the regime: Eurasianists presented the regime as it actually was, not as it tried to present itself. Roman Bäcker's "From the Time of Rejection to the Attempts of Reconciliation, Poles and the Inter-War Eurasian Movement" addresses the problem of the perception of Eurasianists by foreigners, Poles in this case. Vadim Rossman's "Anti-Semitism in Eurasian Historiography: The Case of Lev Gumilev" addresses the problem of transition from early Eurasianism to present-day variations. And he pays considerable attention to the image of the Jews in the Eurasian paradigm.

BIBLIOGRAPHY

Boss, Otto. 1961. *Die Lehre der Eurasier: Ein Beitrag zur Russichen Ideengeschichte des 20. Jahrhundems.* Wiesbaden.
Danilevskii, Nikolai. 1867. *Rossiia i Evropa.* Moscow, 1992.
Fukuyama, Francis. 1992. *The End of History and the Last Man.* London.
Kaiser, Markus. 2004. *Auf der Suche nach Eurasien: Politik, Religion und Alltagskultur zwischen Russland und Europa.* Bielefeld.
Kritika. 2000. "From the Editors," 1, 1.
Laruelle, Marlène. 1999. *L'idéologie eurasiste russe, ou comment penser l'empire.* Paris.
Sarkisyanz, Manuel. 1952. *Russian Ideologies and the Messianism of the Orient.* Dissertation, University of Chicago.
———. 2005. *Rossiia i Messianism k "Russkoi Idee" N. A. Berdiaeva.* St. Petersburg.
Sorokin, Pitirim Aleksandrovich. 1925. *The Sociology of Revolution.* New York: 1967.
———. 1942. *Man and Society in Calamity: The Effects of War, Revolution, Famine, Pestilence upon Human Mind, Behavior, Social Organization, and Cultural Life.* New York.

I. The Orient in Russian Thought at the Turn of the Century

Marlène Laruelle

THE GENESIS OF EURASIANISM

The Orient occupies a unique space in the history of Russian thought. A number of intellectuals have taken an interest in this theme since the nineteenth century in order to define the place of Russia in the world and its relations with Europe. Nevertheless, Orient can have different meanings: Byzantium, Caucasus, the Muslim world, India, China, ... Orient can also be internal to Russia, from the turcospeaking peripheries of the Volga to the Siberian Far East. The position of Russia toward this Orient is ambiguous: doesn't Russia itself constitute an Orient facing Europe? Petr Y. Chadaaev sensed this paradox and was anxious to specify that to be situated at the Orient of Europe didn't necessarily mean to be the Orient (Chadaaev 1970: 205).

As a founding theme in Russian thought of the nineteenth and twentieth centuries, Orient is present in many areas of human thought. The half-century between the 1870s and the 1920s sees the emergence of this theme in Russian geography (the idea of the third continent), historiography (rehabilitation of Moscovy under the Tatar yoke), philosophy (Vladimir Soloviev's pan-mongolism), literature (the decadent symbolists and the theme of Huns and Scythians), and especially art (Nikolai Rerikh's orient-alistic painting) more than in the ideological geopolitical field (the "Oriental" movement). The theme is intrinsically dependent on some classical philosophical and political postulates in the history of ideas in Russia: totality, organicism, spirituality, anti-individualism, death of Europe, empire. Whether considered "internal" or "external," it is another way of thinking about Russia and a possible expression of numerous Russian intellectuals' doubt about the place and the nature of the object "Russia."

Eurasianist ideology is at the heart of reflections on the place of Orient in Russian thought: it endows theories on proximity between Russia and Orient with a scope never reached before. It is also the only ideology that pursues the ambiguousness of the definition: the Orient is at the same time in the "cultural areas" surrounding Russia (Islam, India, China) and an internal entity, organic to Russia, the steppic world. This chapter will try to show the genesis of Eurasianism in the half-century that precedes its birth: the richness of philosophical currents as well as the development of orientalistic fashions in many fields of Russian thought announce the influence that Eurasianism, as a cultural and political movement, will have on the "Orient" (Laruelle 1999).

Everyone who has an interest in post-Soviet studies hears the terms "Eurasia" and "Eurasian." Indeed, interest in Eurasianism and "Eurasia" has grown, and references can often be found in Russian and Western literature. What is Eurasianism? How was the movement and ideology born?

Eurasianism as an intellectual and political trend emerged in 1921 when a group of Russian émigrés published the brochure, "Turn to the East." The movement attracted attention among the Russian diaspora and increased in size. By 1929, it experienced splits with the emergence of the left Eurasianists. By the end of World War II, Eurasianism was known in the USSR, with Lev Gumilev as a major representative. Upon the collapse of the USSR, it became a major ideological tenet of the "red to brown" opposition to the Yeltsin regime. In 2002, under Vladimir Putin, two Eurasian parties were launched.

In the process of political/ideological development, Eurasianism changed and diversified. At the same time, however, all representatives of the movement had a common ideological base. They assumed that Russia-Eurasia is a distinct civilizational unit, different from both Asia and Europe. In some Eurasianists' doctrines, Eurasia included Europe and a good part of Asia proper. In recent years Eurasianism has been discussed, at least briefly, in many articles and books. Still, there is much to be done for a comprehensive study of the movement. To our knowledge there are actually only two book-length monographs that treat Eurasianism at length (Boss 1961; Laruelle 1999). Russian works on the subject often are polemical writings whose major goals are not so much the elaboration of Eurasianism as the promotion of this or that political creed. Even less work has been done on Eurasianism in historical context.

The present work could well be regarded as the first step in showing how Eurasianism emerged and developed over the course of time. The first part of the book deals with historical Eurasianism, the second with the transition from historical Eurasianism to its more recent modifications. The focus here is on the approach to Jews and how Eurasianist views on Jews changed in the course of time.

The chapters by Françoise Lesourd and Ryszard Paradowski provide a focus on Lev P. Karsavin (1882–1952), one of the leading Eurasianist philosophers, whose philosophy provides a good overview of the tenets of the movement. Karsavin discarded Western culture because of its stress on the individual and particular. These aspects of Western civilization were related to the Western political system and ideas of political/social conflicts. Karsavin and in fact all Eurasianists implicitly discarded the notion of Western democracy. To them, it was actually the dictatorship of the elite which manipulated the electorate. In Vilfred Pareto's terms, the Western elite as presented by Karsavin were all "foxes," cunning creatures who manipulate the naïve populace. Karsavin juxtaposed these philosophical and political arrangements to his and many Eurasianists' philosophies in general. He emphasized the holistic totality of society and time as a transtemporal unity. This philosophy constituted the very essence of Russia/Eurasia.

Karsavin, like many Eurasianists, had an ambivalent relationship with the Soviet regime, one that can be understood if we remember how the Soviet elite visualized their relationship to the West, at least in their official propaganda. Soviet leaders promulgated the notion that the regime was a mortal enemy of the capitalist West. This confrontation was due to the fact that the Soviet regime represented the workers and peasants, and was therefore guided by Marxism and later Marxism-Leninism, the revolutionary ideology of the proletariat. Western governments proclaimed that Bolshevik policy, the child of its philosophical creeds, made Bolsheviks outcasts. Some Russian émigrés also emphasized that Bolsheviks were absolutely different from mainstream European civilizations. This was the case with Mensheviks and liberals.

The Eurasianists had a different approach. Some proclaimed that the problem with the regime was not that it had forsaken Western civilization. They saw the root of the problem quite differently: Bolsheviks with their Marxism were perpetrators of Russian Westernism, which was foreign to Russia/Eurasia. Thus, the rise of the Bolshevik regime meant not the end but the continuation of Westernism. At the same time, Eurasianists also discovered anti-Western aspects in Bolshevik ideology and practice. This appreciation of the anti-Western aspect of the Soviet regime increased as time went on and led to Eurasianists' acceptance of Soviet ideology almost in totality.

Karsavin was no exception and, as demonstrated by the above mentioned articles, was ready to accept the Soviet regime. He saw the similarities between Marxism in its Soviet reading and Eurasianism. So when, as Lesourd stated, Karsavin decided not to run from the approaching Red Army, he assumed that the regime would not touch him. His assumption was not due to his notion of the regime's civility. He assumed the regime would regard him as a kindred spirit and not only would not harm him but would allow him even to teach.

Karsavin was mistaken in his belief that the regime would spare him, but he was right from another perspective. Eurasianism and Soviet ideology had a lot in common. Some aspects of Eurasianism (e.g., belief in strong government, emphasis on the organic unity of the ethnic groups of the USSR) were actually identical to tenets of the regime.

The rise of Eurasianism led to interest in ideology among the political/ intellectual elite of neighboring countries. The Polish elite were among these, as Roman Bäcker elaborates in his chapter in this volume, "From Rejection to Attempts of Reconciliation: Poles and the Interwar Eurasian Movement." These elements of the Polish approach to Eurasianism were not accidental. Polish intellectuals were among the first who actually formulated Eurasianist ideas (e.g, that Russians were not so much Slavs as they were a Turanic people). As Bäcker shows, there was a considerable interest in the emerging Eurasian movement in post-World War I Poland. The approach was controversial. Some Polish intellectuals saw Eurasianists as just another group of Russian nationalists who in the case of victory would try to incorporate Poland into the Russian empire. Others saw Eurasianists differently, noting that they deemphasized the importance of Slavic characteristics. For them, Poland was just another country outside the cultural/geographical area of Eurasia, not necessarily part of Russia/Eurasia.

The articles of Vadim Rossman constitute the second part of the book and demonstrate the transition from the classical Eurasianism to its later modifications. The connection/disconnection between classical and modern Eurasianism has been demonstrated in the context of their relation to Jews.

Jews were of interest to early Eurasianists, as were other ethnic groups of Russia/Eurasia. It was true, as Rossman stated, that one could find anti-Semitic ideas in the writing of early Eurasianists. But this was not unique to Eurasian discourse. As a matter of fact, anti-Semitism in this or that form could be found in all European nationalism. It was fairly strong in Russian nationalism, at least in some variations. The interesting point of the classical early form of Eurasianism was the attempt to integrate at least religious Jews into the Russian/Eurasian cultural/ethnic entity. The same could be said about later forms of Eurasianism. This approach can be found, for example, in the work of Aleksandr Dugin, one of the best-known Eurasianists in present-day Russia.

Despite the elements of anti-Semitism in Dugin's writing, one must not overestimate them. Following the line of Bromberg, an early Jewish Eurasianist, he divided Jews into two types. The materialistic Jew became the embodiment of Atlantic civilization, the mortal enemy of Russia/ Eurasia. The story is different with the religious Jews, who, together with Muslims, could be incorporated in the great Eurasian empire.

While Rossman tended to overestimate Dugin's anti-Semitism, he was absolutely right in regard to Lev Gumilev, for whom Jews were a demonic force and the true enemy of the people of Russia/Eurasia. Still, the extreme forms of anti-Semitism are not popular among mainstream Eurasianists. In fact, Rossman states, this downplaying of the importance of race/ethnicity as a divisive factor made possible the attempt to provide an alternative to Communist ideology.

Eurasianism has almost an eighty-year history, and one could raise the question as to whether it has a future. There is no easy answer. There are forces that work both for and against Eurasianism in post-Soviet Russia. It is clear that Eurasianism can play an important role in the future. First, it can compete with Communism as a political force, for it can fill the vacuum created by the slow disintegration of "red to brown" nationalists led by post-Soviet communists. The possibility for Eurasianism to replace Communism lies in the nature of post-Soviet ideology.

According to post-Soviet communists, the major outcome of Yeltsin's regime was the destruction of the USSR, the mighty empire. The great USSR, in the Communist view, was the legitimate successor of Russia. The Bolshevik Revolution and Soviet regime were praised not for the liberation of humanity, but for the creation of the mighty state. Communist opposition has appealed to the memory of the Soviet regime precisely for this reason, which explains the attachment to Stalin, the symbol of Soviet empire, and almost total ignoring of Lenin in the past ten years or so. Communist influence is in decline and an appeal to the Soviet legacy as the foundation of the Soviet/Russian empire has become more and more irrelevant because Communists failed to become a viable opposition to power. And the images of the Bolshevik Revolution and Soviet regime became irrelevant to new generations of Russians who grew up in the post-Soviet era.

Eurasianism could provide a viable replacement to Communist ideology, even in its nationalistic transmogrification. As stated by its founders since the beginning of the movement, Eurasianism can be interpreted as being nothing but Communism with Orthodox Christianity instead of Marxism as a framework. The fact that the new Eurasian party launched by Dugin in 2002 enjoyed the support of authorities and proclaimed its dedication to Vladimir Putin, Russia's president, provided the party with the 1 chance to take part of the electorate from the Communists. Dugin may well be dreaming of replacing Communists completely as the leading corporate-nationalist party.

Eurasianism is also the only viable ideology that provides some legitimization for Russia as a multi-ethnic state, and it enjoys other important characteristics that make it quite useful in post-Soviet Russia. It is a flexible doctrine, as is easy to see. At the beginning of his career, Dugin gravitated toward "red to brown" Communists with their emphasis on deprivatization. Later he asserted that private property could be accepted as a foundation for Eurasianist Russia. The geopolitical combination that stems from the assumption that Russia is a Eurasian power was also manifold.

Eurasianism provided the opportunity for a variety of geopolitical arrangements. The early Eurasianists limited "Eurasia" to the confines of the USSR/Russia. Some even stated that Genghis Khan's excessive ambitions were wrong because he tried to conquer lands outside the historical/geographical context of Eurasia. At the same time, the appeal to Mongol tradition implies a drive for global predominance. Some Eurasianists, such as Georgii Vernadskii, regarded the Mongol drive to dominate the center of geographic Eurasia as a healthy urge. Vernadskii's book elaborating these ideas, written after World War II, implied a blessing on Stalin's great Eurasian empire, poised for global predominance.

In the 1960s and 1970s, Lev Gumilev once again limited the territory which could be regarded as Eurasia and countries with whom Eurasia could be engaged in alliance. China, for example, was excluded and transformed into a mortal enemy of Eurasia. During the Yeltsin era some Eurasianist-minded politicians (e.g., Primakov) started once again to view China as a natural ally of Russia-Eurasia. In post-Soviet Eurasianism, the United States was usually seen as the mortal enemy of Russia/Eurasia. Yet with a little geopolitical imagination the U.S. could be transformed into a complementary country-civilization. These ideas apparently started to emerge among some of Putin's elite when his foreign policy made a sharp turn around after the 9–11 terrorist attack. The confrontational approach was replaced by an announcement that Russia had become the chief U.S. ally. In light of these changes, some Eurasianist-minded intellectuals proclaimed that Russia-Eurasia could be an American watchdog. In their view, Russia-Eurasia and the United States could complement each other well.

Thus there are many reasons why Eurasianism has played an important role in present-day Russia and can continue to do so. At the same time, one must not ignore the potential problems that could devalue Eurasianism in the future. Regardless of its numerous variations, it is essentially an ideology of empire. Ethnic Russians are seen as the backbone of Russia/Eurasia, providing benign geopolitical guidance for a wide variety of people. Russians are, as Dugin put it, "Eurasian Romans," all-embracing groups that include anyone who accepts their geostrategical guidance.

This implies that Russia is a strong, united nation, open to outsiders precisely because of its confidence in its strength. This notion could be questioned as post-Soviet history continues to unfold. Russians have been marginalized, not just in relationship to other nations, but also inside the Russian Federation with the increasing rise of non-Russian people. Russians often cannot compete with the non-Russian minorities and those from the former Soviet Republics. This is especially clear in Russian markets. The number of ethnic Russians is in continuous decline with the increasing spread of AIDS and other diseases. Increasing social polarization has intensified the problems. In these situations seemingly increasing numbers of ethnic Russians feel that Russians cannot hold even the reduced empire, the Russian Federation.

One manifestation is the rising popularity of Russian nationalism, often in extremist form. While mimicking the symbols of Nazi Germany, these Russian nationalists are essentially different. One point of difference between Nazi Germany and most recent Russian nationalists is the question of empire. Nazi Germany was imperial in its core belief that Aryans must dominate globally. Contemporary Russian extremist nationalists often do not entertain the idea of empire and resurrection of the USSR, but rather emphasize cleansing Russia from everything non-Russian. Many would accept a scenario in which Russia would be reduced to the territory populated only by ethnic Russians. They had no apprehension of Eurasianism and called Eurasia "Asiopia"—"Ass Asia"—the term coined by Paul Miliukov, a Russian liberal politician upset by the early Eurasianist anti-European stand.

While Russian nationalists increasingly professed ideas of nationalist exclusion rather than imperial inclusion, the same feeling was professed among non-Russians, mostly Muslim ethnic minorities within Russia. They were regarded by Eurasianists as a major ingredient of Russia-Eurasia, one that made Russian/Eurasian civilization unique and not just another Slavic civilization. Some of these groups seem to have shared the Eurasian quest for building a unique Eurasian civilization of Slavic and non-Slavic.

For example, Saparmurad Niiazov, an ethnic Russian who converted to Islam, created his own party in 2002, the year Dugin created his Eurasian party. Dugin protested and proclaimed that Niiazov must not use "Eurasianism" to define his party. There were many personal issues in their disagreement, for they both compete for political influence, but it is not just personal jealousy that separates them. Dugin followed the traditional interpretation of Eurasianism in which ethnic Russian was "Eurasian Roman," the "big brother" of non-Russian minorities.

Niiazov's vision of Russia/Eurasia is different. For him, Russians must share power with non-Russian Muslim people of the Federation. Logically, he implies that due to the physical decline of the ethnic Russians, they must play the role of "younger brother" in the future. It is clear that most of Russia could hardly accept this scenario, and would rather opt for exclusive nationalism. The pull toward further fragmentation was reinforced by the feelings of most Muslims. While some might dream of Muslim domination in the Federation, most would rather opt for future loosening of their ties to the center, or complete independence.

The cohesiveness of the Federation and therefore the viability of Eurasianism as a political creed is further undermined by the separatist feeling spreading even among ethnic Russians in some provinces who saw Moscow as the colonial power. At the same time, the feeling of estrangement from the provinces is also spreading among Muscovites. Many of them despise provincials, even ethnic Russians who are regarded as foreign entities in the capital. Their view of the provincials is shared by some Russian extremist nationalists. The author of this essay was present at the meeting of one of these neo-Fascist groups. Speakers, while lambasting America as Russia's national enemy, screamed the slogan: "Russia for Russians; Moscow for Muscovites." The first part of the slogan would be accepted by Nazi Germans, who would of course rephrase it as "Germany for Germans." The second part would hardly emerge in the mind of a German Nazi. He would never proclaim that Berlin must be only for Berliners, for that would imply not the greatness of the German empire, but the disintegration of the German state.

Dmitri Trenin, a leading Russian politologist, has proclaimed that what everyone now witnesses is "the end of Eurasia." In Trenin's interpretation, Russia is to be abandoned as a civilization separate from the West and will join the Western civilizations. There is a good point in Trenin's assumptions. Russia, if not in the present, but at least in the future, could cease to be "Eurasia." It could indeed be integrated into a different civilization, but different from that projected by Trenin. If the present trend persists, Russia will quite likely be transformed into a new "Holy Roman Empire." Because that loose confederation is sandwiched between Europe and China, it could be absorbed by the two regions. In this case, "Russia" would indeed join Europe, but most likely only as far as the Ural Mountains. The other part would be under Chinese influence. In this case, instead of "Eurasia," one would find just Europe and Asia. Still, this disintegration is not likely to take place very soon, barring unexpected shake-ups. And until then "Eurasianism" will play an important role in Russian intellectual and political development. This is the reason those who are interested in the Russian past, present, and future should find useful information in this volume.

The notion of Orient has been bound for a long time to the Byzantine tradition, especially in the Slavophiles' view. Is Constantinople European as a Christian city, or oriental due to its Orthodoxy? Appeal to the

Byzantine theme doesn't mean adherence, and anti-Byzantinism inspired by the Enlightenment is still present in the minds of many Russian intellectuals, such as Mikhail A. Bakunin (1819–61), Vladimir Soloviev (1853–1900), and even Slavophiles. The unique convinced defender of Byzantium as a median world between West and Orient is Konstantin Leontiev, leader of the conservative pan-Slavists, whose writings are tinted with admitted conservative turcophile leanings.

During the romantic era, Russian literature focused on a new Orient, the Caucasus. The theme was inaugurated by Aleksandr S. Pushkin (1799–1837) with *Kavkazskii plennik* in 1820–21. All the Romantics, Aleksandr S. Griboedov (1795–1829), Mikhail Lermontov, and Bestuzhev-Marlinski, pursued this appeal as the Russian Empire was progressing in this area. For Russia of the 1930s and 1940s, the Caucasus played the role of revolutionary Greece for Byron or America for Chateaubriand. One can find again this orientalism, close to the western one, with the Decembrists, who were inspired by the oriental style, the Qur'an, and Iranian poetry. Ethnographism, poetic imagination, and popular legends constitute the common fund of pictures evoked by the Caucasus. The latter permits the expression of a still wild and imposing nature, of free and warlike mountain peoples; it exalts a very "oriental," voluptuous, and lazy eroticism, and women as an object of pleasure or desire. With literature, Russia "colonizes" its Empire poetically, integrates it, and makes it a constituent part of its identity. Sometimes the Romantics, especially Pavel I. Pestel (1793–1826) or Ivan I. Orlov (1861–1928), can be accused of sustaining and exciting their government's imperialistic dreams, transfiguring the Caucasian wars in an epic adventure for Russian intellectuals (Layton 1994).

By contrast, the conquest of Central Asia hardly left any traces in the literature. In 1881, Fedor Dostoevskii, in his Journal, criticized Europeans and recommended the conquest of Turkestan and Asia. He is the only famous Russian nineteenth-century writer to develop a discourse on Russia as a link between Europe and Asia, and he defined Orient, not as the Caucasus or Buddhist Asia, but as the Muslim Central Asiatic world. This Persian Orient, rarely evoked in literature, has been present for a long time in Russian popular mythology like a mythical country of abundance. For writers, it is above all the cradle of a refined poetry, discovered at the beginning of the nineteenth century, thanks to French and German translations. Persia permits the expression of a paradoxical feeling present in all Russian orientalist discourse: Orient is the world of wisdom, lyricism, philosophy, and prophecy but also the incarnation of despotism, childhood, and historical opposition to change. For Slavophiles, Islam is in general an ally against the Latin world; for conservatives such as Nikolai Y. Danilevskii (1822–85), it is appreciated for its social stability and spiritual values (Niqueux 1999).

Beyond this Byzantine and Caucasian Orient, Russia also has, inspired by the West, constructed many reflections on China and India as different oriental pictures. In the eighteenth century, Catherine II used the image of China to justify her enlightened despotism like the philosophers of Light. But the country has a negative connotation as much for Slavophiles as for Westernalists, as the symbol of conservatism, stagnation, and militarism. This critical discourse coexisted despite a fad for the art and literature modernists from Japan and the fashionable chinoiseries in French circles. India had her period of glory with the Romantics of the first half of the nineteenth century, after the discovery of Sanskrit: it embodies the mythical place of the origin and unity of humanity, a part of oneself to rediscover. This Indomania will reappear at the turn of the century in the esoteric questions of numerous intellectual Russians.

THE TURN OF THE CENTURY, OR THE CRYSTALLIZATION OF DISCOURSE ON THE ORIENT

Before 1900, Russian intellectuals were anxious to define themselves only vis-à-vis Europe and the rest of the Slavic world: orientalism didn't mean a new fashion of reflection on oneself. In the twentieth century, Russia "was looking for an Asian genealogy" (Nivat 1966: 461) as Asia embodied exoticism in time and space and made the intellectuals dream they were rejecting their own westernization. It is therefore at the beginning of the century that the "Orient question "in Russian thought moved from Byzantium or Orthodoxy toward to the Tatars and Asia: it throws back into question the classical Russian historiography since Nikolai M. Karamzin (1766–1826) and Visarion C. Bilinskii (1811–48), who were thinking that the Mongolian domination justified the backwardness of Russia and her despotism.

The oriental studies development in universities, the success of the Asian Museum, the orientalist section of the Ministry of Foreign Affairs, the impact of important academics such as Aleksandr K. Kazem-Bek (1802–70), Sergei F. Ol'denbourg (1863–1934), and Vasilii V. Barthold (1869–1930) are to be put in parallel with the Russian advance in Central Asia and the Far East. The development of orientalism as a large, European level academic discipline helps orientalistic discourses by giving them scientific, linguistic, or historic arguments. Writers such as Boris Pil'niak or artists as Nikolai K. Rerikh feed their imagination with the documentary reports of orientalists; even Soloviev won't stop referring to French orientalist discourse as scientific discourse and a justification of the imperialistic undertaking, and supplies indirect authority to theories on pan-Mongolism.

Russian interest in Asia and Orient increased considerably with the new century. The Empire reached its limits in the Pacific; the Far East and the Amur gave rise to tensions with China and Japan; the "Great Game" with the British Empire in the Indies didn't permit any further advance toward Afghanistan; the Caucasus, steppes, and the three khanates of Central Asia were pacified. In 1895 appeared the word panturanism, extolling the regrouping of all Mongols and Tatars, from Finland to Manchuria. In the first Duma, a Muslim deputy group declared itself "Turanian." At the same time, therefore, besides the development of a intellectualized and artistic discourse on Asia, the Turkic part of the Russian Empire, and especially its elite, the Tatars, became aware of themselves, developing a political discourse on their unit and the role of Russia in Asia (Benningsen and Lemercier-Quelquejay 1986).

The Revolution of 1905, its defeat, the weakness of successive Dumas, and the general political and social blockage that touched the Russia of Nicolas II brought some intellectuals to an eschatological pessimism, waiting for brutal and bloody changes. The victory of Japan over Russia in 1905, the first Asian military victory over a white empire, had an enormous impact on both Russians and foreigners, even in the West. The "yellow peril" and "decline of Europe," two themes then fashionable, seemed to be not a fantasy but a reality for the new century. The Russian-Japanese war reversed the perspectives of some intelligentsia about the relations of their country with Orient: in order not to disappear, Russia was obliged to find a territory of understanding with a bellicose Asia.

ORIENTALIST MYSTICISM AND THEOSOPHY IN RUSSIA

At the beginning of the century, Russia knew a prophetic and eschatological atmosphere: Nietzsche, Camille Flammarion, and Wells were read, and people were interested in schismatics and the "Atlantides," oriental wisdom, spiritualism, and esoteric mythology. The discovery of psychoanalysis and the Freudian unconscious, combined with the vulgarization of the Nieztschean discourse on the superman and God's death (in Nieztsche's *Zarathustra*) as well as the fashionable Bergsonian vitalism, irrationalism, Schopenhauerian pessimism, and intuition constituted a natural ground for orientalistic fashions. The doubt caused by the supposed omnipotence of sciences and progress, combined with Russian intellectual identitary uneasiness and need to explain a European State but an Asian Empire, found a way out in "Orient," whose qualification varies with a lot of inconsistency: Buddhist, Mongol, Chinese, yellow, Japanese, nomadic, etc.

The famous figure of this mystical fashion was Elena P. Blavattskaia (1831–1891, known in the U.S. as Madame Blavatsky), a Russian who became a naturalized American. She created a Society of Theosophy in 1875 and published numerous books which were supposed to found this new "science" (Guénon 1921). Her inspirations varied from spiritualism and séances to journeys in India. Her so-called powers are often considered trickery, but Russian theosophy in its widest and most philosophical meaning can be defined in three points. It was first of all an attempt at social harmony through a spiritual transformation of the human personality. It then claimed to be an experimental test (by spiritualism, hypnosis, etc.) of "superior" phenomena which are not explainable by faith. Blavatsky finally called for a return to the Orient spiritual inheritance and especially that of Buddhism and Hinduism, the only one to have kept the faith in the man-nature ties. This Russian mysticism claimed to be synthetic: it was at the same time religion, philosophy, and science, and attracted many Russian intellectuals such as, for example, Soloviev.

The mystical fashion that seized Russia at the turn of the century was far from being only popular, it was also founded on such scientific works as those of Aleksei Vertelovskii on the western medieval mystical, on essays of Aleksandr I. Vedenskii (1856–1925), Karsavin, Petr Y. Svetlov (1861–?), on the rediscovery of the mystical current of hesychasm, on the emphasis on Sufism of Georgii I. Gurdjieff (1872–1919), and so on. His orientalist fashion spread through all intellectual circles: a Buddhist church opened in St. Petersburg, attended by the intelligentsia and orientalists, and writers and poets of the Silver Age took on numerous oriental motives. Tolstoy himself succumbed to the orientalist fashion and looked for his inspiration in Buddhism, Confucianism, Taoism, and so on.

The history of the Rerikh family is on this account exemplary. The father, Nikolai K. Rerikh (1874–1947), a painter and archaeologist, former member of the vanguard movement Mir Isskustva, rushed into a very romantic Indomania and went in search of the Shambhala, a mythical place of the Himalayas; he defined an esoteric Buddhist doctrine and announced an eschatological era of peace and justice. He introduced the main pictures of Russian cosmism in his futuristic painting: reevaluation of the Slavic and Scandinavian pagan past, and numerous oriental motives (mainly Buddhist) after his expeditions in High Asia and to Tibet and his settling in India (1923–36). His two sons pursued the double tendency of the paternal work and hesitated between artistic and scientific approaches to Orient: Iurii N. Rerikh enriched Soviet orientalism with his experience of Tibet and India while Sviatoslav N. Rerikh continued to live in India and pursued the orientalist and futuristic painting of his father.

VLADIMIR SOLOVIEV AND THE IDEA OF TOTALITY (*VSEEDINSTVO*)

The philosopher Vladimir Soloviev (1853–1900) also took part, on a more conceptual level, in this effort to develop a mystical syncretism between Orient and West. He created a teaching based on a new spiritual ideal, embodied as "free theosophy," that renewed in a decisive way, by the concept of *vseedinstvo* (totality), the main ideas of Russian cosmism. He opened a new era in Russian philosophy that had important repercussions in the twentieth century as it directly influenced the symbolist movement and a renewed religious philosophy. His ideas were used in the Russian emigration by Nikolai Berdiaev and especially by Lev Shestov, specialist in Kierkegaard and Pascal and philosopher of "the existential interiority."

Soloviev retook for his own use Kireevskii's thesis, from a Schellingian origin, according to which Western philosophy came to its definitive crisis with Schopenhauer and Hartmann. Nevertheless he embodied a double rupture with Slavophiles because he did not depreciate Western thought but on the contrary called for a synthesis of Orient and West, of religion and science. He tried to dig foundations of personalist ethics and estheticism based on relations between art and religion.

He also developed an eschatological religious philosophy, uniting orthodoxy and neoplatonism and calling for ecumenism of all Christian churches. Russia had to give up religious and political nationalism and accomplish the mission that neither Constantine nor Charlemagne could achieve: it embodied a third strength between a rationalistic West and an impersonal Orient. Around the concept of *vseedinstvo*, his philosophy of religious and cultural synthesis, but also the man and the universe synthesis, he provoked a deep interest for the Eurasianists in their search for an original unit, a totality that would form the cosmos and humanity.

THE INHERITANCE OF PAN-SLAVISM: "CIVILIZATIONISM" AND ITS ASSUMPTIONS

Pan-Slavism emerged as a doctrine between the Crimean War (1853–56), which was an intellectual and political shock for Russians, and the Russian-Turkish war in 1878. It was born in the high intelligentsia and got there a real audience: intellectual circles discerned with acuteness the unsolved problem of Russian identity and, if the choice of Europe was obvious for economists and technicians, it has remained, since Romanticism, a painful alienation for people of letters. The Conservative pan-Slavism of the 1870s constitutes one of the intellectual matrices of Eurasianism. If the two currents differ in their national qualification of Russia (Slavic or Turanic), the second borrowed from the first a range of arguments and also the pseudo-scientific discourse of the nineteenth century (Petrovich 1966).

The pan-Slavist Konstantin Leontiev (1831–91) was one of the first authors to introduce naturalist elements in his philosophy of history: according to him, there was one unique law that determined the development of plant, animal, and human worlds, and therefore of history. Convinced of historical fatalism, he denounced European anthropocentrism, the biological weakening of the West caused by democratization. He called Russia to react and claim an autocracy, to refuse social leveling in the name of material well-being. Pan-Slavism also became famous for a philosophy of land and soil, for the research of the"direct," the restoration of an organic integrity between territory, Russian people, and orthodoxy, which we can find especially in Apollon Grigoriev's writings (1822–64). Nikolai Strakhov (1828–96) combined the belief in scientific knowledge and the idea that there are some unconscious elements in the historical process. He developed the paradox of calling for rational knowledge of the world with a Hegelian mind and a bitter antirationalism: the human was a mystery which was not accessible to secularized thought. Greatly influenced by Tolstoy as well as Schopenhauer, he was also the author of *Mir kak tseloe*, published in 1872, whose title reveals his will to conceptualize the totality of Russian pan-Slavism.

However, Nikolai Danilevskii (1822–85) was the leading intellectual who gave a systematic formulation of pan-Slavism, setting up the connection with the Slavophilism of the romantic era: he became very popular in the intellectual circles after the Russian-Turkish war in 1878. In 1869, his book, *Rossiia i Evropa* (Russia and Europe), in a cyclic perspective of the destiny of civilization that prefigures Spengler, clearly evoked the irreducible cultural difference between Russia and Europe and saw in the history of the West since the eighteenth century the irretrievable signs of a decline written in the logic of evolution. Danilevskii transformed the Slavophile mysticism into scientific "theories" inspired by the biologic model. He was one of the Russian philosophers to say that there is a unity between the laws of the nature and history. He rejected the first Slavophiles' Hegelianism and condemned linear development of humanity, a progress of "the idea": there are only closed civilization areas that divide the world, without possible values transmitted from one to the other.

He defined about ten cultural and historical types in the history of humanity and his reducing culturalism was based on the anthropo-racial classifications of that time. According to him, the opposition between Slavs and "Romano-Germans" determined the outcome of history, governed by organic principles and biologic determinism. If humanity is subject to natural laws, Slavic development is predetermined. Unlike the first Slavophiles, he didn't differentiate Western and Eastern Europe: Europe was a Romano-Germanic unit; Ural was a Western metaphor supposed to divide Russia and cause it to be rejected in Asia. Danilevskii then invited Slavs to challenge the Western yoke. If Russians could reestablish the splendor of oriental Rome and have Constantinople as their imperial capital, if they could create a Slavic federation, they would then appear as the only true heirs of the Greeks. The source of Russia's unease would be the strange mistake it committed when trying to westernize itself, whereas the Slavic civilization would carry infinite religious, scientific, artistic, political, and economic virtues.

Eurasianism borrowed many of its historical and philosophical patterns from Danilevskii and other conservative pan-Slavists: cyclic history, areas of closed civilization, irreducible Europe-Russia opposition, philosophy of territory, Platonic existence of a hidden reality "truer" than material appearance. Eurasianism only deeply distinguished itself from Danilevskii's theories by its national characterization of Russia. For the latter, Russia was only Slavic: Mongols and Turks were considered negative agents of history, who episodically passed across its stage and went back into the shade of the no-history. Eurasianism took the assumptions of Danilevskii but let the Turco-Mongols enter the stage, proposing a no longer Slavic but oriental and steppic Russia.

THE IDEA OF A THIRD CONTINENT: THE GEOGRAPHICAL MISSION OF RUSSIA IN THE ORIENT

If Eurasianists drew their intellectual knowledge from the inheritance of Pan-Slavists and Soloviev, they were also heirs of geopolitical currents turned toward Orient. Asia was thus an object of survey for many administrators, state servants, and geographers sent into Caucasus, Siberia, or Turkestan. These administrators and scientists working for the state during the nineteenth century thought about the Russian Empire's specificity. The latter wouldn't stop collecting knowledge on Orient, institutionalizing along the way an official orientalism long before the West, an orientalism of power. Since 1848, wasn't Fedor I. Tutchev (1803–73) dreaming himself, in *Russkaja geografiia*, of a Eurasian Empire for Russia (Hauner 1992)?

In the 1870s, geographer and public law specialist Mikhail I. Veniukov (1832–1901) called Russia to a civilizing mission in Central Asia, one that would respect religious differences and cooperate with the conquered peoples for their well-being. Many academics contributed to the development of doctrines that justified Russian presence in Asia. Vasilii V. Barthold (1869–1930), official historian under both czarist and communist regimes, advocated for a cultural rapprochement between people from different origins, recalled worldwide empires as a historical necessity, and invited Russia to put a lot in Central Asia. According to N. M. Prževal'skii (1839–88), peoples of Mongolia and Sing-Kiang were waiting to be under the domination of the "White Czar."

Even Witte, partisan of Russia as a world aside and different from the West, spoke of the Russian proximity to the Asian worlds. This proximity would take the shape of a pacific colonization by Russians that would follow the construction of the Trans-Siberian railway. The end of the century turned Russian official interest toward the Far East: the "Great Game" with Great Britain between Central Asia and India, the constitution of a State buffer, Afghanistan, between the two empires, invited Russia to look toward Japan and China. The agrarian and populating politics of Petr A. Stolypin (1862–1911) along the Trans-Siberian reinforced this "discovery" of the Amur region of Siberia, illustrated for example by M. M. Bogoslovskii (1867–1929), professor of the future Eurasianist historian Georgii Vernadskii, whose first thesis topic would concern the deep reasons for the Russian advance into Siberia.

In 1903, the St. Petersburg historian Sergei M. Seredonin (1860–1914), in *Istoriceskii ocherk zavoevaniia Rossii aziatskoi*, tended to justify the "need for space" of Russia and its natural orientality. More than a millennium of cohabitation and interpenetration between Russians and Asians, the inheritance of Byzantine empire—antechamber of Asia—and the Mongol yoke, as well as the easy conquest of the cold spaces, caused him to conceive an Asian Russia, oriented toward Orient but not Europe, which was considered as too insular and too populated. Several theoreticians of a "third continent" between Europe and Asia then asserted themselves: Vladimir I. Lamanskii (1833–1914), Vasilii V. Dokuchaev (1846–1903), and the economist Peter B. Struve (1870–1944), professor of the future Eurasianist P. N. Savitskii in St. Petersburg.

Lamanskii, geographer as well as linguist and ethnographer, proposed in 1892 the most developed theory on this topic in his book *Tri mira evro-aziatskogo materika*. Russia did not exist in two continents, European and Asiatic, but in one unique Eurasiatic continent in which three radically different worlds confronted each other: the Romano-Germanic world, the Greek-Slavic world of the middle, and a non-Christian world, Asia. Russia at the same time encompassed the whole and was encompassed by the whole, an empire inside the Greek-Slavic world. Lamanskii marked in that way the passage between one pan-Slavist conception that made Russia the center of a Slavic supra-entity and a vision of the empire as a strictly enclosed geo-cultural totality that will remain in the heart of the Eurasianist thought.

THE ORIENTALS MOVEMENT (*VOSTOCHNIKI*)

In the 1880s appeared the movement called the "Orientals." For these disappointed Slavophiles, the future of Russia was to be bound not to the other regions of the Slavic or orthodox world but to Asia. Nikolai F. Fedorov (1828–1903), for example, theorized the dualism between agricultural civilizations and steppic nomadism and viewed in it the dynamical principle of history, giving Russia a good place in the future of the world. Agriculture would develop saving virtues by avoiding trade and luxury, and Russia, the cantor of the agricultural principle, was called to defend the exploited peoples (in particular India) against Britain and also against nomads. Fedor Fedorovich Martens (1845–1909), jurist in international law, and sinologist Vasilii P. Vasilev (1818–1900) thought the "civilizing mission" of Russia was toward Asian peoples, barbarians who threatened Russia with a new invasion. They published numerous booklets on the advance of China toward Russian territory.

These reflections also attracted such populists as Sergei Iuzhakov (1849–1910) who considered that the peasants of Russia had a mission to save the agricultural nations of Asia and Siberia from their perennial enemy, Turanian nomadic Asia. Russia must pass on the peasant socialism mission to the agricultural *obsinas* of India and China and invite them to fight against Western capitalistic exploitation. Thus, when Asia was positively viewed, it always in terms of the sedentary cultures: the nomadic world that would exalt Eurasianist movement was not yet envisaged.

Later, the small movement "yellow Russia" of Prince Esper Ukhtomskii (1861–1921), the extreme wing of the "Orientals," developed the principle of an organic affinity between Russia and India. Though it was not really representative, this current was not so marginal as it appeared: Ukhtomskii owned several magazines, was close to Witte, and was the tutor of the future Emperor Nicolas II. If he glorified Chinese civilization, his texts remained paradoxically imprinted with a discourse on the "yellow peril." His friend German Brunhaufer developed the fear of a strong Buddhist wave led by Japan. The last big epic figure among those who were attempting to achieve on a geopolitical or culturalist plan proximity with the Orient was doubtless the "mad baron" von Ungern-Schtenberg, who converted to Buddhism in order to protest the decline of European values that would have been revealed by the Russian Revolution. In exile in Mongolia, he proclaimed himself the new Genghis Khan at Ulan-Bataar in 1921, but was stopped quite quickly and executed by the Bolsheviks.

Interest in Asia therefore came from a double paradoxical approach, an appeal for a certain Orient and an attempt to reply to the "yellow peril." Russian imperialism was indeed a defensive reaction to Asia, and the fear of miscegenation of Whites with the Yellow and Turanian races sustained all these reflections. Darwinist and neo-Malthusian theories invited the thought that invasion of the less populated zones such as Russian and especially Siberian territory by yellow peoples whose demographic growth seemed to be without limits, was unavoidable.

THE MONGOLIAN WAVE:
THE ORIENT AND ESCHATOLOGY

At the turn of the century, Russia tried therefore to think about its border with Asia. Questioning was expressed mainly through literature and more precisely through poetry. Soloviev was the forerunner of this current since he prophesied, in several poems such as "Panmongolism" (1894), a new Mongolian invasion. According to him, all humans wanted, at least unconsciously, the Antichrist's universal royalty, introduced by a second Tatar yoke. Facing a pan-Mongolian threat, the solution would be in the union of the Catholic and Orthodox worlds, the rebirth of a unique apostolic church.

Soloviev's article "China and Europe" (1890) challenged China's values, literature, and religions—all an extreme materialism at the opposite extreme of Christian values. China had only one interest, to be the mirror of the attitude of Europe-facing Christian principles. If the latter appeared unfaithful to its principles, China then made itself threatening; if Russia remained loyal, China would return to an historical apathy. *The Short Narration on the Antichrist* (1900) put on stage the invasion of Europe by China and the particular role played by France, which was also the symbol of the "black peril." The power that would come from Asia would serve therefore the Antichrist. This parallel Mongol/Antichrist was not new and already existed in two of Gogol's fantastic narrations (e.g., *Portraite*), where the wizard and the devil appeared with Asian faces and clothes and both had the power to penetrate Russian souls without their knowing (Savelli 1996).

All symbolists were also very interested in that theme: according to them the Mongol peril had a metaphorical significance since the danger was in Russia and its Europeanized intellectuals. Dmitry Merezhkovskii was the most important propagator of this "yellow peril" precedence: the advent of Cham was the reign of spiritual philistinism, positivism, mediocrity, and intellectual nihilism. In *Griadushchii ham* (1906) and *Zhelto-litsye pozitivisty* he affirmed that Russia knew again an Asian temptation and developed the nightmarish vision of a Mongolized Russia occupied by millions of "teeming and tight small things." Asia wouldn't need to invade Europe, which would become sinicised on its own, synonymous with mediocrity and "petit-bourgeois fossilization."

Andrei Belyi (1880–1934) transformed Soloviev and Merezhkovskii's Mongolian allegory into a fantastic and morbid reality. In 1910 he published *Serebriannyi golub*, where a young Russian left his westernized world for an oriental sect that would lead him to death. In *Sankt Petersburg* (1913), Russians were internally and physically colonized by the Mongols. The described world was totalitarian, even on the architectural level (geometric avenues), there was a dense and teeming crowd, yellow became the dominant color. The reaction as much as the terrorist revolutionaries were conscious or unconscious agents of pan-Mongolism. France allied with the menacing Asiats to diffuse the pan-Mongol danger to Russia. Haunted by the feeling of the existence of a fatal crack in the world between Orient and West, Belyi played on the theme of the confusion of notions between Orient and West as only one figure embodied these two destinies.

ESCHATOLOGY REVIEWED BY THE REVOLUTIONARY PRISM

The succession of exceptional events since 1914 in Russia gave rise to millenarist interpretations. The spiritualistic current developed in the wake of Soloviev, the return to a neo-Slavophile climate, some perceptions derived from populism and pessimism inherent to the sociopolitical blockage in the finishing Old Regime drove artists and poets to imagine imminent chaos, a return to barbarism, a tragic but redeeming phase that would precede the advent of the Kingdom. Therefore the Revolution must lead eventually to the realization of the Christian ideals and a reign of justice. All these interpretations somewhat recalled the millennium.

Faced with the Revolution of 1917, there were two possible attitudes, which echo the debate that agitated the Russian culture in the nineteenth century: to accept the revolutionary fact and even to be thrilled about it, in the continuation of a certain populism or even an unavowed Slavophilism, or to refuse it to the name of a Westernalist conviction. Intellectuals rallied to the regime; survivors from the Silver Age believing that people were carrying a vital energy were sensible to the first process.

At that time when the exclusive ideology overwhelming Russian culture affirmed a radical atheism, a religious nature process and thought constituted a foundation of various futuristic utopias. "God's builders,"

Anatolii Lunacharskii (1875–1933), Aleksandr A. Bogdanov (1873–1928), Vladimir Bazarov (1874–1939), and even Maksim Gorkii (1868–1936), for example, wanted to use religious longings to back socialism, the new faith. The new God to construct was the hard-working people themselves, and the energy emanating from their auto-deification would break all their social chains. The cultural and artistic world was impregnated with a scientist cult which combined the poetism of the new industrial world with the religious and eschatological foundations of traditional Russia.

A NEW ORIENT TO WHICH REVOLUTIONARY RUSSIA BELONGS

This religious reflection was accompanied by a narrative displacement of Russia in front of Orient. A conservative neo-Slavophile wave, led by personalities as Sharapov, refuses for example all nationalism and extols the respect of Zionism, pangermanism, pan-Mongolism, etc. Sergei Sharapov (1855–1911) sketches the future Russian geography as four capitals (Moscow, Kiev, Petrograd, Constantinople), and incorporation of most of Asia (Persia, Afghanistan, Turkestan) and Central Europe in the Russian Empire.

With the Revolution was developed the idea of solidarity between Russia and Asia. The Mongol theme was replaced by Scythianism and Eurasianism. The two Revolutions of 1917 reversed the steppic peril: facing Bolshevism and western cultural shock, Scythianism wanted to be an even more virulent Russian nationalism than that of the Slavophiles, endowing Russia with the least possible European past. Asia became a positive, offensive, no longer defensive thematic: if it used to be invading and anesthetic, it was transfigured into a wild and energetic Asia, especially in Blok's (1880–1921) *Skify*. This lyrical symbolist was deeply influenced by Soloviev's thought and convinced that Russia and the world were going to topple during a terrifying Apocalypse from which God's Kingdom would emerge. "Yes, we are Scythians, yes, we are Asiats," exclaimed Blok in his last and most famous poem, calling to the "primitive raw" invasion.

If the expectation of Huns is seen as a self-destructive ecstasy, the Russian intellectuals of the Scythian movement included themselves in these regenerative elementary strengths. In *Na pole Kulikovo* (1908), Blok's Russian steppe was waiting again for these invaders, and whereas the Russian army—the masses' one—was still lying dormant, the Mongolian army was constituted with Russian intellectuals. In Blok's *Skify*, intellectuals carrying the nostalgia of Europe were torn between revolutionary barbarians (Huns) and Europeans. In this poem Blok warned Europe against a revolutionary radicalization that could hide another much more terrifying one: if Europe wouldn't accept the assistance Russia offers, the latter would launch Mongols on her.

In 1905, Vladimir Briusov (1873–1924), a future member of the Scythian movement, also sang in *Griadushch gunny* the death of Europe and the Barbarians' return. His works were a hymn to strength and toughness, to old cruel empires and young warriors impregnated with bravery. The Revolution was glorified as a rejuvenating phenomenon and a wild burst of national energy. The novelist Boris Pil'niak (1894–1937) also described it as the expression of elementary violence, the return of the pagan Russian primitive popular foundation, which was previous to Christianization. The Revolution was a childbirth marked by convulsions, animality, instinct, and sex. In his numerous novels, Pil'niak played the "yellow peril" card while describing Russia as a second China: a Chinese reality was hidden behind every Russian aspect, and Russia appeared as a vast chessboard on which Asia's pawns advanced.

In 1916–17, the manifesto "The Scythians" (Belyi, Blok, Ergenii Zamiatin (1884–1937), Ivanov-Razumnik, Lev Chestov (1866–1938), Sergei A. Esenin, etc.) constituted the most revealing example of this situation reversal: Russians were presented as Asian and non-European warriors and as barbarians from the West; their rural, wild, pagan Russia was the place for eschatology. The Scythian movement wanted to achieve fusion between people and intelligentsia to prepare the advent of the "new City." Its neopopulist ideologist, Ivanov-Razumnik (1878–1946), took Herzen's idea that socialism, as Christianity in its time, would come and sweep over the old world. The end of the latter was guaranteed therefore by Russia's Asiatism. The Revolution was humanity's liberation from materialism, capitalism, and state: the Scythes' anti-westernalism prepared for the National Bolshevism.

Dmitry Merezhkovskii, Belyi, and Blok partook, each in his own way, in this fear/desire of the Mongol surge. If the first hoped for a Christian solution, the second tinged his discourse with Buddhist and Hindu motives, and the third had the least ideologically constructed but most poetically elaborated discourse. The "Turanism" of Belyi, Asiatism of futurists, and "Scythianism" of the poetic vanguard attempted, with this new terminology, to define Russia again through its differences from Europe. They constituted the first achievement of thought about its otherness from Europe and revealed the Asian elements of Russia. Eurasianism would be the second one.

THE AMBIGUITY OF THE PRE-REVOLUTIONARY
RUSSIAN APPEAL TO THE ORIENT

At the beginning of the century the Russian interest in Asia was multiform: if it had some political and scientific aspects (to deepen Russian knowledge of Asia), it expressed itself mainly through literature and the culturalist currents calling for bringing together or even fusion with oriental peoples. These few years marked a turning point in Russian identitary discourse: accustomed to rejecting Europe in order to claim to emanate from the Slavic or Byzantine world, Russian intellectuals turned for the first time, from a symbolic point of view, toward the real "antithesis" of the West, Asia. This thematic, which appeared in Russia in Mongolian terminology, knew a spectacular reversal: born from nightmares of certain thinkers and fear of the "yellow people," it was brutally changed into a symbol of regeneration, an incarnation of a Russianness that would finally be revealed to itself. Asia then became the natural narrative space of Russia.

The idea of a "yellow peril," which was also present in the West at that time, gave Russia a European nation's position in its consideration of Asia, apprehended as foreign, diabolic, and nearly extra-human. The narrative rebirth of Asia under the shape of Scythism made Russia pass on the other side: it became integrated into Orient and opposed the West from then on in the name of a "not civilized" space carrying a regenerative strength. This double movement of nearly physical disgust and mystical attraction toward Asia would be at the center of the Eurasianist contradictions.

Eurasianism would also use the political tradition of pan-Mongolism: Asia always remained bound to the advent of an eschatological and totalitarian kingdom. If the latter was first discerned as a negative phenomenon—Asia announcing the Antichrist's arrival—it thereafter became positive: after the apocalypse would come the time of Christ's Kingdom, of the elected people of God and the renewal. Totalitarianism found not only a religious recognition but an oriental expression and illustration. By its place in literature, art, and historiography of the time, the pan-Mongolism myth constituted one of Russia's restlessness modes: the Mongol was an irrational and fascinating element of Russian otherness in its relation to Europe, a Russia corrupted by an Europeanity that numerous intellectuals viewed as deeply foreign.

THE GENESIS OF EURASIANISM
BEFORE THE REVOLUTION

The stabilization of the Bolshevik regime after the civil war was going to cause, in the emigration, a deepening and theoretical structuring of these orientalizing ideas. The Eurasianist ideology, which was born in exile during the interwar years in Prague, Berlin and in Paris, led by strong personalities such as Prince Nikolai S. Trubetskoi (1890–1938), linguist and ethnographer, and Petr N. Savitskii (1895–1968), geographer and economist, was the Russian emigration's most original thought. It combined philosophy, reflections about identity, and politics. Intellectually extremely fertile, it had violent controversies with its objectors (Berdiaev, Petr Mikhailovich Bitsili (1879–1953), Georgii V. Florovskii (1893–1979), Aleksandr A. Kizevetter, Paul Miliukov (1859–1943), etc.) as well as internal dissensions, in particular when some of its protagonists rallied to the Soviet Union in the 1930s (for example, the "Clamart split" movement, which had been publishing for the Marxist weekly *Evraziia*).

Eurasianists tried to drive this Russian identity quest to its end by expressing it as the cult of an oriental alterity. They deliberately prolonged the Asian fashion of the beginning of the century. Numerous Eurasianists belonged to the generation of the 1890s: they spent their childhoods in Russia and studied there, mainly in St. Petersburg (except Trubetskoi) in the academic liberal circle, where they were receptive to the orientalist theories. Thus, if Eurasianism was formed in 1920–21, some of its partisans of the first generation had begun to publish "pre-Eurasianist" texts ten years earlier. One of the main protagonists of the movement, Trubetskoi, in his introduction to *Evropa i chelovechestvo*, recognized that "ideas which are expressed [in this book] arose in my conscience more than ten years ago" (Trubetskoi 1996: 45) in the Muscovite intellectual circles of the 1910s. These circles based their analysis on a multidimensional Asia, on scientific and mystical aspects. His father, Sergei N. Trubetskoi, a friend of Vladimir Soloviev, took again the theme of the Russian struggle with the Mongol world.

From adolescence, Trubetskoi had been interested in mythology and Caucasian and paleo-Siberian folklore. His orientalistic tendencies appeared in his youth: he compared the paleo-Asian and Finno-Ugrian languages, connected old Slavs more to the Orient than to the West, and in 1905 created the Zyrianic Society, which aimed to preserve the Zyrian language. In 1907 he wrote a work on kamchadals languages and met with paleo-Siberian anthropologists. Between 1910 and 1913 he stayed several times in the Caucasus and gave lectures at Tbilisi about Caucasian language philology, in particular about the Ossete language. In 1912 he got a chair at the university. An active member of the linguistic circle of Moscow, Trubetskoi didn't limit himself to linguistics and literature but widened his researches to mythology, folklore, and ethnography. His first publications announced his future Eurasianist interests: linguistics and folklore, oriental languages of the Empire, Slavism.

Vernadskii also studied in his first thesis the Russian progression into Siberia and elaborated a theory on space and time in Siberia. According to him, different historical times were simultaneously present in the Russian space; so this space could not be placed in a univocal manner on a linear temporal ladder. Thanks to Siberia, Russia would become the biggest continuous territory on the planet under only one power; it would have unique properties, specific to the universe: the farther one sees, the more one goes up in time. Vernadskii also specified a relation between space and time: 1000 verstes distance was equivalent to 100 years back. Russia could thus be an object of astronomical science: Russo-Siberian experience becomes a reference for the rest of the universe. There was not only an asynchrony between center and periphery, which were living at different times, but a spatial and countable materialization of times of Russia (Vernadskii 1914).

Savitskii wrote about Russian Empire specifics as he was still the foreign affairs minister P. B. Struve's secretary, in the General Wrangel government. According to him, two kinds of empire could exist. The first, essentially welded by political relations, was continental and conveyed the model of the Roman Empire; the second, maritime and mainly economic, appeared as a leveler of the cultures it dominated and was based on the British model. Only the first, to which of course Russia was referring, was an imperialism Savitskii considered healthy: it was able to create a supranational culture and contribute to the progress of humanity; it was a particular type of macro-state that widened its national culture beyond its geo-ethnic borders. A number of Eurasianist ethnographical and historiographical discourses used this differentiation between imperialism (positive and Eurasian) and colonialism (negative and European).

The Revolution, civil war, and exile were not the only things that gave birth to Eurasianism. Eurasianism was inspired by the Asian fashion of the beginning of the century but radicalized it. Eurasianists pursued their predecessors' ambiguousness by citing proximity to Asia while refusing it as a model for Russia. This paradoxical game, extolling the rehabilitation of non-European cultures and praising their "absence of civilization," revealed the instrumental and passive character of the discourse on Orient. Eurasianists would innovate, however, by putting in the heart of Russian identity and history the Mongol world, nomadic and formerly rejected to the profit of sedentary Asia.

THE EURASIANISTS' ORIENTALISM AND ITS LIMITS

Eurasianism knew how to create an original interaction between geographist ideology, philosophy of history, and orientalism. It developed a positive but general discourse about Orient: Russia would be closer to Asia than to Europe, Orthodoxy would be an oriental religion, Islam,

Buddhism and Hinduism were appreciated for their mysticism, "fundamentalism," and "organicism."

> Is it possible to find in Russia people who don't have khazar or polovtsi, tatar or bachkir, mordve or tchouvache blood? Are there many Russians who are completely devoided of the oriental mind, its mystic, its love of contemplation, its contemplative laziness? In the Russian popular masses one notices some inclinations toward the popular masses of Orient; by this organic fraternity between the orthodox and the nomad or the Asian, Russia is eventually an orthodoxo-Moslem, orthodoxo-Buddhist country. (Savitskii 1921: 2)

After such a profession of faith, is it possible to doubt the favorable report of the original Eurasianism concerning oriental religions?

Eurasianism of the 1920s constituted many aspects of the unknown Russian version of the western orientalism of the nineteenth and beginning of the twentieth century. It distinguished itself by an anti-western iconoclastic mind with roots in the ambiguous cultural position of Russia toward Europe. According to Russian intellectuals, orientalism was not a simple exoticism and a research of alterity, but an affirmation of its difference with the West. The original Eurasianism was crossed by contradictory ideas as Orient represents a crucial and idenditary topic. All Eurasianists consider themselves more a part of Asia than of Europe. "Our relation to Asia is more intimate and warmer since we have the same origin" (*Evrasiistvo* 1926: 402). It remained to define more precisely ties between Eurasia and Asia and their similarity.

Divergences and polemics then appeared, the most famous and revealing the argument between the Eurasianist movement and the essayist (and specialist on China) Vsevolod N. Ivanov (see Ivanov 1926). The latter contributed to the difficulties in the explanation of Eurasianist thought, which meant to extol Asia while presenting itself as an Orthodox movement. Ivanov thought the only way to have real ideological unity with Asia would be to set Russian religion aside. It would be necessary to notice the duality of Eurasianist discourse. Given the ambiguousness of presenting itself as Asian while actually differentiating itself from it, Eurasianist discourse justified the internal contradiction: According to Eurasianists there were two Russian terms to express the idea of Asia: *aziistvo* or *azia-china*. One could retranscribe this fundamental nuance of Eurasianist thought by differentiating the oriental, built-in, organic, from the Asiatic, outside Russia-Eurasia.

One could notice indeed, in Eurasianist ideas a politicocultural and especially a very clear identitary dichotomy between the Scythian-Siberian world, considered Eurasian, and the near-oriental world judged Asian. The real Asia was an intrinsically foreign world to the Eurasianist identity.

The identity they claim was only constituted by the steppic world: if this world was presented as "typically Asian" (Savitskii 1993: 125), it was only because it actually expressed not Asiatism but Eurasian orientality. There was an outside and an internal Asia to the Russian world, and only the latter embodied the positive picture of Orient. The violence of the religious dismissal (different from spiritual "attraction") in Asia was to be put in parallel with the ambiguous cult of Turanian "civilization absence," as well as with the idea that the third world colonized nations could not identify themselves if they did not have Christian Russia as their leader. Eurasianism cultivated paradoxes and iconoclasm: the "no-culture," "primitivism," "satanism" of non-European and non-Eurasian peoples could be claimed in order to shock the West while being actually rejected by Russia and Orthodoxy.

Relations with Asia weakened Eurasianist thought on the structural unity of the Eurasianist totality: this one was geographically and linguistically presented as enclosed, closed on itself. Actually, two types of relations existed with the non-Eurasian world: total impermeability and discontinuity between Eurasia and Europe, and permeability between Eurasia and Asia. Relations between the latter two hesitated between continuity and discontinuity. The mythified notion of "Orient" permitted a tie to a certain metaphysics and absolute social cult. Asia and its religious realities, a more concrete expression of this "elsewhere" that Eurasianists so much revered, were violently rejected, on the other hand, as a pagan and satanic queerness inassimilable in Russia.

One can thus formalize three Orients in Eurasianist thought: sometimes a near (the third world, the absolute social of the religious) or a foreign (China, the polytheistic religions) Asia; an outside Orient (idential mirror, that meant Iran); and an interior Orient (Turanian world). These three apprehensions of "Orient" allowed Eurasianism to present itself as oriental, to play the Asian card against Europe while preserving a more traditional Orthodox Russian nationalism. It didn't manage to define clearly the border between Eurasia, Asia, Turanism and the Persian world, between identity and alterity in these spaces. This caused the movement to contradict itself, and it was not able to answer the Eurasianist Ivanov's extreme discourse denying the existence of a Eur-Asia. "For Eurasianism, the first and fundamental affirmation in our relations with Orient is the conviction in its autonomous value as another type of culture, whose knowledge is all the more necessary for the Russian conscience since it permits our auto-conscience . . . [because] the Orient for Russia is not exotic or foreign" (Nikitin 1928: 5).

In the first Eurasianist compilation, Savitskii revealed the fundamental paradox of Eurasianism: Russia was already the Orient. Therefore, it could not "go" toward the Orient, but must become more precisely aware of its internal orientality (Savitskii 1921: 1). Eurasianism affirmed the *aziistvo* of Russia but not its *aziachina*, its orientalism but not its Asiatism. Despite the discourse on symbiosis and fusion, Russia's Eurasianists thought Russia did not owe anything to anybody: it was culturally and religiously the Orient by itself. The theory of centrality that was supposed to be elaborated by Eurasianism thus showed some difficulties. Were there two or three worlds? If the Eurasianists' Russia lay midway between "Europe" and "Asia," it was between "West" and "Orient," since the latter was only another formulation of Russia.

The relation to the Orient led to difficult discussions within the Eurasianist movement. In the 1930s, the young generation, politically more committed and less intellectual, challenged the founders' romanticism which no longer matched "the air of the time." "Eurasianism deeply appraises cultures of peoples of Asia but it has never been tempted to consider itself to belong to these cultures" ("Buria nad Aziei" 1932: 2). The nomadic world, without "big" culture, was not the equal of the sedentary world and it was therefore necessary to sustain the Soviet government's sedentarization policy. Savitskii and Alekseev, the last members of the first generation, still wanted to rehabilitate the nomadic world and Orient while remaining more moderate than in the 1920s and recalling that Russia was also turned westward (*Evraziiskie tetradi* 1935: 13–14). The politicization of the movement and its moving closer to Soviet Union were not thus without influence on the iconoclastic and futuristic orientalism of the original Eurasianism.

CONCLUSION

The importance in post-Soviet Russia of identitary thought tying the country to Asia, as well as the revival of geopolitical fashions (geoculturalism and "civilizationism") invites us to question ourselves about older traditions of thinking about Russian imperial expansion: since the second half of the nineteenth century, after the conquest of the Caucasus, Russia has been indissociably binding its imaginary on the Orient with the constitution of a geopolitics that could legitimate the Empire. This geopolitical orientalistic imaginary still remains unknown as it is one of the major stakes of the rediscovery of a memory on Orient anchored in Russia and of epistemological traditions different from the Western traditions. Such a survey permits us to re-place Russian intellectual life in the setting of western intellectual life of this time. It also explains in original ways the traditional debates on the Russian identity: "Orient" is only the reversed mirror of "the West"; the appeal of Asia and discourses on the "yellow peril" reveal the Russian intellectuals' affirmation of a specificity for their country in front of Europe. Russian orientalism is then just one style of thinking about the national identity and is a culturalist cover supposed to legitimize the political orientations as imperialism or authoritarianism.

A better knowledge of the heterogeneous Russian imaginary on the Orient that preceded the foundation of the Eurasianist movement gives a missing historical and theoretical depth to contemporary Russian political questioning, to the nostalgia of the Empire as well as to the new "Eurasianist" legitimations of some post-Soviet states, and the reappropriation of Eurasianist ideas by Turco-Muslim elites in Tatarstan and Central Asia.

The study of the genesis of Eurasianist ideology permits us to avoid clichés and to question ourselves about the intellectual evolution of the Russian world. Eurasianism belongs to currents of thinking with roots in the Russian nineteenth century: the ambiguous relation to the Byzantine empire, conservative pan-Slavism, the "yellow peril" myth at the time of the Russian progression toward Far East, literary pan-Mongolism and Asiatism at the beginning of the century, movements of the Conservative Revolution in the 1920s, and so on. Eurasianism rephrases in its own terms, often in ways disconcerting to western thought, the Russian intellectuals' questioning of the founding of the identity of their country and their own identity. The resurgence of this movement with the downfall of the Soviet Union fits into the European conservative renewal that started in the United States and the West at the beginning of the 1980s.

BIBLIOGRAPHY

Benningsen, Alexandre and Chantal Lemercier-Quelquejay. 1986. *Sultan Galiev, le père de la révolution tiers-mondiste.* Paris.

Boss, Otto. 1961. *Die Lehre der Eurasier: Ein Beitrag zur russischen Ideengeschichte des 20. Jahrhunderts.* Wiesbaden.

"Buria nad Aziei." 1932. *Svij put'* 2 (April).

Chadaaev, Petr Y. 1970. "Nous sommes situés à l'Orient de l'Europe, cela est positif, mais nous ne fûmes jamais l'Orient pour cela." In *Lettres philosophiques adressés à une dame.* Paris.

Evraziiskie tetradi. 1935. 5: 13–14.

Evraziistvo. 1926. *Evraziistvo: Opyt sistematicheskogo izlozheniia.* Paris.

Guénon, René. 1921. *Le théosophisme: Histoire d'une pseudo-religion.* Paris, 1921.

Hauner, Milan. 1992. *What Is Asia to Us? Russia's Asian Heartland Yesterday and Today.* London.

Ivanov, Vsevolod N. 1926. *My Kul'turnoistoricheskie osnovy rossiiskoi gosudarstvennosti.* Kharbin.

Laruelle, Marlène. 1999. *L'idéologie eurasiste russe ou comment penser l'empire.* Paris.

Layton, Susan. 1994. *Russian Literature and Empire: Conquest of the Caucasus from Pushkin to Tolstoy.* Cambridge.

Nikitin, V. P. "My i Vostok." *Evraziia,* 24 November.

Niqueux, Michel. 1999. "Les différents Orients de la Russie." *Slavica occitania.*

Nivat, Georges. 1966. "Du panmongolisme au mouvement eurasien: Histoire d'un thème millénaire." *Cahiers du monde russe et soviétique.*

Petrovich, Michael B. 1966. *The Emergence of Russian Panslavism, 1850–70.* New York.

Savelli, Dany. 1996. "Le péril jaune et le péril nègre: éléments pour une représentation de la France et de l'Allemagne chez V. Soloviev et A. Biély." In *Transferts culturels triangulaires France-Allemagne-Russie*, ed. Katia Dimtrieva and Michel Espagne. Philologiques 5. Paris. 257–72.

Savitskii, P. N. 1921."Povorot k Vostoku." In *Iskhod k Vostoku: Predchustviia i sversheniia.* Sofia.

——. 1993. "Step' i osedlost'." In *Rossiia mezhdu Evropoi i Aziei.* Moscow.

Trubetskoi, Nikolai Sergeevich. 1996. *Evropa i chelovechestvo.* Trans. Patrick Sériot, *L'Europe et l'humanité.* Liège.

Vernadskii, Georgii V. 1914. "Protiv solntsa: Rasprostranenie russkogo gosudarstva k Vostoku." *Russkaia mysl'* 1.

II. Eurasianism as a Reaction to Pan-Turkism

Stephan Wiederkehr
Translated by Barbara Keller and Ellen Simer

In his 1925 booklet "Nasledie Chingiskhana: Vzgliad na russkuiu istoriiu ne s Zapada, a s Vostoka" (The Legacy of Genghis Khan: A Perspective on Russian History Not from the West but from the East), Nikolai Sergeevich Trubetskoi criticized the Imperial government's policy of forcible Russification in the following words:

> as they merged with the Russian tribe, the Russified Turanians imparted their own characteristics to the Russian people and introduced them into the Russian national psychology, so that together with the Russification of the Turanians there occurred a simultaneous Turanianization of the Russians. From the organic merger of these two elements there arose a new, unique entity, the national Russian type, which is in essence not pure Slavic but Slavo-Turanian. The Russian tribe was created not through the forcible Russification of "indigenous peoples," but through the fraternization of Russians with those peoples. . . . Artificial, government-inspired Russification was a product of complete ignorance of the historical essence of Russia-Eurasia, the result of forgetting the spirit of her national traditions. Consequently, this seemingly nationalistic policy did great damage to Russia's historical interests. (1925b: 248)

In the same year he published an essay entitled "O turanskom elemente v russkoi kul'tur" ("On the Turanian Element in Russian Culture"), in which he wrote:

> Drawing the conclusions of all that has been said about the role of the Turanian ethnopsychological traits in the Russian national character it can be said that altogether this role has been positive. . . . We are rightfully proud of our Turanian ancestors no less than of our Slavic ancestors and we are obliged to gratitude to both of them. The consciousness of not only belonging to the Aryan but also to the Turanian psychological type is indispensable for any Russian striving to personal and national self-knowledge. (1925a: 375)

Why did a leader of the Eurasian movement take such a positive attitude toward Turan and Turanians? And what does this have to do with the official policy toward non-Russian nationalities in the Russian Empire and, let me add, in the Soviet Union?

The explanation that I should like to offer is that Eurasianism can be understood as a reaction to Pan-Turanian and Pan-Turkic ideas, which in the first quarter of the twentieth century were discussed in Russia as well as in Western Europe and the Ottoman Empire. After spreading among the Turkic Muslims of Russia in the second half of the nineteenth century, Pan-Turkism was perceived as a danger to the territorial integrity of Russia both by politicians and in public debate. In the aftermath of World War I, when Eurasianism arose, the multinational Habsburg and Ottoman Empires had collapsed and the Russian Empire was likely to fall apart into its national constituents as well. At the same time, supra-national ideologies such as Czechoslovakism and Yugoslavism had led to the formation of states. In these circumstances, I argue, the Eurasians consciously constructed an ideology intended to safeguard the territorial integrity of the multinational Russian Empire despite its takeover by the Bolsheviks, thereby integrating its Turkic population by redefining the term Turan to fit their own aims. In this sense—as an ideology intended to undermine potential secession demands of Russia's Turks—I consider Eurasianism a reaction to Pan-Turkism.

With this new interpretation, I do not intend to question either rec-ognized work on the intellectual roots of Eurasianism or the argument of Patrick Sériot, who relates the emergence of Eurasianism to the emer-gence of structuralism in linguistics (see Böss 1961; Riasanovsky 1967; Luks 1986; Hagemeister 1989: 417–57; Alevras 1996; Vandalkovskaia 1997; Laruelle 1999; Wiederkehr 2000. See also the exhaustive bibliog-raphy *O Evrazii i evraziitsakh* (1997: 73–91); Sériot (1999. I intend rather to add an aspect that has been largely overlooked until now (see Urchanova 1995; Laruelle 1999: 294; Doronchenkov 2001: 138).

Modern research makes an analytical distinction between Pan-Turkism and Pan-Turanianism. The former refers to the idea of the unification of all peoples of Turkic origin; the latter refers to the unification of Turkic peoples w ith the Finno-Ugric peoples, for whom a common ancient homeland in "Turan" is ascribed. This Urheimat of Turan is to be found in an imprecisely defined region of the Central Asian steppe (Landau 1995: 1f).[1] The logical consequence of both ideologies was the ultimate disintegration of the Russian Empire due to the secession of its Turkic (and possibly Finno-Ugric) peoples, and their uniting with the Turkic peoples of the Ottoman Empire to form one state. Pan-Turanianism in the modern sense of the word has not achieved any political significance,

---

[1] On the etymology and geographical and political use of the term Turan, see Minorsky (1934); Yalçinkaya (1997: 431–33). In the nineteenth century some linguists presumed a Turanian language family, a position Minorsky (954) already called outdated.

and the importance of Pan-Turkism was also overrated (on Pan-Turanianism in Hungary, see, however, Kessler 1967).

These recent findings, however, are less relevant to my approach than is contemporary perception. (See Landau 1995; Geraci 1997: 151; Hyman 1997; Roy 1997: 75–78; Adam 2000. On Pan-Turkism in the Russian Empire and the Soviet Union see also Arsharuni and Gabidullin 1931; von Mende 1936; Hostler 1957; Arnakis 1960; Zenkovsky 1967; Önder 1977; Mukhammetdinov 1996. The Armenian point of view is reflected in Zarevand 1926, 1930, 1971.) In late nineteenth- and early twentieth-century sources the term Pan-Turanianism was often used in the sense of Pan-Turkism. There was no clear distinction between the two ideologies among their proponents and contemporary observers. This is also true for the writings of the Eurasians, in which reference is usually made to "Turan," "Turanian," and "Pan-Turanianism."

If Eurasianism was a reaction to Pan-Turkism, which is my contention, it was a reaction to the way the latter was perceived at the beginning of the twentieth century. Therefore in the first section of this chapter, after an overview over Pan-Turkism on the basis of current research, I have to reconstruct its contemporary image on the basis of Russian and Western language sources. These influenced Russian consciousness more than publications in widely unknown Turkic languages could.[2] In the second section I analyze the Eurasians' attempts to redefine the term Turan, to create a supranational ideology, in order to integrate the multinational Russian Empire and at the same time delegitimize the idea of uniting all Turks in one state.

PAN-TURKISM—THREATENING THE RUSSIAN EMPIRE? PAN-TURKISM AND MODERNIZATION OF RUSSIA'S MUSLIM TURKS: THE EMERGENCE OF PAN-TURKISM IN RUSSIA

Pan-Turkism emerged in the second half of the nineteenth century as a diaspora ideology among the Turks of the Russian Empire. It originated in resistance to the imperial government's Russification and "civilization" policies (on the imperial government's "civilization policy," see Baberowski 1999). Propagated by the liberal Turkic *intelligentsiia*, it was from the beginning directed against autocratic rule and connected with modernization and secularization (Landau 1995: 7–10; Mukhammetdinov 1996: 27; Baberowski 2000: 392–94). At the turn of the century, Turkic peoples

---

[2] As I am not able to read Turkic languages I am in the same position as most observers of the Pan-Turkic movement at the beginning of the twentieth century.

made up some 11 percent of the population of the Russian Empire. Around 85 percent of Muslim Russia was Turkic, and about 90 percent of this population was Muslim (Zenkovsky 1967: 9; Landau 1995: 7). Thus Pan-Turkic and Pan-Islamic activities went hand in hand (Zenkovsky 1967: vii; Adam 2000: 204).

In the second half of the nineteenth century, a portion of the Tatar bourgeoisie and a few members of the liberal, western-educated Turkic *intelligentsiia* came to believe that the Turkic and Muslim populations of the Russian Empire would be able to preserve their own identity among the Russians only if they could overcome their traditional social order and develop a common national consciousness. The creation of a common Turkic literary language and the development of a secular education system in this language seemed to them to be a decisive means of modernization. The Crimean Tatar Ismail Bey Gasprinskii (1851–1914) was a particularly active spokesman for this idea through his newspaper *Tercüman* (*Interpreter*), founded in 1883. Gasprinsky's outspoken attitude toward the Russian state was conciliatory in the last decades of the nineteenth century. In his *Russkoe musul'manstvo* (*Russian Islam*) and "Russko-Vostochnoe soglashenie: Mysli, zamietki i pozhelaniia" ("Russo-Oriental Relations: Thoughts, Notes, and Desires"), he emphasized that belonging to Russia was advantageous to the modernizing projects of its Muslim Turks (Gasprinskii 1881, 1896; see also Fisher 1988; Lazzerini 1988, 1989; Ortayli 1991; Iordan and Chervonnaia 1994).

As a consequence of the 1905 Revolution, newspapers, magazines, and journals written in Turkic languages and containing Pan-Turkic ideology were founded in great numbers and given the opportunity to expand in the Russian Empire (Bennigsen and Lemercier-Quelquejay 1964: 47–52). As a result of the three Muslim Congresses in 1905 and 1906, a political party representing the interests of Russia's Muslims in the newly created Duma was founded: Ittifak-ul-Muslimin (Zenkovsky 1967: 40–54; Landau 1995: 11–13). The social base of a modern Turkic national consciousness, however, a secularly educated middle class, remained underdeveloped. Most Turkic Muslims were hardly affected by modernization. They continued to live in traditional nomadic and agrarian societies. The majority of the Muslim clergy strongly resisted the secularization of the educational system and opposed the "new method" (*usul-i cedid*) (Zenkovsky 1967: 35–36, 272; Baberowski 2000: 405–6). Within the Western-educated Turkic *intelligentsiia*, Pan-Turkism competed with liberal Pan-Islamism and the narrower national constructs of individual Turkic peoples such as the Volga Tatars, Crimean Tatars, or Azeri (Allworth 1990: 240–5; Altstadt 1992: 69–71; Swietochowski 1996; Kirimli 1996; Kendirbay 1997); Yémelianova 1997; Noack 2000).

Thus, until World War I, the Russian Pan-Turkists, aware of their own weakness (and writing under Czarist censorship), adhered to a policy of Realpolitik, making no secession demands and striving instead toward totally equal rights within a future democratic Russia. Therefore a close collaboration arose in the Duma between the liberal Kadets and the Ittifak Party (Amaeva 1998: 9 and passim). The main focus of Pan-Turkism prior to 1914 was the spiritual and cultural union of all Turkic peoples, existing state borders for the moment not being challenged. While (re)writing their own past and creating a national myth, the Pan-Turkists revalued the tribes of the steppe, drawing a heroic picture of Genghis Khan and other Mongol leaders (Zenkovsky 1967: 109; Mukhammetdinov 1996: 95, 114–15).

PAN-TURKISM IN THE OTTOMAN EMPIRE

In the Ottoman Empire prior to 1908, Pan-Turkism was less important than Ottomanism and Pan-Islamism. After the Young Turk Revolution, however, several influential Pan-Turkic organizations and publications (*Türk Dernegi, Türk Bilgi Dernegi, Türk Yurdu, Türk Ocagi*) were founded (Landau 1995: 39–42) The territorial losses in southeastern Europe during the Balkan Wars (1912/1913) enhanced their impact on the new government (Landau 1995: 47–49). A number of prominent Turkic Muslims, who had emigrated from the Russian Empire after autocracy had again tightened in 1907, played a central role (Dumont 1974; Georgeon 1988; Adam 2002).

One of them, the Tatar intellectual leader Yusuf Akçura (1876–1935), proposed the first political manifesto of Pan-Turkism as early as 1904. In his article "Les trois systèmes politiques" ("Three Systems of Government"), anonymously printed in Cairo, he rejected Ottomanism and Pan-Islamism in favor of Pan-Turkism, designating Russia as the only, and surmountable, impediment to the unification of all Turkic peoples (Akçura (1904), 105–6). Azeri Turk Ahmet Agayev (1869–1939) became an active polemicist for Pan-Turkism in Turkey as well. Ali Hüseyinzade (1864–1941), an Azeri teaching at the Military School of Medicine in Istanbul, wrote a poem, "Turan," which Ziya Gökalp (1876–1924) later called the "first manifestation of the ideal of Pan-Turanism" (Gökalp 1923: 5). A writer and sociologist born in the Ottoman Empire and a leading figure of the Pan-Turkic movement, Hüseyinzade, published "Turan" in 1911, stating that

> For the Turks, Fatherland means neither Turkey, nor Turkestan.
> Fatherland is a large and eternal country—Turan! (quoted in Landau 1995: 37)

The outbreak of World War I changed the prospects of Pan-Turkism as all its ideological objectives seemed suddenly achievable by political and military means.

WORLD WAR I, THE RUSSIAN REVOLUTIONS, AND AFTERWARD

In another poem, written in the first months of World War I, Gökalp openly called for the destruction of the Russian Empire:

> The land of the enemy shall be devastated
> Turkey shall be enlarged and become Turan. (quoted in Heyd 1950: 128)

In 1915 Tekin Alp (really M. Cohen), an author close to the Young Turks, explicitly advocated the destruction of the Russian Empire with the support of Germany in order to achieve a "union of all Turks of the world" under the leadership of the Ottomans (Alp 1915: 12). He stated that the Russian Turks

> expect only one thing from the Ottoman Turks: . . . The development of a national culture and a national civilization requires . . . an independent government. If Russian despotism is overthrown by the opposing German, Austrian and Turkish armies—which is to be hoped—then thirty to forty million Turks will have their independence. Together with the ten million Ottoman Turks this amounts to a sizeable population of fifty million that can grow into a great, new civilization. . . . All of the desires of the Turkic nation are aimed at this high objective, the establishment of a new, national Turkic civilization. (97)

According to Alp's pamphlet, the alliance between the Ottoman Empire and Germany in World War I was the conscious expression of an unconscious thousand-year-old brotherhood in arms against their common enemy, the Slavs (46). The Young Turk proclamation on the entry of the Ottoman Empire into the war contained Pan-Turkic statements. The military offensives in the Caucasus in 1914/1915 and after the Russian Revolution proved that these statements were not merely rhetorical (Swietochowski 1985: 76–77; Landau 1995: 53). Akçura, Hüseyinzade, and other emigrants from Russia were propagating their Pan-Turkic ideals in Western Europe during World War I (Landau 1995: 54; Kirimli 1996: 203–7).

Following the February 1917 Revolution, the majority of Turkic Muslims still seemed to prefer autonomy within a democratic Russian state to secession (Zenkovsky 1967: 279–82; Iskhakov 1999: 429). But there was a chain of anti-Russian or anti-Soviet uprisings lasting from the Central Asian revolt of 1916 to the Basmachi movement in the early 1920s. Various ephemeral local Turkic governments passing declarations of autonomy or independence after the October Revolution created a confused situation (cf. Pipes 1964; Smith 1999). After World War I the state ideology of Kemalism and the idea of an independent national state in a reduced territory took the place of Pan-Turkism in Turkey. Matters were far from clear, however.

Evidence of this confusion were the actions of former Ottoman minister of war Enver Pasha, who changed sides. Enver was sent to Central Asia by the Bolsheviks after his participation in the Congress of the Peoples of the East in Baku (1920). Instead of fighting anti-Soviet resistance, Enver turned into its leader, under whom Turkish troops fought in the southern territories of the former Russian Empire. He was killed in action against the Soviets in 1922 (Hostler 1957: 154–55; Dumont 1975; Masayuki 1991). There were also Pan-Turkic ideas within the Bolshevik Party, where they were condemned as bourgeois nationalistic deviations. The most prominent was Sultan Galiev's idea of a Socialist Republic of Turan, intended to be a springboard to spread the revolution in Asia (Hostler 1957: 160–68; Bennigsen and Lemercier-Quelquejay 1960; Bennigsen and Wimbush 1979: 62–68; Landau 1995: 16–19; Smith 1999: 126–30, 228–38).

The Pan-Turkist vision of uniting all Turks in one state, which implied the destruction of the Russian Empire, was never realized. In retrospect, we can say that it was never even close to being realized. In the early 1920s when the Eurasian movement emerged, however, the future was still open. Neither the Soviet Union nor Kemalist Turkey had consolidated, and military operations in Central Asia had not ended.

CONTEMPORARY PERCEPTIONS OF PAN-TURKISM IN THE FIRST QUARTER OF THE TWENTIETH CENTURY

Modern research emphasizes the weakness of the Pan-Turkic movement (see Mukhammetdinov 1996: 30; Geraci 1997: 150–52; Roy 1997: 75–78; Adam 2000). At the beginning of the twentieth century, however, it was familiar to the public in Western Europe and Russia. Its potential for breaking up the Russian Empire, whose collapse many feared and others hoped for, was debated in important magazines and newspapers. In 1907 Hungarian orientalist Armin Vambéry warned of the immense consequences of the possible unification of all Turks in one nation of 50 million people (Vambéry 1907: 91; see also 1905, 1906). On the eve of World War I the French *Revue du Monde Musulman* presented its readers with a series of well-informed articles on Pan-Turkism and related political ideologies in Russia and the Ottoman Empire (among others, X 1912, 1913). One of these articles—quoting Akçura—openly stated that the realization of Pan-Turkic ambitions presupposed the collapse of the Russian Empire (X 1913: 200).

Western attention to and writing on the Pan-Turkic movement reached its peak during and immediately after World War I, when the multinational empires collapsed and new states with new borders were created. In this connection the impact of Alp's French and German pamphlets on European perception of Pan-Turkism cannot be overrated (Risal 1912; Alp 1915). Those who did not promote Pan-Turkism linked the Ottomans' fighting on the side of Germany to Pan-Turkic aspirations as Alp had done:

> Of course the Pan-Turanians recognized that anything like a realization of their ambitious dreams was dependent upon the virtual destruction of the Russian Empire. . . . They realized that Germany and Austria were fast drifting toward war with Russia and they felt that such a cataclysm, however perilous, would also offer most glorious possibilities. These Pan-Turanian aspirations undoubtedly had a great deal to do with driving Turkey into the great War on the side of the Central Empires. (Stoddard 1921: 167)

In Western eyes there was no doubt that the aim of Pan-Turkism was the destruction of the Russian Empire in order to unite all Turks in one state (Turkey 1917: 112, 131; Mouvement 1917: 174, 181; Manual 1918: 11); Pears 1918: 377). Critics of Pan-Turkism often repeated that it only served Germany's expansionist ambitions (Mouvement 1917: 182; Turkey 1917: 100–102; Czaplika 1918: 9). The realization of the Pan-Turkist program was not seen as the most probable outcome (X 1913: 200; Manual 1918: 222–22; Turkey 1917: 125); Czaplika 1918: 108–10; Wipert 1922: 210, but it was certainly discussed as a realistic possibility.

Russian publicists and the Czarist government saw a threat in Pan-Turkism, too. Interior Minister Petr A. Stolypin initiated a "Special Meeting for Working Out Measures to Counteract the Tatar-Muslim Influence in the Volga Region," which took place in 1910. The report on this meeting copiously used the terms "Pan-Turkism" and "Pan-Islamism," proposing several measures against the spread of these ideas (Geraci 1997: 142–43). In a secret internal circular sent to the governor of the Tavrida guberniia in 1911, Stolypin called for the expulsion of "emissaries of the Young Turks" who were allegedly spreading Pan-Turkic propaganda while disguised as merchants and pilgrims (Kirimli 1996: 189–91). Muslim intellectuals and publishers accused of disseminating Pan-Turkic or Pan-Islamic ideas were repressed. In a 1912 show trial the heads of a reformist Muslim school were sentenced for teaching "Pan-Turkic and Pan-Islamic ideas" (Geraci 1997: 150–52; Noack 2000): 370–71).

Within state administration, the existence of a strong Pan-Turkic and Pan-Islamic movement was taken for granted (Mouhammetchine 1996; 89–92; Adam 2000: 195–96 points out that before World War Russian authorities perceived Pan-Islamism as more dangerous than Pan-Turkism). An internal circular of the Department Politsii dated 1911 stated:

The most important principle around which the Pan-Islamic movement is gathering and which is so to speak its soul is the unification of the whole Muslim world in political and economic respects under the lead of Turkey aiming ultimately at founding a Pan-Turkic republic. At the moment the leading Turkish and Russian Muslim publicists have more than ever increased their efforts to find tribes belonging to the same race as they do, in order to arouse hatred against Russia in them and leading them into a future common Muslim federation. (quoted in Noack 2000: 363)

A report of the same department the following year noted that

All of the sympathies of the Muslims of the North Caucasus and Transcaucasia are on the side of Turkey and Persia as countries of the same religion, with whom they dream of uniting at the first favorable opportunity. (quoted in Arsharuni and Gabidullin 1931: 109)

In the Duma, deputy Sadri Maksudov stood up for the interests of Russia's Muslim Turks in a number of speeches rejecting the accusation of Pan-Turkic aspirations and disloyalty toward the Russian state (Amaeva 1998: 98 and passim). In the parliamentary debate of February 26, 1911 he declared:

The right-wing parties . . . denounce us with the government as if our educational movement had an anti-state character; they ascribe to us certain anti-state objectives, they accuse us of . . . (a voice from the right of Pan-Islamism) . . . that's it, they accuse us of that, us, the Muslims, of connections with certain foreign organizations—Pan-Islamic and Pan-Turkic ones—and so on. I assure you, however, that among the Muslims there are no such secret organizations that pursue anti-state objectives; I assure you of that and if any of you here or of the government representatives who are absent now assert only one single fact proving that there exists any such organization among the Muslims . . ., I shall give you my hand to cut off in the true sense of the word. (Amaeva 1998: 155)[3]

The emotional tone of Maksudov's statement as well as the interruption are evidence of Pan-Turkism being debated with commitment in late Imperial Russia. A 1909 article in *Russkaia mysl'*, one of the *tol'stye zhurnaly*, dealing with the "Muslim question" warned of the unwanted effect of anti-Muslim and anti-Turkic measures of the Russian government, which would strengthen the common consciousness of Russia's Muslim Turks (Alisov 1909: 42–43). In this context the author emphasized that the unity of Russia's Muslims was based not only on common religion but also on common language and nationality: "there exists a common Turkic consciousness and it gives a wonderful natural ground for a unification movement" (39).

---

[3] Another of Maksudov's speeches was interrupted by a deputy crying "Go to Turkey" (Amaeva 1998: 75).

The Saint Petersburg journal *Mir islama* informed its Russian readers on Pan-Turkism at length ("Panislamizm i Pantiurkizm" 1913). Among many other things, they were told that

> a large number of students [in Turkey] with pleasure call themselves "true and legitimate descendents of Genghis" . . . they are enthusiastic about the idea that Genghis and Timur were not barbarians, but on the contrary, founding fathers of civilization. (617)

There certainly was a Pan-Turkic movement crossing the borders of the Ottoman and Russian empires at the beginning of the twentieth century. Its potential for breaking up the Russian state, however, was much exaggerated by its contemporaries. Some modern authors argue that Russian preoccupation with Pan-Turkism served other political ends (Altstadt 1992: 70; Geraci 1997: 150–52; Yalçinkaya 1997: 432–33). On contemporary Muslim reactions see Adam (2000: 194–94). Nevertheless, the Eurasian movement emerged in a period of great uncertainty. During World War I, Pan-Turkic ambitions had come closer to realization than ever before. Russia was still likely to follow the fate of the Habsburg and Ottoman empires, which had collapsed as new states with new borders formed in their former territories. So, creating a new ideology aimed at integrating the Russian Empire by undermining potential secession demands of Russia's Muslim Turks seemed opportune to Russian emigrants at the time (see Nikitine 1922).

EURASIAN NATION-BUILDING AGAINST THE CHALLENGE OF PAN-TURKISM: THE EURASIAN PERCEPTION OF PAN-TURKISM

The Eurasians did not mention Pan-Turkic authors in their works and rarely polemicized against Pan-Turkism directly. They were, however, aware of the Pan-Turkic movement from the beginning. There are a number of plausible reasons for this assumption.

First, the pre-revolutionary Russian debate on the issue was conducted in important publications as well as in the Duma and state administration, to which the Eurasians had close family ties (Adam 2000: 189–90). Second, the leading Eurasians are highly likely to have learned about Pan-Turkism through their scholarly work. Trubetskoi devoted his earliest writings to the folklore of the non-Slavic peoples of Russia, showing a strong scholarly interest in their affairs (Liberman 1991: 298–304). Petr Nikolaevich Savitskii, who introduced geopolitical categories into Eurasianism and was preoccupied with long-term socioeconomic trends, must have been aware of the prospects of Turkic modernization. In addition, Russia's possible loss of Central Asia was a main topic in geopolitical writing of the time (Hauner 1992; Alevras 1996). Third, the Eurasians became eyewitnesses to the Pan-Turkic activities of Russia's Muslims on their emigration route. Like many other white emigrants, they stayed in the Crimea or in Transcaucasia for some time during the war and the Russian Revolutions, and ultimately passed through Constantinople before reaching their final destinations of exile. There they came across Pan-Turkic emigrants from the former Russian Empire (Mukhammetdinov 1996: 40; Doronchenkov 2001: 30–31, 69, 116; see, e.g., Trubetskoi's letter to Jakobson, 12/12/1920; 1975: 4 or the memories of Togan 1997: 471). Fourth, as mentioned earlier, when they arrived in exile, the Western European debate on Pan-Turkism had just reached its peak.

There is a further, decisive argument for Eurasian familiarity with Pan-Turkism and the idea of Turan from the beginning. In the very first text of the Eurasian movement, Trubetskoi spoke out against any kind of "pan-isms," referring to Turanians. His "Evropa i chelovech-estvo" ("Europe and Mankind") (1920) ended as follows:

> the intelligentsia of all the non-Romano-Germanic nations . . . must never . . . be distracted by nationalism or by partial, local solutions such as pan-Slavism and other "pan-isms." One must always remember that setting up an opposition between the Slavs and the Teutons or the Turanians and the Aryans will not solve the problem. There is only one true opposition: the Romano-Germans and all other Peoples of the World—*Europe and Mankind*. (Trubetskoi 1920: 104/1991: 63–64, italics original)

"TRUE" AND "FALSE" NATIONALISM— THE EURASIAN POINT OF VIEW

The questions of national self-knowledge (*natsional'noe samopoznanie*) and national self-awareness (*natsional'noe samosoznanie*) took a central place in Eurasianism, which was both a kind and a theory of nationalism. The Eurasians were obviously seeking an ideology integrating the multinational Russian Empire, as they stated in the introduction to their first collection, *Iskhod k Vostoku* (*Exodus to the East*) (Savitskii 1921):

> In worldly matters our mood is the mood of nationalism. But we do not want to confine it within the narrow bounds of national chauvinism . . . we direct our nationalism not merely toward "Slavs," but toward a whole circle of peoples of the "Eurasian" world, among whom the Russian people has the central position. This inclusion of a whole circle of East European and Asian peoples into the mental sphere of the culture of the Russian world has its roots, it seems to us, in even measure, in a secret "affinity of souls"—which makes Russian culture comprehensible and close to these peoples and conversely establishes the fecundity of their participation in the Russian enterprise—and in the commonality of their economic interest, the economic interrelationship of these peoples. Russians and those who belong to the peoples of "the Russian world" are neither Europeans

> nor Asians. Merging with the native element of culture and life which sur-
> rounds us, we are not ashamed to declare ourselves *Eurasians*. (Savitskii
> 1921: vii, slightly modified; trans. *Exodus* 1996: 4, italics original)

A passage in Trubetskoi's letter to Roman Jakobson written the same
year makes clear how consciously Eurasian ideology was constructed to
achieve political aims: "the term "Eurasia" [is] maybe not very felicitous,
but it catches the eye and [is] therefore suitable for purposes of agita-
tion" (Trubetskoi to Jakobson, 28/7/1921/1975: 21).

Trubetskoi contributed an essay entitled "Ob istinnom i lozhnom natsionalizme" ("On True and False Nationalism") to the first Eurasian collection. In this article he justified Eurasian nationalism by refining his
general theory of nationalism formulated for the first time in "Europe
and Mankind" (Trubetskoi 1920/1991; cf. Riassnovsky 1964). Advocating
radical cultural relativism, Trubetskoi repudiated the notion of a "universal human culture," which according to him was nothing but disguised "Roman-Germanic [Eurocentric] chauvinism," based on "egocentric
psychology" (Trubetskoi (1920: 71–72/1991: 66–67; cf. Trubetskoi
1920/1995 passim. The "non-Romano-Germanic" nations, on the other
hand, suffered from "excentricity"; that is, they considered "Romano-
Germanic" culture a landmark and objective to achieve instead of striving toward self-knowledge. As Trubetskoi put it,

> The first duty of every non-Romano-Germanic nation is to overcome every
> trace of egocentricity in itself; the second is to protect itself against the
> deception of "universal human civilization" and against all efforts to become
> "genuinely European" at any cost. These duties can be expressed by two
> aphorisms: "Know thyself" and "Be thyself." (1920: 72/1991: 66)

The distinction of true and false nationalism results from these presup-
positions. According to Trubetskoi, true nationalism is based on self-
knowledge expressed in a "unique national culture" (1920: 75). The
majority of existing forms of nationalism, including prerevolutionary
Russian nationalism and pan-Slavism, are false nationalisms, for "The
only kind of nationalism which can be acknowledged as true, as morally
and logically justified, is a nationalism that has its origins in a unique
national culture or is directed toward such a culture" (1920: 79/1991: 73).

Among the types and examples of false nationalism Trubetskoi enu-
merated was also the idea of "national self-determination" of "'small'
nations" whose "efforts are directed towards achieving national independence regardless of the cost" (1920: 79–80). In a 1921 letter to Jakobson,
he wrote, "'National self-determination' as understood by former president
Wilson and various separatists like the Georgians, the Estonians, the
Latvians and so on is a typical kind of false nationalism" (Trubetskoi to
Jakobson, 7/3/1921, 1975: 14).

The way the concept of true nationalism based on self-knowledge is applied to Russia by the Eurasians reveals the postulated link between Eurasianism and Pan-Turkism. True Russian nationalism must acknowledge the "Turanian element in Russian culture," as Trubetskoi put it in his 1925 essay:

> the living together of the Russians with the Turanians is a recurring *motif* throughout Russian history. If the association of Eastern Slavs and Turanians is the fundamental fact of Russian history . . ., then it is perfectly obvious that for a correct national self-knowledge we, Russians, have to take into account the presence of the Turanian element in ourselves, we have to study our Turanian brothers. (1925a: 351–52)

The same idea was expressed already in *Exodus to the East*:

> Thus from an ethnographic point of view, the Russian people are not purely Slavic. The Russians, the Ugro-Finns, and the Volga Turks comprise a cultural zone that has connections with both the Slavs and the "Turanian East," and it is difficult to say which of these is more important. The connection between the Russians and the Turanians has not only an ethnographic but an anthropological basis: Turkic blood mingles in Russian veins with that of Ugro-Finns and Slavs. And the Russian national character is unquestionably linked in certain ways with the "Turanian East." (Trubetskoi 1921b: 100/1991: 96)

The political intention behind such statements became manifest in the very first Eurasian collection, too:

> in order for Russian Culture to be completely "ours," it must be closely linked to the unique psychological and ethnographic characteristics of Russian national life. Here one must bear in mind the special properties of Russianness. We have often heard that it is Russia's historical mission to unite our Slavic "brothers." But it is usually forgotten that our "brothers" (if not in language or faith, then in blood, character, and culture) are not only the Slavs, but the Turanians, and that Russia has already consolidated a large part of the Turanian East under the aegis of its state system . . . Russian culture . . . must not be based exclusively on Eastern Orthodoxy but must also manifest those traits of the underlying national life that can unite into a single cultural whole the diverse tribes that are linked historically with the destiny of the Russian people. (Trubetskoi 1921a: 102–3; trans. slightly modified 1991: 99).

Eurasianism was clearly an attempt at nation-building. The Eurasians' intention was to legitimize the future existence of one single state on the territory of the former Russian Empire by providing it with a new ideology, which stressed both its multinational character and the bonds uniting the peoples inhabiting it and repudiated competing ideologies possibly leading to its disintegration as false nationalisms (see the Shnirel'man-Karlov controversy: Shnirel'man 1996, 1997); Karlov 1997a, b). Among these, Pan-Turkism was attributed a prominent place, for example, in Georgii Vernadskii's 1934 sketch of Eurasian history:

> Pan-Turkism was particularly strong, when it could be linked to Pan-Islamism in practice . . . through the rupture of Pan-Turkism and Pan-Islamism in Ottoman Turkey the political position of Pan-Islamism is rather weak. As to Pan-Turkism, how far its objective is to tear away the Turkic peoples of Eurasia from their political union with the latter, such a downfall of Eurasia (if it were possible) would first of all be extremely disadvantageous for the Turkic peoples themselves, who now belong to Eurasia. (Vernadskii 1934: 24–25)

The idea of Eurasian nation-building was never more explicitly expressed anywhere than in Trubetskoi's "Obshcheevraziiskii natsionalizm" (Pan-Eurasian Nationalism) (1927). This essay dealt with the question whether there was a factor "capable of knitting the state [the former Russian Empire] together" after the revolution (Trubetskoi 1927: 26; 1991: 235). The desirability of this objective was a presupposition that went unquestioned by Trubetskoi and his fellow Eurasians. In his opinion the answer to the problem was Eurasianism:

> For the separate parts of the former Russian Empire to continue as parts of a single state there must exist a single substratum of statehood . . . A stable and permanent unification is . . . feasible only on the basis of an ethnic (national) substratum . . . *the only national substratum of the state formerly known as the Russian Empire and now known as the U.S.S.R. can only be the totality of peoples inhabiting that state, taken as a peculiar multiethnic nation and as such possessed of its own nationalism. We call that nation Eurasian, its territory Eurasia, and its nationalism Eurasianism.* (1927: 28; 1991: 239, italics original)

In this connection Pan-Turanianism was mentioned and rejected as "violence against nature" (!) because of its centrifugal potential:

> Eurasianism, rather than pan-Slavism for Russians, Pan-Turanianism for Eurasian Turanians, or Pan-Islamism for Eurasian Muslims, should become predominant. These "pan-isms," by intensifying the centrifugal energies of particular ethnic nationalisms, emphasize the one-sided link between the given people and certain other peoples by only a single set of criteria; they are incapable of creating any real, living and individual multiethnic nation. But in the Eurasian brotherhood, peoples are linked not by some one-sided set of criteria, but by their common historical destiny. Eurasia constitutes a geographical, economic, and historical whole. The destinies of the Eurasian peoples have become interwoven with one another, tied in a massive tangle that can no longer be unraveled; the severance of any one people can be accomplished only by an act of violence against nature, which will bring pain. This does not apply to the ethnic groups forming the basis of pan-Slavism, Pan-turanianism, and Pan-Islamism. Not one of them is united to such a degree by a common historical destiny. . . . Pan-Eurasian nationalism . . . is not only pragmatically valuable; it is nothing less than a vital necessity, for only the awakening of self-awareness as a single, multiethnic Eurasian nation will provide Russia-Eurasia with the ethnic substratum of statehood without which it will eventually fall to pieces, causing unheard-of suffering in all its parts. (1927: 29–30; trans. slightly modified 1991: 242)

This passage is important in another respect. In concise form it reflects an important conceptual difference separating the Eurasians from contemporary nationalist thinkers including Pan-Turkists. According to them, Eurasian unity is based not on common origin but on historically acquired similarities: the peoples of Eurasia have converged in history, and they are still converging because they have been living in the same geographical milieu and in permanent contact for centuries.[4] Following on older theories, the Eurasians refined the idea of historical convergence and similarity due to contact, particularly in geography by the concept of *mestorazvitie* and linguistics, where Trubetskoi together with Roman Jakobson developed the theory of Sprachbund.[5]

The Eurasians were aware that replacing descent from one origin by development from different starting points toward the same *telos* as the founding principle of nationalism was neither obvious nor common. They did not expect the majority of their contemporaries to understand their complex reasoning. Rather, they charged a small elite with reeducating the masses—it need not be pointed out how much this idea lacked democratic spirit and how close the Eurasians thereby came to the role the Bolsheviks attributed to themselves in Soviet society:

> For Pan-Eurasian nationalism to function effectively as a unifying factor for the Eurasian state, it is necessary to re-educate the self-awareness of the peoples of Eurasia.... The individuals who have already fully recognized the unity of the multiethnic Eurasian nation must spread their conviction.... It is necessary to re-examine a number of disciplines from the point of view of the unity of the multiethnic Eurasian nation, and to construct new scientific systems to replace old and antiquated ones. In particular, one needs a new history of the Eurasian peoples including the history of the Russians. (1927: 30/1991: 242–43)

In *The Legacy of Genghis Khan* Trubetskoi himself gave a good example of constructing new scientific systems (see also Logovikov 1931) and rewriting history by applying them. In the very first sentence he repudiates the "point of view generally accepted in history textbooks ... that the foundations of the Russian state were laid in so-called Kievan Rus" (1925: 211/1991: 161). The alternative interpretation of Russian history he then outlines is founded on geographical determinism:

> The territory of Russia ... constitutes a separate continent ... which in contrast to Europe and Asia can be called *Eurasia*. ... Eurasia represents an integral whole, both geographically and anthropologically.... By its very nature, Eurasia is historically destined to comprise a single state entity. From the beginning the political unification of Eurasia was a historical inevitability, and the geography of Eurasia indicated the means to achieve it. (1925: 213–14/1991: 164–65, italics original)

---

[4] According to the Eurasians, the most important areas of convergent development were folklore, language, socioeconomic life, and political organization.

[5] As Savitskii (1927: 29) defined *mestorazvitie*, "The socio-historic milieu and its territory have to merge ... into one whole, into a geographical individual or landschaft." For Sprachbund, see Sériot (1999).

Therefore, the foundations of the Russian state are to be found in the Mongol Empire of Genghis Khan, who was the first to unite Eurasia and fulfill the mission predestined by geography:

> Eurasia is a geographically, ethnographically, and economically integrated system whose political unification was historically inevitable. Genghis Khan was the first to accomplish this unification. . . . In time the unity of Eurasia began to break up. Instinctively the Russian state has striven and is striving to recreate this broken unity; consequently, it is the descendant of Genghis Khan, the heir and successor to his historical endeavors. (1925: 216/1991: 167)

In this way Genghis Khan, glorified in anti-Russian Pan-Turkic historiography, was integrated as a positive actor into Russian-Eurasian history by the Eurasians (Khara-Davan 1929: 9 and passim; cf. Laruelle 1999: 263–66). He was more than just an individual: he came to represent the Turanians, whose history was an integral part of Eurasian history:

> The political unification was first accomplished by the Turanians in the person of Genghis Khan; these Turanian nomads were the first bearers of the idea of a common Eurasian state system. Later . . . the idea of a common Eurasian state passed from the Turanians to the Russians, who became its inheritors and bearers. It was now possible for Russia-Eurasia to become a self-contained cultural, political, and economic region and to develop a unique Eurasian culture. (Trubetskoi 1925: 258–59/1991: 221)

Trubetskoi even claimed a revival of the Turanian element in Russian culture in his days:

> everywhere we can see the genuine Russia, historical Russia, ancient Russia, not an invented "Slavic" or "Slavo-Varangian" Russia, but the real Russo-Turanian Russia-Eurasia, heir to the great legacy of Genghis Khan. . . . In Russian physiognomies . . . one is beginning to notice something Turanian. In Russian language itself one is beginning to hear new sound combinations that are also "barbarous," also Turanian. (1925; 261/1991: 224)

This statement once again led him to the conclusion that the future existence of one state on the territory of the former Russian Empire including its Muslim Turkic population is historically determined by the "fact" that Turan is located within Eurasia, that Turanian history is part of Eurasian history, that Turanians belong to the Eurasian peoples:[6]

---

[6] Trubetskoi (1927: 29; trans. slightly modified 1991: 240–41) had a kind of *matrioshka*-like nationalism in mind: "Every nationalism contains both centralist elements (the affirmation of unity) and separatist elements (the affirmation of uniqueness and distinctiveness). Inasmuch as ethnic entity is contained in another . . . there may exist nationalism of various amplitudes. . . . These nationalisms are . . . contained in each other like concentric circles. . . . For the nationalism of a given ethnic entity not to degenerate into pure separatism, it must be combined with the nationalism of a broader ethnic entity. With regard to Eurasia this means that the nationalism of every individual people of Eurasia

The legacy of Genghis Khan is inseparable from Russia. Whether Russia wants it or not, she remains forever the guardian of this legacy. . . . Even during the period of the antinational monarchy [in the post-Petrine era] . . . Russia was compelled by the very nature of things to continue the historical enterprise of uniting Eurasia into one state—the enterprise of Genghis Khan. The annexations of the Crimea, the Caucasus, the Transcaspian region, and Turkestan . . . were all steps along the path toward reunification of the scattered parts of the Eurasian *ulus* of Genghis Khan's empire, while the colonization and cultivation of the steppe . . . consolidated the transfer of the Eurasian state idea from the Turanians to the Russians. (1925: 261f/1991: 225)[7]

As I have pointed out so far, the Eurasians included Turan in Eurasia in order to repudiate potential secession demands of Russia's Turks and legitimize the continued existence of a single state on the territory of the former Russian Empire. Trying to give their political conviction the impression of scientific correctness, they use one more type of argument. According to the Eurasians the terms Turan and Turanian refer not simply to a geographical location or ethnic group but to a *mestorazvitie*, the complex structure of a geographical milieu and people inhabiting it. The orientalist Vasilii Petrovich Nikitin therefore could argue in his essay "Iran, Turan i Rossiia" ("Iran, Turan, and Russia") that the traditional opposition of Iran and Turan is based on a difference of psychological type and socioeconomic lifestyle rather than ethnic origin. Because, in his eyes, some Northern Iranian tribes became Turanians due to their nomadic lifestyle, Russia in her relation toward Iran became Turan in the course of history (Nikitin 1927: 90; "Redaktsionnoe primechanie" 1927: 77–78). In the same historical process Russian national character incorporated the characteristics of the Turanian psychological type, which—according to the Eurasians' writings—exists within the former and plays a positive role without being independent from it ("Redaktsionnoe primechanie" 1927: 80; Trubetskoi 1925: 368–70; 1927: 28–29).

In sum, the Eurasians answered the challenge of Pan-Turkism by taking up two of its key elements and giving them new meanings.[8] By

---

(the contemporary U.S.S.R.) should be combined with Pan-Eurasian nationalism, or Eurasianism." Cf. Laruelle (1999: 230).

[7] See also (1925: 262/1991: 226): "Russia is still being forced . . . to put into practice . . . that fraternization with the peoples of Eurasia which is an inevitable consequence of the historical mission of Russia, the political unifier of Eurasia and the heir and descendant of Genghis Khan. The gravitation of the various peoples of Eurasia toward a common state structure that unites them into a single family compels them to look upon the Russian state as their own, as theirs by birth."

[8] Subsuming Russians among Turanians or assuming a Turanian element in Russian culture was not absolutely new. Duchin'ski (1864) and Martin (1866: ii–iii) promoted it in Western Europe; Gasprinsky and Konstantin Leont'ev were among nineteenth-century precursors in the Russian Empire. On the latter, see Kosik (1997: 123).

claiming the legacy of Genghis Khan as their own, Russian Eurasians stressed the common historical destiny of Russians, Finno-Ugrians, and Russia's Muslim Turks in one state. By pointing out the Turanian element in Russian culture, they tried to remove the ethnic barrier between the Slavic, Finno-Ugric, and Turkic populations of the former Russian Empire. They ideologically undermined the Pan-Turkic movement and its disintegrating potential, for citing the Turanian origin of the Turkic peoples and idealizing Genghis Khan's role as their unifier did not exclude living together with the Russians in one state.

CONCLUSION

Eurasianism was a consciously constructed ideology of integration intended to safeguard Russia as a multinational empire, despite its takeover by the Bolsheviks and the collapse of the Habsburg and Ottoman Empires. By making the idea of Turan their own, the Eurasians ideologically undermined the emerging Pan-Turkic movement, which was basically anti-Russian and strove toward the liberation of Russia's Turks from Russian domination, either by autonomy and equal rights within Russia or by independence and unification with the Turks of the Ottoman Empire. Although the Pan-Turkic movement of the late nineteenth and the early twentieth centuries lacked mass support and competed with other identity constructs among Turkic elites, Russians, and Western European contemporaries perceived the Pan-Turkic movement as a threat to the territorial integrity of the Russian Empire.

At this early stage of Turkic nation-building, the Eurasians reacted to the Pan-Turkic challenge by using and redefining its anti-Russian key terms to stress the unity of Turks and Eastern Slavs. They replaced the Pan-Turkists' Turan myth by their own, emphasizing the common historical destiny of Turanians and Eastern Slavs. They shared the Pan-Turkists' heroic picture of Genghis Khan, but saw in him a ruler uniting not only the Turkic-Mongol tribes but the whole of Russia-Eurasia. Yet the Eurasians failed to gain the support of Russia's Turks for their idea of a multinational Eurasian nation. They were just as unable ideologically to integrate Russia's Turks as the Pan-Turkists themselves, who in their turn did not succeed in creating one single nation embracing all branches of the Turkic linguistic family. It was the Bolsheviks' power that prevented the Turks of the former Russian Empire from seceding and it was their policy of nationalities which resulted in the formation of several Turkic nations within the Soviet Union.

BIBLIOGRAPHY

Adam, Volker. 2000. "Auf der Suche nach Turan: Panislamismus und Panturkismus in der aserbaidschanischen Vorkriegspresse." In *Caucasia Between the Ottoman Empire and Iran, 1555–1914*, ed. Raoul Motika and Michael Ursinus. Wiesbaden. 189–205.

——. 2002. *Russlandmuslime in Istanbul am Vorabend des Ersten Weltkrieges: Die Berichterstattung osmanischer Periodika über Russland und Zentralasien.* Frankfurt a. M.

Akçura, Yusuf. 1904. "Les trois systèmes politiques." 1904. Reprinted in François Georgeon, *Aux origines du nationalisme turc: Yusuf Akçura (1876–1935).* Paris, 1980. 95–106.

Alevras, N. N. 1996. "Nachala evraziiskoi kontseptsii v rannem tvorchestve G. V. Vernadskogo i N. Savitskogo." *Vestnik Evrazii* 1: 5–17.

Alisov, G. 1909. "Musul'manskii vopros v Rossii." *Russkaia mysl'* 30, 7: 28–61.

Allworth, Edward A., ed. 1988. *Tatars of the Crimea: Their Struggle for Survival. Original Studies from North America, Unofficial and Official Documents from Czarist and Soviet Sources.* Durham.

——. 1990. *The Modern Uzbeks: From the Fourteenth Century to the Present: A Cultural History.* Stanford.

Alp, Tekin (pseudonym of M. Cohen). 1915. *Türkismus und Pantürkismus.* Weimar.

Altstadt, Audrey L. 1992. The *Azerbaijani Turks: Power and Identity Under Russian Rule.* Stanford.

Amaeva, L. A. 1998. *Musul'manskie deputaty Gosudarstvennoi Dumy Rossii. 1906–1917. Sbornik dokumentov i materialov.* Ufa.

Arai, Masami. 1992. *Turkish Nationalism in the Young Turk Era.* Leiden.

Arnakis, G. G. 1960. "Turanism: An Aspect of Turkish Nationalism." *Balkan Studies* 1: 19–32.

Arsharuni, A. and Kh. Gabidullin. 1931. *Ocherki panislamizma i pantiurkizma v Rossii.* Moscow.

Baberowski, Jörg. 1999. "Auf der Suche nach Eindeutigkeit: Kolonialismus und zivilisatorische Mission im Zarenreich und in der Sowjetunion." *Jahrbücher für Geschichte Osteuropas* 47: 482–504.

——. 2000. "Nationalismus aus dem Geiste der Inferiorität: Autokratische Modernisierung und die Anfänge muslimischer Selbstvergewisserung im östlichen Transkaukasien 1828–1914." *Geschichte und Gesellschaft* 26: 371–406.

Bennigsen, Alexandre and Chantal Quelquejay. 1960. "Les mouvements nationaux chez les Musulmans de Russie." In *Le "Sultangalievisme" au Tatarstan.* Paris, 1960.

Bennigsen, Alexandre A. and S. Enders Wimbush. 1979. *Muslim National Communism in the Soviet Union: A Revolutionary Strategy for the Colonial World.* Chicago.

Böss, Otto. 1961. *Die Lehre der Eurasier: Ein Beitrag zur russischen Ideengeschichte des 20. Jahrhunderts.* Wiesbaden.

Czaplika, M. A. 1918. *The Turks of Central Asia in History and at the Present Day: An Ethnological Inquiry into the Pan-Turanian Problem, and Bibliographical Material relating to the Early Turks and the present Turks of Central Asia.* Oxford.

Doronchenkov, A. I. 2001. *Emigratsiia "pervoi volny" o natsional'nykh problemach i sud'be Rossii.* St. Petersburg.

Duchin'ski, F.-H. 1864. *Nécessité des réformes dans l'exposition de l'histoire des peuples aryâs-européens & tourans, particulièrement des slaves et des moscovites: Peuples aryâs et tourans, agriculteurs et nomades.* Paris.

Dumont, Paul. 1974. "La revue Türk Yurdu et les Musulmans de l'Empire Russe 1911–1914." *Cahiers du Monde Russe et Sovietique* 15: 315–31.

——. 1975. "La fascination du Bolchevisme: Enver Pacha et le Parti des soviets populaires 1919–1922." *Cahiers du Monde Russe et Sovietique* 16: 141–66.

Fisher, A. W. 1988. "Ismail Gaspirali, Model Leader for Asia." In Allworth (1988: 11–26).

Gasprinskii, Ismail Bey. 1881. *Russkoe musul'manstvo.* Reprint Oxford, 1985.

——. 1896. "Russko-Vostochnoe soglashenie: Mysli, zametki i pozhelaniia" (Russo-Oriental Relations: Thoughts, Notes, and Desires). Bakhchisaray: Tipo-Litografiia Gazety Perevodchika, 1896. Trans. Edward J. Lazzerini in Allworth (1988: 202–16).

Georgeon, François. 1988. "La montée du nationalisme turc dans l'État ottoman (1908–1914). Bilan et perspectives." *Revue du Monde Musulman et de la Méditerranée* 50: 30–44.

Geraci, Robert. 1997. "Russian Orientalism at an Impasse: Tsarist Education Policy and the 1910 Conference on Islam." In *Russia's Orient: Imperial Borderlands and Peoples, 1700–1917*, ed. Daniel R. Brower and Edward J. Lazzerini. Bloomington. 138–61.

Gökalp, Zia. 1923. *The Principles of Turkism*. Ed. R. Devereux. Leiden, 1968.

Hagemeister, Michael and Nikolai Fedorov. 1989. *Studien zu Leben, Werk und Wirkung*. Munich

Hauner, Milan. 1992. *What Is Asia to Us? Russia's Asian Heartland Yesterday and Today*. London.

Heyd, Uriel. 1950. *Foundations of Turkish Nationalism: The Life and Teachings of Ziya Gökalp*. London.

Hostler, Charles Warren. 1957. *Turkism and the Soviets: The Turks of the World and Their Objectives*. London.

Hyman, Anthony. 1997. "Turkestan and pan-Turkism Revisited." *Central Asian Survey* 16: 339–51.

Iordan, M. V. and S. M. Chervonnaia. 1994. "Ideia tiurko-slavianskogo soglasiia v nasledii Ismaila Gasprinskogo." In *Tsivilizatsii i kul'tury*, vol. 1, *Rossiia i Vostok: tsivilizatsionnye otnosheniia*. Moscow. 239–49.

Iskhakov, S. M. 1999. "Pervaia mirovaia voina glazami rossiiskikh musul'man." In *Rossiia i pervaia mirovaia voina: Materialy mezhdunarodnogo nauchnogo kollokviuma*. St. Petersburg. 419–31.

Karlov, V. V. 1997a. "Evraziiskaja ideia i russkii natsionalizm: Po povodu stat'i V. A. Shnirel'mana 'Evrazijskaja ideja i teorija kul'tury.'" *Etnograficheskoe obozrenie* 1: 3–13.

———. 1997b. "O evraziistve, natsionalizme i priemakh nauchnoi polemiki." *Etnograficheskoe obozrenie* 2: 125–32.

Kendirbay, Gulnar. 1997. "The National Liberation Movement of the Kazakh Intelligentsia at the Beginning of the Twentieth Century." *Central Asian Survey* 16: 487–515.

Kessler, Joseph A. 1967. "Turanism and Pan-Turanism in Hungary, 1890–1945." Ph.D. dissertation, University of California, Berkeley.

Khara-Davan, Erenzhen. 1991. *Chingis-Khan kak polkovodets i ego nasledie: Kul'turno-istoricheskii ocherk Mongol'skoi imperii XII–XIV vv*. 1929. Elista.

Kirimli, Hakan. 1996. *National Movements and National Identity among the Crimean Tatars, 1905–1916*. Leiden.

Kosik, V. I. 1997. *Konstantin Leont'ev: Razmyshleniia na slavianskuiu temu*. Moscow.

Landau, Jacob M. 1995. *Pan-Turkism: From Irredentism to Cooperation*. London.

Laruelle, Marlène. 1999. *L'idéologie eurasiste russe ou comment penser l'empire*. Paris.

Lazzerini, Edward J. 1988. "Ismail Bey Gasprinskii (Gaspirali): The Discourse of Modernism and the Russians." In Allworth (1988: 149–69).

———. 1989. "Reform und Modernismus (Djadidismus) unter den Muslimen des Russischen Reiches." In *Die Muslime in der Sowjetunion und in Jugoslawien: Identität, Politik, Widerstand*, ed. Andreas Kappeler et al. Köln. 35–47.

Liberman, Anatolii. 1991. "Postscript: N. S. Trubetzkoy and His Works on History and Politics." In Trubetzkoy (1991: 295–389).

Logovikov, V. (pseudonym of N. Savitskii). 1931. "Nauchnye zadachi evraziistva." *Tridcatye Gody: Parizh*: 53–63.

Luks, Leonid. 1986. "Die Ideologie der Eurasier im zeitgeschichtlichen Zusammenhang." *Jahrbücher für Geschichte Osteuropas* 34: 374–95.

A Manual on the Turanians and Pan-Turanianism. 1918. Compiled by Geographical Section of the Naval Intelligence Division, Naval Staff, Admiralty. London.

Martin, Henri. 1866. *La Russie et l'Europe*. Paris.

Masayuki, Yamauchi. 1991. The *Green Crescent under the Red Star: Enver Pasha in Soviet Russia, 1919–1922*. Tokyo.

von Mende, G. *Der nationale Kampf der Russlandtürken: Ein Beitrag zur nationalen Frage in der Sovetunion*. Berlin, 1936.

Minorsky, Vladimir. 1934. "Turan." *Enzyklopädie des Islam* 4: 951–57.

Mouhammetchine, Rafiq. 1966. "L'apport de quelques sources russes officielles à l'historiographie du djadidisme chez les tatars de la Volga (aux Archives centrales d'État du Tatarstan)." *Cahiers du Monde Russe* 37: 83–96.

"Le Mouvement pantouranien." 1917. *L'Asie Française* 17 (October-December): 174–82.

Mukhammetdinov, R. F. 1996. *Zarozhdenie i evoliutsiia tiurkizma iz istorii politicheskoi mysli i ideologii tiurkskikh narodov; Osmanskaia i Rossiiskaia imperii, Turtsiia, SSSR, SNG 70–e gg. XIX v. -90–e gg. XX v.)*. Kazan'.

Nikitin, Valentin. 1927. "Iran, Turan i Rossiia." *Vestnik MGU* Ser. 9: *Filologija* 5 (1992): 61–90.
Nikitine, Basil. 1922. "Le problème musulman selon les chefs de l'émigration russe." *Revue du Monde Musulman* 52: 1–53.
Noack, Chriatian. 2000. *Muslimischer Nationalismus im russischen Reich: Nationsbildung und Nationalbewegung bei Tataren und Baschkiren 1861–1917.* Stuttgart.
O Evrazii i evraziitsakh: Bibliograficheskii ukazatel'. 1997. Petrozavodsk.
Önder, Z. 1977. "Panturanismus in Geschichte und Gegenwart." *Österreichische Osthefte* 19, 2: 93–101.
Ortayli, Ilber. 1991. "Reports and Considerations of Ismail Bey Gasprinskii in Tercüman on Central Asia." *Cahiers du Monde Russe et Sovietique* 32, 1: 43–46.
"Panislamizm i Pantiurkizm." 1913. *Mir islama* 2, 8–9: 556–71, 596–619.
Pears, Edwin. 1918. "Turkey, Islam and Turanianism." *Contemporary Review* 114 (October 1918): 371–79.
Pipes, Richard. 1964. *The Formation of the Soviet Union: Communism and Nationalism 1917–1923.* Rev. ed. Cambridge.
"Redaktsionnoe primechanie." 1927. *Vestnik MGU* Ser. 9: *Filologija* 6 (1990): 77–80.
Riasanovsky, Nicholas V. 1964. "Prince N. S. Trubetskoy's 'Europe and Mankind.'" *Jahrbücher für Geschichte Osteuropas* 12: 207–20.
———. 1967. "The Emergence of Eurasianism." *California Slavic Studies* 4: 39–72.
Risal (pseudonym of M. Cohen). 1912. "Les turcs à la recherche d'une âme nationale." *Mercure de France*, 16 August, 673–707.
Roy, Olivier. 1997. *La nouvelle Asie centrale ou la fabrication des nations.* Paris.
Savitskii, Petr Nikolaevich. 1921. *Iskhod k Vostoku: Predchuvstvie i sverzheniia.* Sofia. Trans. Ilya Vinkovetsky, *Exodus to the East: Forebodings and Events.* Idylwild, Calif.: Schacks, 1996.
———. 1927. *Rossiia—osobyi geograficheskii mir.* Prague.
Sériot, Patrick. 1999. *Structure et totalité: Les origines intellectuelles du structuralisme en Europe centrale et orientale.* Paris.
Shnirel'man, V. A. 1996. "Evraziiskaia ideia i teoriia kul'tury." *Ètnograficheskoe obozrenie* 4: 3–16.
———. 1997. "Evraziistvo i natsional'nyi vopros. Vmesto otveta V. V. Karlovu." *Ètnograficheskoe Obozrenie* 2: 112–25.
Smith, Jeremy. 1999. *The Bolsheviks and the National Question, 1917–1923.* Basingstoke.
Stoddard, Lothrop. 1921. *The New World of Islam.* London, reprint 1932.
Swietochowski, Tadeusz. 1985. *Russian Azerbaijan, 1905–1920: The Shaping of National Identity in a Muslim Community.* Cambridge.
———. 1996. "National Consciousness and Political Orientations in Azerbaijan, 1905–1920." In *Transcaucasia, Nationalism, and Social Change: Essays in the History of Armenia, Azerbaijan, and Georgia*, ed. Ronald G. Suny. Rev. ed. Ann Arbor. 211–34.
Togan, Z. V. 1997. *Vospominaniia: Bor'ba musul'man Turkestana i drugikh vostochnych tiurok za natsional'noe sushchestvovanie i kul'turu.* Moscow.
Trubetskoi, N. S. 1920. "Evropa i chelovechestvo." In Trubetskoi (1995: 55–104). Trans. "Europe and Mankind" in Trubetzkoy (1991: 1–64).
———. 1921a. "Ob istinnom i lozhnom natsionalizme." In (Savitskii 1921: 71–85). Trans. "On True and False Nationalism" in Trubetzkoy (1991: 65–79).
———. 1921b. "Verkhi i nizy russkoi kul'tury (ètnicheskaia osnova russkoi kul'tury)." In Savitskii (1921: 86–103). Trans. "The Upper and Lower Stories of Russian Culture: The Ethnic Basis of Russian Culture" in Trubetzkoy (1991: 81–99).
———. 1925a. "O turanskom èlemente v russkoi kul'ture." *Evraziiskii vremennik* 4: 351–77.
———. 1925b. "Nasledie Chingiskhana: Vzgliad na russkuiu istoriiu ne s Zapada, a s Vostoka." In Trubetskoi (1995a: 211–66). Trans. "The Legacy of Genghis Khan: A Perspective on Russian History Not from the West but from the East" in Trubetzkoy (1991: 161–231).
———. 1927. "Obshcheevraziiskii natsionalizm." *Evraziiskaia khronika* 9: 24–31. Trans. "Pan-Eurasian Nationalism" in Trubetzkoy (1991: 233–44).
———. 1995. *Istoriia, kul'tura, iazyk.* Ed. Nikita I. Tolstoi, L. N. Gumilev, and V. M. Zhivov. Moscow.

Trubetzkoy, N. S. 1975. *N. S. Trubetzkoy's Letters and Notes*. Ed. Roman Jakobson. The Hague.
——. 1991. *The Legacy of Genghis Khan and Other Essays on Russia's Identity*. Ed. A. Liberman. Ann Arbor.
"Turkey, Russia and Islam." 1917. *Round Table* (December): 100–138.
Urchanova, R. V. 1995. "Evraziitsy i vostok: pragmatika liubvi?" *Vestnik Evrazii* 1: 12–31.
Vambéry, Arminius. 1905. "The Awakening of the Tatars." *Nineteenth Century* 57: 217–27.
——. 1906. "Constitutional Tatars." *Nineteenth Century* 59: 906–13.
——. 1907. "Die Kulturbestrebungen der Tataren." *Deutsche Rundschau* 132: 72–91.
Vandalkovskaia, M. G. 1997. *Istoricheskaia nauka rossiiskoi èmigratsii: "Evraziiskii soblazn"*. Moscow.
Vernadskii, Georgii V. 1934. *Opyt istorii Evrazii s poloviny VI veka do nastoiashchego vremeni*. Berlin.
Vinkovetsky, Ilya and Charles Schlacks, Jr. 1996. *Exodus to the East. Forebodings and Events. An Affirmation of the Eurasians*. Idylwild, 1996.
Wiederkehr, Stefan. 2000. "Der Eurasismus als Erbe N. Ja. Danilevskijs? Bemerkungen zu einem Topos der Forschung." *Studies in East European Thought* 52: 119–50.
Wipert, K. 1922. "Der Turanismus." *Neue Orient* 4 (December): 202–10.
X. 1912. "Les courants politiques dans la Turquie contemporaine." *Revue du Monde Musulman* 21: 158–221.
——. 1913. "Le Panislamisme et le Panturquisme." *Revue du Monde Musulman* 22: 179–220.
Yalçinkaya, Alaeddin. 1997. "The Frontiers of Turkestan." *Central Asian Survey* 16: 431–38.
Yémelianova, G. M. 1997. "The National Identity of the Volga Tatars at the Turn of the Nineteenth Century: Tatarism, Turkism, and Islam." *Central Asian Survey* 16: 543–72.
Zarevand. 1926. *United and Independent Turani: Aims and Designs of the Turks*. Leiden, 1971 (originally published in Armenian 1926, Russian trans. 1930).
Zenkovsky, S. A. 1967. *Pan-Turkism and Islam in Russia*. 2nd ed. Cambridge, Mass.

III. Karsavin and the Eurasian Movement

Françoise Lesourd
Translated by Jack Pier

A certain side of modern Russian thought, coming from the Slavophiles, has traditionally tended to place the future of Russian culture outside Europe. The circumstances around 1917—military defeat, vacancy of power, and then the Revolution—touched off a grave crisis of identity and anxiety as to the future of the Russian state, all of which fed an ancient culturological reflection based on Russia's geographical position between West and East and on the eastward extension of the Russian empire.

This anxiety showed itself starting with the early years of the Revolution, when Aleksandr Blok responded to this situation of profound disarray with his poem, "The Scythians." During the 1920s, however, the historical context changed: the Bolshevik Revolution seemed to have won a durable victory and the Soviet regime to have established itself for an incalculable period of time.

Whether expelled from the USSR or émigrés, numerous representatives of the Russian intellectual world found themselves in exile. This situation, painfully experienced by many, caused them to look for a profound historical necessity in the highly particular destiny of Russia and at the same time to attempt to renew the bond, severed by emigration, with the real Russia, the Soviet state. The Eurasian movement represents the clearest manifestation of this intellectual stance, for it sees what is specifically Russian in Russia's intermediate position between Europe and Asia, and in Soviet power the realization of this specific calling.

For many, the need to gain a new hold on what was really going on in Russia was to be found in this attitude, the ambiguity of which lay in "acceptance of the Bolshevik Revolution" (Hauchard 1996: 359) together with that of the new power, but refusal, more or less radical according to the "Eurasians," of its ideology. This was the position of the philosopher Lev Karsavin (1882–1952), who played an important although brief part in this movement. Many years later he was to state that in the beginning he was hostile to the Revolution, but "in 1918–19, I understood that Soviet power was a popular and solid power. However, the ideology of the new power did not correspond to my vision of the world" (L.Y.A.: July 12, 1949).

Keep the regime but change the ideology—this was the aim of the intellectual world and of their practical action. Karsavin summed it up this way: the Eurasian movement

> based its ideological program on acknowledgment of the October Revolution and of the Soviet regime established in Russia, but rejected communism, setting itself the goal of replacing it with Greek Orthodoxy and a specifically Russian culture.
>
> In place of the socialist regime, the Eurasians favored a society without the dictatorship of the proletariat, a society based on harmonious coexistence between its various classes.
>
> In the economic field, it favored the existence of a private sector alongside the state sector. The aim of the Eurasian organization was thus to replace the communist ideology by the Eurasian ideology while at the same time keeping the Soviet regime. In my opinion, this replacement was conceived as a change from communism into Eurasianism thanks to a natural evolution of communism. (L.Y.A.: Sept. 23, 1949)

Numerous former "Eurasians" returned to Russia of their own free will (Klepinina-Lvova) or by force (Savitskii, arrested in Prague by the Soviets at the end of the war), were to pay a price for this ambiguity. During their interrogations in prison, they acknowledged having been led into subversive action against the Soviet regime and enlisted by the NKVD (Klepinina-Lvova). There was in fact a "rightist" Eurasian current that favored restoration of the monarchy.

EURASIAN CONNECTIONS

In the beginning, nothing could have foreseen the participation of Karsavin, a historian of Western culture, in the Eurasian movement. All of his works prior to the Revolution, including his first dissertation, *Ocherki religioznoi zhizni v Itali XII–XIII vekov* (1912a; *Essays on Religious Life in Italy in the XII–XIII Centuries*), his second dissertation, *Osnovy srednevekovoi religioznosti v XII–XIII veka* (1912b; *Foundations of Medieval Religious Faith in the XII–XIII Centuries*) (both written at the University of Saint Petersburg under the guidance of Professor Grevs), and his books *Monasestvo v srednie veka* (*Monachism in the Middle Ages*), *Katolichestvo* (*Catholicism*), and *Kul'tura srednikh vekov* (*Culture in the Middle Ages*) deal with Western spirituality.

He did, however, publish a book in 1922 in Petrograd entitled *Vostok, zapad i russkaia ideia* (*The East, the West and the Russian Idea*), which gave some idea of a preoccupation, new in his work, with the historical destinies of Russia and a desire to think over the situation of Russian culture from a perspective that could bring him closer to the Eurasians. On the other hand, the article "Evropa i Evraziia" ("Europe and Asia"), published in Berlin in 1923 in *Sovremennie Zapiski*, is, at least in appearance, full of sarcasm with regard to the pathos, terminology, and themes of the Eurasians: their pompous predictions about the "catastrophic crisis of culture" as compared with the age of "great migrations of peoples" (1923b: 297) hide a permanent confusion, according to Karsavin, between the objective facts and what is dictated to them by their subjectivity. This is what, in 1922 in his *The East, the West and the Russian Idea*, he had already reproached all those for who, after the Revolution, lost themselves in prophecies as to the future of Russia.

The very necessity of the term "Eurasia" did not seem obvious to him. Were the Eurasians ashamed to say they were Russian? For them, was everything thus to perish—what is "European" just as what is "Russian"—in order to be replaced by a so-called "Eurasia," a "face (*obrazina*) coming from who knows where?" Karsavin's answer is clear:

> In this case, I, a Russian, don't give a damn about their Eurasia and would rather die with my Russian people, Orthodox. When the going gets rough, it does not suit me to renounce my native language and my original name. (298)
>
> Let's save Russia! Let's spit on Europe, let's create Eurasia. . . . Why spit on Europe? . . . And why create a "Eurasia" unknown to everyone while it is Russia that interests us? (301)

Karsavin is acting here a bit like a psychoanalyst, discovering under a sometimes confused language their worries and their pain, which is at the same time his own. More generally, the irony he pours out so unsparingly in this article is a form of modesty he took on when entering into the gravest subjects. Furthermore, it shows that the idea of Eurasia has nothing new about it, as Russia has always been a melting pot for various peoples.

The merit of the Eurasians, however, was to have occasionally brought out the specificity of Russian culture among the other major national cultures (cf. Souvtchinski's work on Leskov, *Znameniia bylogo*). But on the whole, this was all idle speculation, similar, according to Karsavin, to the "wild imaginings" (*gadaniia*) of Spengler. This was also one point on which he would never agree with the Eurasians, even during the time of his active participation in the movement: the "decline of the West" seemed to him neither likely nor desirable.

Particularly comic is his summary of an essay by Petr Savitskii, "The Continent-Ocean," according to which the cultural center of the old world is moving from one millennium to the next toward countries where the average temperature is colder and colder. Going by this, concludes Karsavin, we will soon wind up at the North Pole, but it is probable that the only thing found there will be Kifa Mokievich (the whale).

While Savitskii went to great effort to put on airs of being a "philosopher," Karsavin remarked ironically, "Is it really worth all the trouble ... to go and disturb philosophy by digging up the annual average of temperatures in the *Julius Hahn Handbuch der Klimatologie* in order to create 'hopes' that may be 'legitimate' but not really convincing?" (303).

An article by Prince Trubetskoi, "The Peaks and Depths [*verkhi i nizy*] of Russian Culture," is subjected to the same treatment. It supposedly demonstrates that "the religious terminology of the Slavic languages is closer to the religious terminology of the Iranian languages, while the Slavic languages coincide with the Indo-European languages essentially in the field of daily life and technology." Karsavin performs a sort of "bearing out of the device" (*obnazenie prioma*): "their soul is drawn toward the Indo-Iranians and their body toward the Western Indo-Europeans. Here is 'food for fantasy'" (306).

This irony is a way of lancing the sore while at the same time showing the inadequacies of their argument, saying in effect that in spite of the validity of their movement, they must "curb their prophetic outbursts" (307). "The Eurasian themes," stated Karsavin, "can be well founded only by a philosophical and metaphysical reflection" (307). He went on to give a germ of this reflection, proposing indirectly a sort of program: their conception of culture as "a unit [*vsedinyj subekt*], concrete and in constant evolution" is sound, as there exists no abstract "subject" of culture (310). Equally sound is their conception of the "people," of the "collective person," bearer of this culture, changing over the ages while maintaining certain features in common. These intuitions need shoring up, however, with serious philosophical reflection.

The Eurasians are right too in linking culture to a specific place ("which need not be called Eurasia—Russia is much more pleasant to say!" (309) or to an ethnological type, but on condition that this be scientifically well founded. It is possible that under our very eyes is being born, "a new subject of Russian culture," observed Karsavin, but these are not "revelations" that can take stock of this new subject in a credible way.

Lack of philosophical basis and of scientific reliability—this is what he reproached the Eurasians with and what he was to attempt to change during his Eurasian period. But in his eyes, things would not really change, which explains in part the brevity of his collaboration with the Eurasians.

In the same article, he showed concretely how to enter into dialogue with Soviet thought by setting out his personal approach to the philosophical system then holding sway in Russia: dialectical materialism. It is not possible, he affirmed, "to cast [it] off with a shrug" (312).

Historical materialism is false, claimed Karsavin, but not entirely. It is correct in affirming that without matter the spirit does not exist, that "the material aspect of life can make it possible to judge life in its entirety." It is wrong when it makes of the material aspect the only principle, reducing spirit to matter and affirming that "the material side of life is not spiritual in its essence." This also implies, however, that one cannot "separate spiritual culture from economic culture" (311), which was also Karsavin's opinion.

This approach to historical materialism was already an attempt to reestablish an intellectual contact between Russia on the inside and the Russia of the émigrés. He was to take this up again in 1946 in a letter to the Minister of Higher Education in the USSR in order to say that he could teach in Soviet Lithuania.

The question of the death of cultures so often brought up in Eurasian literature gave him the opportunity to affirm his profound attachment to the culture of Europe: the Europeanization of Russia that had taken place earlier meant that Russian culture contained a "coming into being" (individual realization) of this totality that European culture represents. To be Russian is also to be European, for each of us is "an individualization of a superior person that encompasses Russia and Europe" (312).

Is the West in the process of perishing? This is not something to rejoice in, said Karsavin, as in this case it is we Russians, too, who are lost in part, even if this were not to prevent us from developing our own culture. We should not jump to conclusions about the death of European culture. It does appear to be in a crisis, but nothing suggests that it has exhausted its resources.

To those Eurasians who thought they were creating something new by rejecting both Europe and a certain Russian past in splendid isolation, he pointed out, amicably and with mild irony, "you are not alone, even though you may think so!" (314). In fact, this article was a sort of hand held out, and it was so understood when Petr Souvtchinski, one of the founders of the movement, paid him a visit in 1924. After that, Karsavin was for several years to put his philosophy of history into the service of what seemed to him a just cause.

When Souvtchinski got in touch with him, he was living in Berlin after being forced into exile by Lenin in 1922 on the famous "boat of philosophers" along with a number of outstanding figures of Russian intellectual life who were not communists. Through this article, recently published in *Sovremennie Zapiski*, and through his reputation as a historian of culture and philosopher of history, but thanks also to his reflection on the place of Russia in relation to Western culture in *The East, the West and the Russian Idea*, he came to be the perfect ideologue of the movement.

SEPARATION FROM THE EURASIAN MOVEMENT

In July 1926, Karsavin moved to Paris (more precisely to Clamart, a nearby suburb where a large number of Russian exiles were living) which, along with Prague, was one of the two principal centers of the movement. In that year, the first congress of the Eurasian movement took place, the only one he was to take part in. He drew up their Essay of Systematic Statement ("Evraziistvo") and directed the "Eurasian seminar" held on the rue de Magdebourg (Hauchard 1996: 361).

Although he was included in the two governing bodies the movement set up (the "board" and the "political bureau"), he was quick to take his distance from them, for he "was not in agreement with the goals they set themselves" (L.Y.A.: Aug. 10, 1949). Further on, we will see which goals he was speaking of.

In 1927 Karsavin turned down a proposal apparently made by Prince Sviatopol-Mirsky, himself a leading figure of the Eurasian movement, to teach at Oxford (Hauchard 1996: 365); he accepted a proposal to teach at the University of Kaunas (capital of independent Lithuania) sent by his former colleague at the University of Saint Petersburg Vassili Sezeman, who himself had taken part in Eurasian publications without having really been engaged in the movement (L.Y.A.). Needless to say, the departure for Lithuania was "a way of initiating a return towards the East (*iskhod k Vostoku*) and Russia" (Hauchard 1996: 365). On January 28, he took up his duties in Kaunas.

During 1927–28, he continued to hold lectures (in Brussels) for a group of Eurasians. However, he did not take part in the meetings of the "political bureau" in Paris in 1928 or in Evian in 1929. In 1929, the breakup of the group was proclaimed in Clamart due to fundamental divergences between the "rightists" (Savitskii, Trubetskoi, Malevich, Arapov), with monarchist leanings, and the "leftists," represented in Paris by Souvtchinski, S. Efron, and Karsavin. An attempt by Savitskii in Prague in 1932 to bring it back to life came to nothing (L.Y.A.: Oct. 27, 1949). The review *Evraziiskaia Khronika* did, however, continue to appear throughout the 1930s.

Even though he maintained his links with the Eurasians (Souvtchinski was his son-in-law, having married his second daughter Marianna), his new obligations, which were fairly heavy (for example, he had to agree to give his course on the history of European culture in Lithuanian), distanced him from them as much as a fundamental disagreement with the leftist Eurasians, the only ones with whom he felt any affinity, but who tended to accept Marxism, while Karsavin was totally anti-Marxist. Letters from Rodzevitch (L.Y.A.: letter of Oct. 28) asking him to distribute "Eurasian" literature in Lithuania and a letter from Souvtchinski (L.Y.A.: Oct. 29) requesting an article for the review *Evraziia* apparently remained without follow-up (L.Y.A.: interrogation of Nov. 29, 1949). And when Savitskii went to Kaunas in 1932–33, Karsavin refused to receive him (L.Y.A.: interrogation of Oct. 27, 1949).

It seems that Karsavin was particularly put off by the compromises with the various secret services that a number of Eurasians allowed themselves to get involved in. Colonel Zaitsev, who apparently helped a number of "emissaries" from the Eurasian movement to slip into the USSR, was expelled from the "board" of the organization in 1926, apparently because he was close to General Koutepov, the leader of the ROVS (L.Y.A.: interrogation of Sept. 23, 1949).

Early on, the movement was suspected of being infiltrated by the NKVD. But by "public knowledge," it was also financed by the Intelligence Service through an Englishman, Spolding, who, under the pseudonym "Old," paid 300 pounds a year. On this matter, Karsavin spoke of a collusion between "English business circles in Moscow" and "oppositionists in Russia" (L.Y.A.: interrogation of Nov. 19, 1949).

This type of financing, the adventurism of certain Eurasians (fantastic and unbelievable episodes, undercover voyages to Russia by Savitskii, who slipped across the border between Vilnius and Minsk before reaching Moscow) (L.Y.A., interrogation of Savitskii), the weakness of their theoretical position, Karsavin's rejection of Marxism (for which the "leftist" Eurasians had a penchant)—all this led him to quickly take his distance.

SOVIET EXPERIENCE

Karsavin was to be caught up with his past in Vilnius in 1949, however. When his daughter Irina was arrested in this same city in 1948, it was for having gotten in touch with her sister, Marianna (then living in Paris), and her husband, Souvtchinski (one of the principal players in the Eurasian movement), through the Minister of Foreign Affairs of the Soviet Republic of Lithuania, Rotomskis. Moreover, from an official voyage to Paris, Rotomskis had brought back to her three issues of *Temps Modernes*, the content of which was judged subversive (L.Y.A.: Memorandum: 5).

Karsavin himself was arrested at the beginning of July 1949, and from July to November he underwent twelve interrogations in the Vilnius prison. Although certain official set phrases were obviously not his own, the minutes of these interrogations give a fairly accurate idea of his exact participation in the Eurasian movement.

It is on this subject that the main part of the accusation weighs, as can be seen from the minutes and the final draft of the accusation. Of seventeen counts, nine bear directly on the Eurasian movement, and it is these counts that led to his being sentenced to ten years in the labor camp in Abez, north of Vorkouta, where he died of tuberculosis in July 1952.

His personal situation in itself was enough to make him a potential victim of the terror: exiled from Soviet Russia in 1922 and a former teacher in "bourgeois" Lithuania, he refused in 1944–45 to flee this country when it became Soviet. Bit by bit, he was led to leave the University of Vilnius, and although this was of his own free will, official statements had it that he was fired: "by myself, without being forced by anyone or being subjected to any pressures whatsoever, I handed in my resignation to the rector for reasons of health" (L.Y.A.: Memorandum: 4). Then, on December 16, 1946, he was forced out of the Vilnius Institute of Fine Arts, where he taught after leaving the university. It appears that, in spite of a genuine effort to be loyal to the new power, the incompatibility of his thought and behavior with Soviet models made him suspect.

Seen in this way, his tragedy turned out to be that of many Eurasians: no matter what the cost, they wanted to enter into dialogue with the Soviet authorities, but were unable to understand that this was a type of power for whom all debate was ruled out. Reports by the secret police show that Karsavin's deeds and acts were under close surveillance starting on October 10, 1944 and bear witness to his efforts to serve the Soviet regime without going back on what he said and did.

In a letter to the Minister of Higher Education of the USSR in January 1946, he stated:

> I do not consider myself a Marxist. . . . But my vision of the world is not idealist and does not run counter to Marxism, or in any case does not contradict its sociological conception which historical explanations in Soviet universities is based on. . . . Questions of general philosophy, which I resolve in my own way, I do not expound in my courses, for I teach neither philosophy nor even the methodology of history, and the specific features of my vision of the world . . . make it possible for me to regard the historical process from a materialist point of view and, without compromising my conscience as a scholar, to follow the established program to the letter and to apply it scrupulously. (L.Y.A.: Memorandum: 5)

He had to admit, however, that his intellectual activity by itself was incompatible with the regime: "I am currently writing a universal history, but my conceptions are unacceptable for the age," he once confided in private (L.Y.A., Memorandum: 6). Too late, he understood that the trap had closed on him and that he could neither teach nor publish his works: "He lost the hope of seeing them appear in the USSR; the idea occurred to him that the only solution was to send his works abroad and publish them there under a pseudonym" (L.Y.A.: Memorandum: 8). His last trip to Moscow, which he took in order to try to release Irina from the grasp of the MGB as much as to try to find work again, seems to have been followed by a moment of despair (according to testimony given by his daughter Suzanne).

His effective participation in the Eurasian movement was the only concrete element on the basis of which an "affair" could be assembled. A list of persons to be arrested for collaboration with the Germans (L.Y.A.: Memorandum: 6) shows that starting from 1944 he was among a number of persons to be arrested, since he was a professor at the University of Vilnius during the German occupation, but his conversations with informers and his personal correspondence under MGB supervision did not make it possible to give a basis to any accusation whatsoever of collaboration or even to some sort of sympathy for the Nazi occupiers. His participation in the Eurasian movement that so interested the examining magistrate appears to have been rather meager, with no practical implications, and it is quite difficult to grant this participation any particular importance.

It still remains that his refusal to leave when Lithuania became Soviet (even though those who were close to him urged him to do so) and his attempts at loyal cooperation with the regime gave evidence of the same attitude as that in 1924, when he agreed to take part in Eurasian initiatives. From this point of view, it might be said that Eurasian movement is revealing of his entire existential attitude and that it played a decisive role in his destiny.

We have seen that prior to his forced emigration in 1922 and in his past as a historian of culture, nothing would seem to indicate that Karsavin was prone to take part in such a movement. Not even in the works from his Eurasian period did he show the characteristic interest of the members of this organization in linguistic speculations, or "geosophy." In the article for *Sovremennie Zapiski*, he even made a point of his incompetence in linguistics.

The only indications explicitly referring to this movement are the use of the term "Russia-Eurasia" in his writings during 1925–29 to designate the cultural and geographical unit he was talking about (a term that often aroused a smirk of irony in him and seems to have been something of a concession) and the highlighting of everything negative that Western European influence might have had as a formative principle of modern Russian culture: if it was possible to speak of the "decline of European culture," this decline was taking place within Europeanized Russian culture.

RUSSIAN CULTURE AND RELIGION

It is this latter point that was the true subject of the book written in 1922, *Vostok, zapad i russkaja ideia* (*The East, the West and the Russian Idea*), which announced two articles relating to the destiny of Greek Orthodoxy: "O sustsnosti pravoslaiia ('On the Essence of Orthodoxy'") and "Uroki otretsennoi very" ("Lessons of a Repudiated Faith"). The title may lead one to believe that what was at issue was a problem related to one debated by the Eurasians: the place of Russia between "east" and "west." In part, this is true, but the treatise took up once again a notion already developed in works that Karsavin had devoted to religious faith in the Middle Ages: "the ambivalence of the religious consciousness," which can devote itself to saving the world (faith materialized in works) or, on the contrary, can flee the world for one's own salvation (hermitism).

In this article, he modified the formulation. One of these tendencies, which, after Khomiakov, he called "theism," places God outside the world; the other, called "pantheism," sees God as immanent in the world. In the pre-Christian world, these tendencies were clearly situated: the first in China, but also in Hellenism and in Rome (1922: 75); the second in Brahmanism, Buddhism, and Taoism (81).

For the first, as God is thought of as being outside the world, all "authentic knowledge of the absolute" (76) is impossible. Man's relation to the divinity, finding no other possible expression, is modeled after that of man to others or to things. This religious attitude involves a high level of ritualism, with the accent falling on "works." As God is not accessible, attention is concentrated on the physically sensible, and human life and its organization end up by acquiring an absolute value, independent of the relation to God.

The second tendency affirms that "an immediate contact with the divine" is possible and that it has a feeling for "the immanence of the absolute" (81). Man is able to enter into intimate fusion with the divinity, placed at the very heart of the physically sensible. This presence of the divinity brings about a relation to the physically sensible that is contradictory: either the physically perceptible can be accepted passively, without any desire to transform the real, or it can be totally rejected as unworthy of its divine content. This attitude leads to asceticism and flight from the world, to hermitism.

Christianity, a superior form of religious belief, brings about a synthesis of these two tendencies, and it comprises a specific geographical area that includes the West and Russia: contrary to what is affirmed by the Eurasians, Russia is thus not located between the East and the West. Russia is in the West if, by "West," Christianity is meant. Here, the term "east" designates "Eastern Christianity," that is, Greek Orthodox Christianity. It has nothing to do with Asia. From a religious point of view, it must also be pointed out that the Eurasians themselves always affirmed their attachment to Greek Orthodoxy.

For Karsavin, "non-Christian" or "pre-Christian" types of religious faith can enter into competition with Christianity. It is "ridiculous" to speak of the "yellow threat" the way "pan-Mongolism" (one of the precursors of Eurasianism) did: so long as the East remains faithful to itself, it cannot overstep its boundaries. And if it does change, it can only become Christian, that is, merge into the unit formed by the West and Russia (85).

The synthesis brought about by Christianity between the two fundamental tendencies of religious consciousness does not mean that these tendencies are expressed everywhere in the same way: the West seems to have privileged the "ritualist" side, whereas Russia (Eastern Orthodox Christianity) shows a clearer attachment to "pantheism," with its mystical and ascetic tendencies.

The essential dogma for Christianity is the Trinity, which is the basis of man's relation with the absolute, with totality. It is in the dogma of the Trinity, such as it is formulated by the Credo, that the fundamental divergence between Christianity of the East and West is expressed, with the latter replacing "by" (the Holy Spirit proceeding from the Father "by" or "through" the Son) with an equivalent of "and": "qui ex patre *filioque* procedit." It is thus that a particular bi-unity is created, the Father and the Son, which seems to "lessen" the Spirit (94). While the West distinguishes the three persons of the Trinity, the East sees them in their dynamic union. "The unity . . . of the hypostasis can be understood only in the sense that each of them is in itself the other two—that is to say, the complete Divinity, which gives the possibility of a full absolution of being created by the Father through the Son and sanctified by the Spirit" (125). This "absolution of being" means that the created world is made divine thanks to the person of Christ incarnated, sacrificed and restored in its unity with the Father thanks to the Spirit. The divine humanity of Christ makes it possible to preserve the link between the physically perceptible and the absolute. With it, it makes all of humanity divine, which has nothing to do with "buying back" sins.

In the West, as a consequence of the *filioque*, this direct link between the physically perceptible and the absolute is lost. Faith and reason are dissociated, and they control two domains that remain distinct. Faith has ceased to be a collective affair, which has thus lost its visible and present relation to the absolute. It has become a purely private affair.

When he discusses the *filioque*, Karsavin may give the impression of wanting to do the work of the theologian, but this is not really his aim: when he reflects on the destinies of Russia, it is as a historian of mentalities, and dogma is a concrete material, a creator and vehicle of mentalities, that enables the historian to think about the future and the present of cultures while remaining within the domain of facts and avoiding the gratuitous "prophecies" with which he reproached Pierre Struve in 1922 (42), and that he later the Eurasians.

The profound rupture between the two tendencies in religious consciousness was consummated during the Renaissance. It was then that the collective reference to the absolute was abandoned, leading to "rejection of the dream of an inaccessible celestial life and absolutisation of terrestrial life in an ideal of universal empirical prosperity" (1922: 100). The Russian Revolution, by pretending to realize this ideal of universal happiness without reference to the absolute, is the extreme outcome of the secularization of Western culture at which the Catholic conception of the Trinity logically arrives: it represents the tragedy of Europe inside Europeanized Russia. Paradoxically, the Russian people, because they belong by their cultural type to the "East" of Christianity, are characterized by their feeling for the absolute. If they attempt to realize the Western dream of earthly happiness, they do it in their own way—extremist and sacrificial, prompted to renounce themselves because of this abnegation, this exceptional receptivity to the other that had been noted by Dostoevskii (129). National self-glorification must not be sought here, however, as intuition of the absolute and feeling for a "divine filiation" do not ward off "the turpitudes of the prodigal son," noted Karsavin ironically (108).

This notion of a collective relationship to the divine is essential, but it must not be confused with a return to Medieval "unanimity," such as described by Nikolai Berdiaev in *A New Middle Ages*. A highly characteristic preoccupation of his time seems to run through his entire work, which is to seek out what lies at the basis of the possibility of our knowledge. The mere fact that a phenomenon is apprehended or that a sign is deciphered presupposes a faculty of generalization that rises out of this "relation to the absolute," and this is one of the main themes of Karsavin's *Filosofiia istorii* (1923a: *Philosophy of History*). The shortcoming of modern Western civilization is that it deliberately puts the collective relation to the absolute aside, a relation which does not disappear, however, since all action and all knowledge are impossible without it, even though it proves to be ignored and is thus often led astray. This observation takes on the full weight of its significance if it is remembered that Karsavin was writing at the dawn of the rise of totalitarianisms.

The treatise of 1922 was also in response to a precise historical situation: on what bases, in the new historical context, could a possible reunification of the churches be realized with the Revolution having modified the relations between church and state (Ju. K. Gerassimov)? This reunification must be realized, stressed Karsavin, by respecting the specificity of each of the denominations. The Uniate solution, for instance, is deceptive: why adopt the "Eastern rite" while keeping the quintessence of Western spirituality, the *filioque* clause? Due to the weakness of the Russian church at this time, attempted reunifications could be disastrous for it. Furthermore, it seemed that Soviet power at the time favored Catholic proselytism.

The intensification of threats weighing on the Russian Orthodox Church no doubt explains Karsavin's criticisms with regard to Catholicism, which grew in virulence between 1922 and 1925, the year *Uroki otrechennoi very* (1925a: *Lessons of a Repudiated Faith*) appeared. In this article, not only is the *filioque* condemned, but so is papal infallibility, the dogma of Immaculate Conception, and even the Eucharist, such as it is presented by Catholicism. In spite his allusions to Dostoevskii or Khomiakov, however, Karsavin no doubt took a position that was different from theirs. First of all, he considered Catholicism from the inside, something like a fan of theological jousts, and if he criticized it violently, as he did at the end of *Lessons of a Repudiated Faith*, this was because he expected a great deal of it, with these" (1925a: 142). The traditional aggressiveness of the Russian with regard to the Catholic Church is due to the fact that this Church is the "other" through which he defines himself by opposing it (89). On the other hand, these criticisms must be looked at in light of the historical context mentioned above. Taking them as such comes down to also taking as such his humorous description of the Sistine Madonna by Raphael, intended to reveal the weakening of spirituality in Western art after the Renaissance. In the same way, his highly critical reflection on the Sacré Cœur (perhaps more justified) should not allow us to forget the very different use that he made of this theme in "Poem of Death."

Neither before the Eurasian period nor, it seems, afterward did he show hostility toward Catholicism. On the contrary—for in his studies on Franciscan religious faith, he described an exceptional meeting between the two fundamental tendencies of religious consciousness. His book *Katolichestvo* (1918b; *Catholicism*) presents this religion in a favorable light and limits discussion of the *filioque* to one line. Later, in the 1930s, his correspondence with Father Wetter, counselor at the Vatican for questions concerning Soviet ideology, and the circumstances of his death in 1952 at the Abez camp (it is sometimes said that he "converted" to Catholicism, as he received the last sacraments from a Catholic priest) show a mind free of all denominational narrowness. But if, during the 1920s, he insisted on what separated, this was because the principal rupture was at work within Russian culture, imperiling its very existence. The violence of expression (the Catholic Church, "if it remains impassive to the distress of the persecuted Russian Church, repudiates Christ crucified in it") stems from this near certainty that "the Russian Church is in the process of dying" (154).

The East, the West and the Russian Idea, written when Karsavin was still in Russia, can thus be considered a Eurasian work before its time. The second work that shows evidence of this meeting with Eurasianism is the article, "The Essence of Orthodoxy," published in the 1924 collection *O suscnosti pravoslaviia* (1924; *Problems of Russian Consciousness*), and the third, as already seen, "Lessons of a Repudiated Faith."

These three publications show that for Karsavin the essential point—and no doubt the one that was a determining factor in his membership in the Eurasian movement—was defense of the Greek Orthodox religion wherein he saw the quintessence and the guardian of the Russian mentality and of its specific values.

The book of dialogues, *O somnenii, nauke i vere*, was also published in 1925 by the Evraziistvo publishing company. In 1926 there appeared three articles on partial, secondary subjects in *Evraziiskaia Kronika* and in *Put'* as well as a treatise intended to be a systematic exposition on the question, *Evraziistvo*, that seems to be collectively inspired (Hauchard 1996: 361).

From this point of view, the most interesting years are 1927–28. It was during these years that lengthy articles appeared setting forth his positions of principle: "Osnovy politiki" ("Foundations of Politics") and "Fenomenologiia revolijucii" ("The Phenomenology of Revolution"), which appeared in *Evrazijskij Vremennik*, as well as a treatise entitled *Cerkov,' licnost' i gosudarstvo* (*The Church, the Person and the State*). An article entitled, "K poznaniju russkoj revoljucii" ("Knowledge of the Russian Revolution"), which was written during those years, was apparently not published at the time. However, an article on the same subject, written in Lithuanian ("Prie Rusu revoliucijos pazinimo") was to appear in the first issue of the journal *Vairas* in 1929. Six articles appeared in 1928 in the reviews *Evraziia* and *Versty*. In 1929, the review *Evraziia* published fifteen of Karsavin's articles, all on political and religious subjects.

This production then came to an abrupt and near total halt. In 1934, an article entitled "Valstybe ir demokratijos krize" ("The State and the Crisis of Democracy"). appeared in Lithuania in a Catholic journal, *Zidinys*. An article on the French Revolution that did not appear at the time and, it seems, took inspiration from "The Phenomenology of Revolution," resulted in an article published in 1939 in the Lithuanian journal *Naujoji Romuva* under the title, "Didzioji Prancuzu revoliucija ir vakaru Europa." The Eurasian period of Karsavin's work was very short, but its production was abundant.

THEORY OF CULTURE

As for the "Eastern" inspiration as such, it seems that reflection on the cultures of the East in a broad culturological perspective was to appear only quite late in his work and that it was not published. During the last years leading up to his arrest, he studied the history of the ancient East, demonstrating (not without veiled reference to Stalinist times) that it was characterized by "collective creation, with the personification of society under the traits of Pharaoh" (L.Y.A.: Memorandum, 7).

In themselves, the "Eurasian" works show no fundamental difference from the rest of Karsavin's thought, which appears to be quite consistent, certain aspects being dealt with more deeply but without ruptures. His theory of state and revolution is based on the general principles of his philosophy and belong to the "non-Eurasian" part of his work. At the end of the 1920s, his philosophy of history was put into the service of the Eurasian movement without any reorientation. His general principles, verified through concrete study of the phenomenon of revolution, made it possible to sketch a completely new ideology that was intended to replace the communist ideology.

The 1926 and 1927 articles "Foundations of Politics" and "The Phenomenology of Revolution" are thus fully complementary. The first summarizes the essentials of his philosophical positions. It reviews the basic principles that are expounded in detail in *Philosophy of History* (1923) and in the treatise "Apie Tobulybe" ("On Perfection"), written in Lithuanian in the camp at Abez in 1951. These positions are based on the doctrine of "wholeness-unity," "symphonic person," and "coincidence of contraries," the last inherited from Nicolas de Cues.

The second article compares the French and Russian Revolutions in order to establish their formal resemblances and to draw out the "inner dialectics" of "revolution" as a phenomenon. One single element can make it possible to reconstitute the entire process. This is the way he put it in 1922: "Like a paleontologist [who], on the basis of only the jaw of an unknown animal, reconstitutes its entire skeleton, so a historian, starting with a single act of the subject of evolution, can . . . imagine its other manifestations and the possibilities of other manifestations" (1922: 66). The unity of this structure implies, in passing, that the historian is responsible for elucidating the present and the immediate future as an interpretation of the past. It is the responsibility of the historian to determine the "destiny" of a culture.

The same reflections were to be taken up briefly two years later in "Knowledge of the Russian Revolution," which adds nothing that is fundamentally new, but insists on the fact that revolutions have a recognizable "form," making it possible to distinguish them from a coup d'état, for example (1928: 65). Conversely, a revolution can appear not to be a revolution: what the French Revolution produced was achieved peacefully by the other countries of Europe.

In the beginning is the idea of "perfection," of "absolute totality of everything that is, that has been and that will be—wholeness." Herein lies the fullness of reality, in space and in time; and yet, it does not belong to the domain of the empirical, which is the domain of division and separation where each moment and each individuation never comes about except as one of the potentialities contained in infinite number within the "whole."

"Persons," who bring certain potentialities of "perfection" into being, are called "symphonic" because they contain in capacity a multiplicity of possibles that are in harmony with each other which, in turn, come into being for a given period of time in other "persons" of lower rank. There is a hierarchy of unities, but this is not only a hierarchy of values: the individual represents a certain unity at the lowest level, and in the sphere immediately higher (e.g., one's family), he represents another unity, and so on and so forth, to arrive at that "higher symphonic person" which is the culture of humanity. In each and every one is preserved the singular features of the "person" situated at another hierarchical level.

In this hierarchical construction, the higher "person" represents the unity and the conjunction of those that are lower. Conversely, it is these lower unities that bring the "person" into being, that materialize it in its concrete qualities. Thus, the "symphonic person," or "culture" (the culture of humanity as a whole), comes into being in various national cultures which, in turn, takes the form of "state," "religion," "type of social organization," and so on. In this way, the last level of coming into being is reached: the individual. It is only because he is integrated into this succession that the individual is a living organ of this "wholeness" represented by culture.

The "symphonic person" is not a sum total. It is a principle of unity, a multiplicity now in "retraction," like a circle reducing into its center, now in "expansion," projecting outward from this center to achieve a certain "quality," a certain possible of this center which contains them all in capacity (*kachestvovanie*). The relation between two "symphonic persons" of differing rank which comes into being through expansion and retraction is thus not a static relation, but a dynamic one, a relation that is in permanent movement.

At the same time, this movement is a continuous succession of deaths and rebirths: just as the multiplicity comes into being in the individual, so the individual returns to the unity to vanish there, then to be reborn in another form, in another coming into being which is at the same time a "retracted" multiplicity (*stiazennoe*). For Karsavin, the permanent succession of deaths and rebirths characterizes both the inner life of the individual (feelings, moods, thoughts of my "self" vanishing ceaselessly to be reborn in other feelings, etc.) and the existence of individuals in the most usual sense, but also the existence of social groups, states, and so on.

This conception of wholeness implies that "I" both exist and do not exist at the same time, since I am both the "I" come into being in a given circumstance at a given "moment" and the multiplicity of my "qualities," but in capacity, in retraction. In particular, "I" am, or can be, the particular and momentary coming into being of all "symphonic persons" of higher rank and of which I am a projection—family, social group, culture, and so on (1927: 12). In the physically perceptible, however, the various instances of coming into being of a same individual are mutually exclusive while at the same time they are coexistent. The coincidence of contraries lies at the very heart of reality (1991: 22).

On these basic principles, Karsavin builds up his theory of culture, state, and law, applied to the Russia of the future ("Foundations of Politics") and verified through the study of recent revolutionary events ("The Phenomenology of Revolution").

The highest "symphonic person," or the culture of humanity, comes into being in different national cultures. The "wholeness" of each national culture determines the unity of the domains in which a given people manifests its existence: state, society, economy, etc. It is here that the philosophical doctrine of the "person" is found, determining the "subject of culture," that is, a culture as the whole of its concrete manifestations and the individuals that materialize it. It is a "collegial" (*sobornyi*) subject, a term that seems to be nearly synonymous with "symphonic": it brings together the individual level and the supra-individual level.

Karsavin defined the essential spheres of culture as follows: state (or political), spiritual, material (1927: 28). They exist in hierarchical relation with one another.

The material sphere concerns relations with nature—its transformation, its "spiritualization." However, it would be wrong to take values thus created for values that are exclusively and strictly material. They express culture in its wholeness in the same way as do law, social organization, and so on. Economy, which lies at the limits of the material domain because it provides intercommunication, must be under the control of the state, for it is not independent of the totality of culture, and the state is the vehicle and guarantor of cultural values. For this reason, it is necessary for the ruling class to participate in economic activity, that is, there must be a state economy alongside individual economic activity, even though it cannot exist alone. Although the principles set out here are rather general and disinterested, one has a feeling, in the definition of power and of its fields of activity, that the reality of power in Soviet Russia was being taken implicitly into account, such as it appeared at the time (prior to the rise of Stalinism).

The most original point is in fact this articulation between principles which, ultimately, are not in contradiction with the Soviet system and the central position given to Greek Orthodoxy. The domain of the relation to the absolute, that is, the sphere of spiritual activity, in fact occupies a primordial position in the theory of the state formulated by Karsavin. To his way of seeing things, it is in the Greek Orthodox Church that the state is materialized. The spiritual sphere presupposes, as do the others, the participation and directive activity of the state (of the ruling class) because it is the bearer of the "wholeness" represented by culture as a superior unity.

Culture is not a sum total of its principal components, the state being one of them. Culture is a principle of unity that takes form in each of these spheres, even if it can be said that the nature of the state is the privileged expression of the type of culture. Moreover, these spheres are in a relation of mutual dependence, as the responsibility of the state, with regard to culture, is immense. It is the state that "determines the existence of this subject as a person," that gives the subject its form. On the state depends the free "organic" development of culture, that is, the creation, development and preservation of values. It is within the framework of culture that "the relation of the subject . . . to its perfection, that is, to its moral and religious activity" becomes manifest (but also that it fulfills its destiny, seen as a completed form). The domain of law is also a function of the nature of the state, since it is through the law that the state acquires its full sense and through it that the state causes norms to be interiorized by the individuals that constitute the state, rather than be made up of a set of empty forms. They are the emanation and the particular coming into being of one and the same totality—a culture.

As each given culture represents the coming into being of this "higher symphonic person" represented by the culture of humanity, the destiny of each particular culture concerns all human cultures (1927: 11). The various types of culture are individual instances of humanity coming into being, of the "higher symphonic person," although each nation materializes a given type of culture in its own way (1927: 22). The other levels of this "person" (e.g., within the nation, that of the "ruling stratum") can be put into correlation with instances of coming into being of the same level (ruling classes) within other nations: this is what determines a multinational culture.

Russia, as a national culture, is located at the junction between two higher supranational levels: European culture and Asian culture. The

Russian Revolution, which sets the space of Russia/Eurasia in play, brings the historic mission of Russia into the open: it concerns Asian cultures, with their new awareness of themselves, as much as it does European culture, which must come out of its current individualist crisis, or die.

The origin of this crisis resides in the alteration of relations between the individual and the collective. Western institutions bear the mark of this: on this point, the anti-Western character of the Eurasian positions come out fully in Karsavin's works. "Parliamentarism" presupposes a lack of union, the absence of common goals and unified organization, but it also presupposes the "state of class," which is no more viable, as it ignores true social diversity. Nor do the famous "rights of man" find grace in his eyes, since for him they were only an "abstract, doctrinaire phraseology, concealing aims that are entirely concrete, practical, . . . a self-serving will to domination and 'bourgeois' self-sufficiency." As Karsavin noted quite correctly, defense of the rights of man is relative to "degrees longitude and latitude"! (1926: 58).

"Fraternity," he was to state in "Knowledge of the Russian Revolution," is illusory, since in the parliamentary system the people are in fact put at a remove from real power by institutions (1928: 72). What characterized the Russian Revolution, by contrast, is the fact that it was a social revolution: it raised the question not of formal liberties, but of real liberties, of their concrete content. Justice overrides an "equality," which is at any rate impossible.

Because it is the expression of no individualized will, the compromise of democracy is an abstraction. The separation of powers is first and foremost a fiction, before being an evil. It generates absurd and debilitating bureaucratization. It reduces the people to a formless "population," devoid of cohesion (1928: 43). Elections do not ensure a permanent contact between electors and their representatives, but result in depriving people of political rights and in excluding them from effective government.

In this context, only the multiplicity of parties protects the state from despotism, not its deep nature. The balance between parties and their multiplicity leads to irresponsibility and insignificance, since "the most unheard-of fantasies" will in any case be corrected. A political party and its program should express a relation to the truth, to the absolute, for it is thus that the government, through the ruling stratum, can become the "symbol" (the sign or, in *Philosophy of History*, "the abbreviator") of the popular will.

The purpose of the concept of "symphonic persons" and their hierarchical construction is to make it possible to overcome this rupture between individual and community. What is truly individual in the individual, according to Karsavin, is to realize the supra-individual consciousness or will in a particular manner. If this consciousness or will is eliminated, the individual himself can no longer exist. The richer in content the "higher" sphere is, the more complete individual existence is. On the other hand, without these individual instances of coming into being, the "higher" cannot exist, as it reveals itself only through them.

The theory of social relations is inseparable from a theory of the "ruling stratum." By "ruling stratum" (which is not a class), Karsavin meant not only the government and those who from far or near participate in it, but "all of cultivated society, from government to the extremist of revolutionaries" (1926: 11). The "ruling stratum" is thus quite close to the notion of "intelligentsia" and is often even combined with it.

The relations of supremacy (the idea of a power that is strong and personal) result from the organization peculiar to the "collegial person." Being "collegial," although multiple, the "collegial person" possesses nonetheless a single will, and this is one of the elements that it is the task and function of the "ruling stratum" and its leader to exteriorize (1926: 16).

Under nonrevolutionary conditions, the "ruling stratum" is a "microcosm" that expresses the "popular cosmos" and vice versa. This organic relation can also take on a variety of forms—those of "despocy" (a neologism of Karsavin) as well as those of "extreme forms of democracy." Under certain conditions that announce either revolution or decline, the "ruling stratum" loses its organic link with the "people," that is, with the concrete unity of culture.

REVOLUTION

Revolution is nothing other than a sign: it shows that the "symphonic" relation between the various components of society and the "ruling stratum" has been severed. The more the gulf between the "ruling stratum" and the people broadens, the more the "ruling stratum" congeals into a "class." In principle, except during periods of crisis, the "ruling stratum" is neither a state nor a class. Its transformation into a class is a sign of decline, of the loss of its "organic" link with the rest of society (1926: 19).

Karsavin rejected the opposition between society and power in which the seed of the revolutionary process is often seen: in reality, the struggle of the "ruling stratum" (otherwise called "society") with power means nothing other than its self-destruction (1926: 18). Under conditions where military defeat threatens the state (e.g., the Russian-Japanese War of 1904), when the "ruling stratum" is no longer able to cope, "the lower classes, which possess a powerful instinct for preserving the state, can, when the conditions are favorable, destroy the corrupt summit" (19).

In spite of appearances, the people do not really intervene in this destruction. The people are content to let the "ruling stratum" destroy itself without intervening (1926: 22). The occasional defects of the leaders (lack of will, preoccupation with routine) are in fact organic features of the "ruling stratum" before and during revolutionary periods (23). No burst of action, no person out of the ordinary, stated Karsavin, would be capable of preventing the triggering of revolution.

The first phase of revolution is thus the death of the former "ruling stratum." Then comes "anarchy" or even, as Karsavin called it, "pan-archy"—the struggle between all possible different "orders" among themselves. When faced with the unchaining of "egoisms," of territorial or social idiosyncrasies that threaten the very existence of the state, the vital necessity is to create new forms of the state rapidly, and that is the reason for this violence that expresses itself in the proletarian state. The interests of the community may then disappear completely behind the explosion of idiosyncrasies.

When individualism (as it is found in the West) is developed to the extreme, it destroys the individual. The solution is to reestablish both the conscious and collective relation to the absolute and the uninterrupted chain of "individuations" from one "higher symphonic person" to another, from culture to the state and up to the individual, in order for the concrete, perceptible link between the state and the various "collegial persons" that correspond to its instances of coming into being not to be lost. This is this new way that is sought by Eurasian thought, a new way opened up to it by the institution of the Soviets and the appearance of a new type of "ruling stratum."

Karsavin granted particular importance to the Soviet system (1927: 39) because through the type of responsibility that it implies, through its hierarchical unity and its methods for the transmission of power, this system represented both diversity and living unity, the basic principles of which it set out.

Indirect elections, which are rather cooptations, take account of a "living personality . . . expressing a collegial consciousness" (1927: 40). However, its representative in particular, even outside the period of elections, always remains responsible before the lower level of which he is an emanation. Through him, the "lower strata" (*nizy*) participate actively and effectively in the action of the state.

The Soviets bring about a sort of cut in society, from top to bottom. They are "the living trunk" that plunges its roots "into the depth of the popular continent." There is thus identity between the "ruling stratum," its sole ideology, and the "popular will," with "totality," its "unconscious ideology," expressing itself in this manner (1927: 46). In theory, at least, the rupture between "ruling stratum" and popular masses is overcome, and their relation can become the expression of the relation to the absolute.

Faced with Soviet power, Karsavin's position is clear: the Soviets are to be preserved, as they are capable of being the authentic expression of a strong and popular power. What must be eliminated is the out-dated communist ideology. which, above all, has the erroneous aim of eliminating the question of the relation to the absolute, recreating the scourge of Western ideologies.

Social groups appear and disappear as particular and momentary individuations of a same higher unity do—society. A given group (the "ruling stratum," for example, during a revolution) disappears only to leave place for other groups. As for individuals, they are mobile and pass from one group to another, also creating "transitory groups." Some may be ephemeral (a scientific expedition), but they show that what constitutes the group is always a goal, an action or a common predisposition of mind (1927: 26). These "ephemeral creatures" ensure intercommunication within the higher "collegial subject," that is, society.

Karsavin's representations always have a highly visual character, and for this reason, social existence is conceived of dynamically as myriads of "subjects" that gather together to constitute new "persons"—"persons" who in turn split up and disappear, as in the visible universe. The dwindling away of this intercommunication, the extreme atomization of society into an "anarchical individualism," is a sign of decay, of entropy.

Empirically, the various individual spheres limit each other and stand in mutual opposition. The "whole" never appears in its plenitude and completeness. Institutions of state are required to take account of the relative character which is peculiar to the physically perceptible (1927: 18), which is the domain of division and separation—separation of classes from one another and of humanity from nature, but especially separation of humanity from God (19).

For Karsavin, this is also the danger par excellence of ideology, for it risks fixing relations once and for all between the various instances of "coming into being" of this higher "person," even though these relations are in perpetual transformation. Knowing how to control this practical domain where all instances of coming into being are in movement and taking account of this perpetual evolution—such is the responsibility of the politician.

The internal dynamism of this "symphonic person" that society represents implies a certain amount of violence, whether this violence is accepted or not: renunciation of oneself is inevitably involved through return to unity within a higher collegial person that organization of "symphonic persons" presupposes. This paradox was to be affirmed by Karsavin many times, whether it was relative to individual existence or to the life of societies, for the affirmation of self is truly complete when one arrives at sacrifice. This explains the importance that the person of Christ and the mystery of the Trinity held for Karsavin.

On the hand, by refusing to renounce "oneself," the individual becomes lost. The very possibility of consciousness shows that man is capable of ceaselessly going beyond the limits of his individual self by turning to a unity of the supra-individual type. This necessarily implies the sacrifice of a part of one's self—of one's former convictions, for example.

The origin of revolution resides in the refusal to renounce oneself. The "ruling social group" condemns itself by becoming fixed in its privileges, by cutting itself off from other social classes, and in the same way, a people condemns itself to perishing when it closes in on itself (1927: 20). We fulfill ourselves by losing ourselves. The Karsavian philosophy, then, is a philosophy of dispossession.

The fact that "these processes express themselves only through individuals and in [individuals]" reveals the articulation between the history of cultures (blossoming, violent death, reappearance in other forms) and the *apologia* of the "will to die" (adherence to one's own disappearance, which is the ideal of the self, as expressed in "Poem of Death"). Like Toynbee, Karsavin puts the kenosis of Christ into relation with the transformations of cultures, but he is clear in showing how the two levels, individual and collective, overlap, and he does so through the teaching on the hierarchy of "symphonic persons" and their relations of expansion toward an infinite circumference and of retraction toward the center which is also unity.

After the death of the former "symphonic person" is born a new "individuation of the higher person" (1926: 52). The historical process represents a series of deaths and rebirths of a same "higher symphonic person" (different individuations of a same culture). However, it can occur that death is not followed by a new birth, and it is then the end of the "higher symphonic person," the disappearance of a nation, its transformation still possible into a "mere ethnographic material" (this expression belongs to Danilevskii 1867: 21).

The question of death, and of a death that is accepted, a sort of voluntary sacrifice, is at the heart of this thought about culture. Karsavin never lost an opportunity to stress that, as a member of the old Russian intelligentsia in exile, he was part of a culture that was condemned, and that if he was lamenting death, it was in fact his own that he was mourning: "we do not wish to see it [that the former world is irremediably condemned] because everything old is dear to us as something that belongs to us, like ourselves—because it is we ourselves who are dying in its death" (1925: 83). After recognizing the truth and validity (*pravda*) of what had taken place, it was necessary to put it into practice, "by renouncing what was dear to us, but that which is nonetheless condemned to disappear" (85). To accept one's own disappearance as a cultural subject was, then, to adhere to the alternation between deaths and rebirths so that Russian culture could be born in another form.

This new Russian culture was based on the revivication of Greek Orthodoxy. The crisis of European culture was first of all a crisis of the collective relation to the absolute, and if this crisis encountered such an echo in Russia, it was because the relation of the Russian mentality to the absolute was not the same as in Western Europe: it took on an exacerbated character which finally brought about the loss of the former lay world in the person of a Europeanized Russia.

In Russia, it was during the Time of Troubles at the turn of the sixteenth century, a time of profound upheavals between the reign of Boris Godunov and that of the first Romanov, that the vital problem of religion began to stand out, for it became necessary "to find an absolute foundation, that is to think through again the vision of the world proposed by Greek Orthodoxy" (1926: 59). At the time, Russia was unable to reestablish the life of the nation on new religious bases in forms that were peculiar to it. This failure "resulted in a forced Europeanization, begun under Peter the Great and finding its peak with communism."

It was then that the rupture between the "ruling stratum" and the "people" took root. The "ruling stratum" became foreign by adopting an imported culture, Western culture, and the wider the gulf grew between the "ruling stratum" and the people, the more "the passage from the first to the second became linked to the loss of the national character and to adaptation to the outside" (1928: 67).

The Russian Revolution, a disaster of European Russia, crystallized the failure of European culture as a whole. In each case of revolution, the external manifestation of a profound vice, the forms of state have been received from the outside (1927: 35). Hence, Europe received its forms of government from England, and Russia received its forms of government from Europe, so that in no case were these forms the product of an organic development.

The religious question, as developed by Karsavin in this theory of the state (the absolute necessity of a state religion), is no doubt the most disturbing point, the most difficult to accept for the modern way of thinking. The very least of our acts, he maintained, implies a relation to the absolute. This relation, whether it is willfully ignored or not, kept in an unconscious state (which is always the case in modern lay societies), goes astray, and because it is not conscious, it takes unchecked despotic power over the individual. It is especially important to elucidate the relation to the absolute and to give it an external form—the domain of the religious. It is possible, of course, to speak of "theocracy" in order to define the form of state advocated by Karsavin. However, what appears to be most necessary in his eyes is that the relation to the absolute be made visible, that it be made the object of public debate and no longer "repressed" (this term belongs to a field that Karsavin never took up, yet it is the term that comes to mind when he defines the collective relation of Western societies to the notion of the absolute).

However, it must not be forgotten that what is involved here is a set of theoretical reflections whose modes of realization yet remained to be discovered. In order to measure what he meant when he spoke of the place of religion in the state, it might be necessary to elucidate the precise and concrete place of religion in his life. On this matter, we have extremely contradictory information. He came from artistic circles in Saint Petersburg that were indifferent to the problems of religion, and it seems that he came to religious faith on his own initiative. In a letter written by M. Dobuzinskii in 1920 there appears an astonishing sentence: "I'll be going with the Verejski to the Vvedenskaja church where Karsavin is to give the sermon." Deeply attached to Greek Orthodoxy as an institution, it seems he was not (if we are to believe his close relations) a churchgoer. There are "vague" memories of seeing him in church on Holy Friday, etc., although his life in the camp at Abez, as related by Vaneiev, leaves a different impression.

The originality of this approach is that while he proposed creating an ideology for the new Russian state, it turns out to be a study of the various revolutionary ideologies and of the ways in which they appeared. A great deal of the demonstration (in the two articles, but especially in *The Phenomenology of Revolution*) describes how a new ideology is born which may not always be viable, as the various episodes of the French and Russian revolutions show. The thinker of a new ideology for the Russian state, Karsavin, as in his early works on Western spirituality, remained attentive to the difference between what can be called a mentality (a profound, organic, largely unconscious phenomenon) and a full-fledged ideology, even though the two can be closely linked and are not totally independent from one another.

What characterizes a mentality is that it acts as a pivot between the possible and the realized, between power and act, between the "person" in retraction or in expansion. Hence, it may be that the ideal formulated by Dostoevskii, the famous "universal receptiveness" of the Russian national character, will become a reality (as believed by some) in "the religious and moral principles according to which the Russian people determine their conduct" (1922: 70). It is equally possible, however, that

the "maximum coming into being of this potentiality is indeed the ideology of Dostoievski." Mentality brought into being in one of its potentialities—this is ideology.

In spite of appearances, revolutionary ideology is only an outdated
ideology, belonging to the old regime (1926: 56). But "nature abhors
vacuums," and it is vital that a new regime be created that is truly
viable. The new stage, and the most essential one, is thus "the [authen-
tic] ideological creation" that is something other than a "phraseology"
and that reflects "awareness and definition of popular ideals, their explanation and religious justification" (56). Involved is the return from an
ideology that is more or less artificial to the deep sources of mentality.

The appearance of a revolutionary ideology can be explained by its
social support. After the first stage of revolution, the most violent and
anarchical, "the torturers, the ambitious and the fanatics" come to power
or, before the revolution, the "expropriators," that is, propagators of acts
of banditry intended to feed the coffers of the party that takes part in
it (perhaps an allusion to Stalin) (1926: 30).

In itself, however, this new "ruling stratum" contributes nothing. It is
merely an emanation of the former stratum, heir to the previous regime,
and the ideology that appears to be new is in fact only a former ideology,
a marginal ideology in times past. Karsavin stresses that revolution in
itself is the emanation of a morbid past and creates nothing new, as the
"new governing bodies" are in fact only the former ones in disguise.

Revolutionary ideology is superficial, consciously adapted to the needs
of the moment and primitive, and a "means of consolation for justifying political actions." It is distinct from "mentality," which, as we saw
above, is deep and organic.

And yet, "to various degrees, ideologies reflect popular mentality
[*mirosozercanie*], although always very imperfectly so." "Whether a good
or an evil, ideology attempts to express the absolute foundations of culture, of the people, of the state" (1926: 31). Even though survival of the
nation might be ensured by a "governmental party" that is popular and
strong, the essential thing is this party's link with a popular will characterized as "unconscious." This is the feature that is peculiar to the
phenomenon "mentality."

Ideology as such remains relative, anchored in a precise moment, and
must be treated as such and able to evolve. Its transformation into a
"compulsory principle" (into the absolute) is a sign of "senility," according
to Karsavin (1926, 31). In any case, he did give clear expression to the
historical stage that the Soviet state was experiencing at the time and
which led, if not to "senility," at least to terror.

When "life itself demands abandonment of the old ideologies," begins the last sentence, then people come to power who have lost all ideology, "and with it their modest reserve of conscience" (1926: 42). Rather than "ideological gangsters," it is "gangsters pure and simple" who settle in.

The destiny of this new "ruling stratum," which borrowed heavily from the former administration, followed that of the model of the French Revolution: the "swamp," a hodgepodge of the old and the new, but without ideological motivation. At this stage, ideology degenerates into "phraseology" and becomes a mere "placard" no longer having anything to do with the concrete. The decisive point for an ideology is to know just how far it is dictated by the real necessities of the life of the state.

The initial actions of revolutionary Russia were motivated by concrete national necessities: requisitions, the fight against free trade, "Sovietization," and so on. On the other hand, the struggle against the NEP and the planned economy were only the "noxious products of an abstract ideology" (1926: 37), and they showed in particular that doubt had crept into the minds of those who proclaimed them. When poverty and famine revealed the limits of the new order of things, it became possible to divert attention by persecuting the Church, by fighting against "bourgeois prejudices," and so on The essential sign of the moment was the ideological vacuum that set in.

Under these conditions of ideological vacuum, terror was no longer justified by anything. Hence, the departure of Robespierre could have been peaceful, claimed Karsavin two years before the "great turning" (he compares the French and Russian Revolutions), if he had not felt the need to continue justifying ideology with terror. During this period, tyranny was all the more on the agenda in that the revolutionary chiefs became useless. However, "the appearance of a tyrannical party and the reconstitution of an apparatus of state are the only way possible for revolutionary 'anarchy' to pass over to a new national spirit" (1926: 41).

At this stage in the development of the new power, ideology represents a necessity and a danger—the necessity for a single ideology that serves as a motor for the life of the state, but also the danger of a rigid ideology transformed into a phraseology that becomes all the more constraining in that it has no links with life, with the authenticity of concrete tasks.

A new ideology, one whose role was to replace communist ideology, was thus to be discovered. In order to be truly productive of new values, this ideology needed above all to be national. This stage was the first one to be really creative because it expressed a profound popular and national will, the will to be reconstituted into a state. In Russia, the people finally defended the Reds and thus put the national spirit on their side, but this was not because the Russians defended communism (1926:

43). It was because the Bolsheviks were the only ones capable of this strong power (refusing concessions at the price of considerable sacrifice), a power for which the country had a vital need at that particular time.

Did the people become "tired" of politics and revolution at this time, as has been said of the Directory? (1926: 44) A "tired" people, answered Karsavin, does not conduct victorious wars. On the contrary, people give the best of their strength during such times. Phenomena of fatigue appear before revolution, caused by the anxiety generated out of vital and unresolved problems. What happens is simply that after a moment of tension when political matters concern everyone in a way that is out of the ordinary, this tension subsides and politics once again becomes "the dullness of an everyday job" (45), the business of specialists.

There was a return to national reality, and it was then that vital problems appearing before the revolution could be solved. "Ideas vital for the nation and based on the absolute sank their roots into the depths of the popular consciousness, . . . and the revolution could do nothing else but help to find these solutions." The task that now became imperative was "to produce a founding ideology of the state that [was] also a national ideology" (1926: 47). Devising this founding ideology for a new noncommunist Russian state was the task that Karsavin set himself.

The new birth of the "symphonic person" reestablishes the links, severed by revolution, with its past or, more precisely, it rediscovers the "absolute ideas" that "form the foundation of its new life and give it a meaning"—both in its past and in its present. This was the reason why it was possible to see a renewal of the idea of nation.

This new national/popular consciousness expressed anew, or should have expressed, the collective relation to the absolute that has been forgotten by modern Western cultures. It was to be felt as a mission to be fulfilled for the people concerned, a mission within a "supra-national unity, which is a higher symphonic person." Here, Eurasia acted as a metamorphosis of the Russian empire achieved thanks to Soviet power.

Contrary to the ideal of bourgeois democracies, the goal of the future Russian state was not to achieve universal prosperity but, rather, "to realize as well and as completely as possible the idea of culture." Berdiaev saw the misfortune of Russian culture in the fact that it is not a culture of material happiness, of "incarnated values." (1918: 25) It is not that Karsavin reveled in the "Russian misfortune," but for him a culture cannot have general well-being as a goal. The new Russian culture must be the guarantor of the relation to the absolute that Western cultures have relegated to the private domain, resulting in the "individualist" crisis that reached its paroxysm in Russia.

THE NEW RUSSIAN STATE

The end of the upheaval brought about by revolution was to rediscover the specific vocation of the Russian people. However, the definition of this vocation had nothing to do with the gratuitous wild imaginings of the publicists on the future of Russia. It was based on concrete observations and on the theoretical framework provided by the historian of cultures. The "task to be realized" was what "informs" a culture, what determines its future. At this stage, the comparison with the paleontologist can be understood better: elements of this "form" of a culture that are contained in the past must make it possible to reconstitute its future starting with factual bases.

This vocation to be realized excludes the typically Western idea of progress (1928: 47) as well as the equivalent one of a communist "paradise." For Karsavin, all of this is "poor metaphysics," for if culture bears witness of a relation to the absolute, it is not itself absolute because its form is never definitively achieved. "Faith in progress" seems to be in search of a sort of immobility, to implicitly devalue time and in particular the present to which one aspires (and it is thus with all of lived reality). The "perfection" toward which individual or collegial "persons" strive (and with them the state) is supra-empirical in nature: "foundation and source of religious and moral activity," this "perfection" can be defined as a sort of higher mission to be fulfilled by the collegial personality (1928: 49), no matter at what ontological level it is located—a "mission" that gives it form as it comes into being. While this perfection is the effective, concrete realization of moral precepts, it has a value in terms of destiny: to strive toward one's "perfection" is to strive toward the full and entire realization of one's destiny, a sort of *amor fati*.

Unique, this ideology was not, however, contrary to liberty. No longer the emanation of a privileged class but of all people, it expressed the unity of culture, that is, of the "subjects" of this culture. It presupposed living interaction between the parts of the whole and thus liberty, but a liberty different from that postulated by individualism, which claims to believe in no final "truth," believing however in its own truth as an absolute. The accusation of despotism that the existence of a single ideology might attract is tempered by the permanent becoming in which the state is involved, presiding over the perpetual creation of new social forms.

Karsavin showed a certain sympathy for fascism (as a national and popular regime) in its beginnings, but never for Nazism. Just as other Eurasians, he criticized Western bourgeois institutions starting with Parliamentarism, for in his eyes it was a parody of popular power. As for fascism, it is "deprived of religious ideology, it lacks a foundation in the absolute." The spirit of the new governmental idea in Russia was fundamentally religious, even with its wayward consequences to the contrary and even with its militant atheism. In its very revolution, which Karsavin considered a "sin," the Russian people remained profoundly religious, and he refused to see in it an "initiation to the mysteries of evil." (1926: 60). Like other thinkers (e.g., Berdiaev 1955), he saw the religious side of Russian atheism. It was not a matter of a "struggle against the Church," but of "religious tension" which revealed itself in all of the horrors of the "sin of an entire people" (*vsenarodnyi grekh*) (60). A "ruling stratum" must exercise a single will, and it is that gives its acts a "concrete" character—something essential in Karsavin's eyes, whence the necessity for a single party. A single party must endow new institutions with this legitimacy which, in the eyes of "the popular element," it lacks in order for these institutions "to take root in life," to rediscover its "organic link" with the popular element.

When everything that is traditional "has gone through the test of the fire of revolution" (1926: 48) the creation of a new "governmental/state" party put a check on the threat of absolute disorder and of annihilation of the nation. Karsavin never really condemned Stalin, for he saw in him a force capable of warding off the threat of entropy.

The crisis of European culture caused the appearance of a "ruling stratum" of a new type in Russia and in Italy, and for Karsavin these crises of the state signal the growth and degeneration of cultures, but also their possibilities for renewal. The Italian Fascist Party and the Russian Communist Party were the two parties that had already got the better of the "individualist reality" represented by Parliamentarism and the separation of powers and which perhaps showed a new way.

It was the compromises in the West that rendered tyranny inevitable, so that in the midst of ideological confusion, only despotism was capable if maintaining a firm grip on all of the components forming the unity of the state. Here, "only the absolutely tyrannical power of a party that has taken everything into its hands makes it possible for a modern state to open up to new forms of the state" (1928: 38). Party dictatorship—if transitional—can make it possible to evolve toward living unity, for the state must not limit itself to being one of the functions of culture, as in Western democracy, which seeks to restrict its field of action as much as possible. The state must express the totality of culture, its unity.

CONCLUSION

This is how Karsavin's participation in the Eurasian movement can be explained, as well as his rapid abandonment of it (*The Foundations of Politics* was written two years before the "great turning"). Before the arrival of Stalin, it seems that he believed in the true possibility of a new type of government in Russia, thanks to the system of the Soviets. "The elementary force roused by revolution" had now retired to its bed, and it was necessary to learn how to think about the new state that had appeared.

The Russian state had been preserved in its integrity. The cult of popular "energy," so characteristic of the whole period with its cult of force, seemed predominant among all Eurasians (Kluchnikov 1997: 48) who, after the threats of the revolutionary age, were greatly concerned with affirming Russian grandeur and preservation of the empire. Karsavin's angle was rather to devise a future for Russia and to avoid the splitting up of the empire and anarchy. In Stalin he saw above all "a firm hand." His kindliness with regard to the Soviet regime at this time was due to the fact that it had managed to preserve the integrity of Russia following the danger of split-up during the Revolution.

Stabilization of the revolutionary process, however, did result in unexpected developments. He was quick to take note of the incommensurable distance between the prospects opened up by the revolutionary process (even those based on rigorous observations) and the new and unthinkable reality that came to light bit by bit. The rapid abandonment of the Eurasian movement was no doubt a manifestation of lucidity. At the beginning of the 1930s, an article published in the Lithuanian journal *Židinys* under the title, "The State and the Crisis of Democracy," affirmed that "there exists in the USSR no true democracy, that the Soviet constitution in fact exists only on paper and that there are no true civil liberties" (L.Y.A.: interrogation of 18 Nov. 1949). And it is interesting to note that, starting from the end of the 1930s, he was to seek analogies with the contemporary epoch in the "Pharaonic" undertakings of the ancient Orient.

As is, this exposition of the principles that were to found the new Russian state and to serve as an alternative ideology to communism is strikingly strange: rejection of the usual principles of the democratic Western state (separation of powers, the principle of representation) were not to prevent him from displaying a preoccupation fundamentally that of the West— liberty—and, while renouncing democracy, to aspire to an authentically popular power. The exposition of principles appears to be a meeting between the system of the Soviet state that had just been created and a memory of social rumblings and experimentations with religious connotations that preceded the Renaissance.

Some people were brought to see the immediate future of the Russian state modeled after that of France following the revolution: taking of power by the army or restoration of the monarchy (the aspiration of the rightist "Eurasians"). At the time the revolution was calming down, "the most active elements were concentrating in the army." Karsavin, however, gave no particular importance to the Red Army. Military empire and imperialism are not to be wished for, he thought, as they would only result in substituting external and nonorganic tasks for vital internal tasks that the age called for.

For those who brought up possible restoration of the monarchy, Karsavin replied that the authentic Russian traditions, *zemskii sobor* and autocracy, had in any case disappeared. The Russian monarchy had been discredited beyond redemption, and restoration would be popular only in appearance, as it remained an empty form (1926: 54).

There is one factor whose impact Karsavin, because of his lived experience and perhaps because of his character, seemed incapable of conceiving: terror and the inner transformation it brought about in individuals. Much later, after the war, it seemed that he had a better understanding of this. In May 1949, on his return to Moscow where he went to make arrangements for freeing Irina, it appears that he arrived at an accurate assessment of the corruption of an entire generation brought about by a regime of terror and penury. Was he well informed of the impact of terror up to that time? It seems not. His behavior in Lithuania on the arrival of Soviet troops after 1944 would suggest that he had underestimated this phenomenon. If he chose not to leave Lithuania, this was because he thought that things had changed in a positive way, that the Soviet authorities "had changed for the better." To those who implored him to leave, he replied "we're not in the Middle Ages."

Karsavin's Eurasian works are a combination of theoretical reflections on the nature and function of the state and the meaning of revolution for the purpose of staking out a future program and, initially, to establish a convergence between the émigrés and the current state of affairs in Russia. A true desire to renew a sort of dialogue with the new power in order to reorient it is proved by a number of attempts to take up contacts with governmental circles in Russia. During 1924–25, the heads of the Eurasian movement (Savitskii, Trubetzkoi, Souvtchinskii, Arapov, and Malevskii-Malevitch) met a certain Langovoi in Berlin who was thought to be close to governmental circles and at the same time a sympathizer with regard to the Eurasians. In order to establish contacts within the country, it seems that between 1925 and 1927 Savitskii and Arapov went to Moscow illegally (L.Y.A.: interrogation of 23 Sept. 1949).

The movement (but not individuals) did in fact receive a serious hearing. It has been shown that the transformations in the course of action followed by Soviet power at the end of the 1930s, especially with the return to national values, had something in common with Eurasian theories (Kluchnikov 1997: 25–26).

Karsavin's relations with Soviet Russia, as can be seen in his passage through the Eurasian movement, was not unique, even though it is striking because of its reflective, systematic and theoretically-based aspect. During the Second World War, the philosopher Berdiaev and the emigrant writer Ossorgin behaved like Russian patriots, in spite of being cut off due to forced emigration.

In Karsavin's work, the Eurasian period is the only time that Russia occupied a central and explicit place. Exactly what did Russia represent for him? Of the real Russia, he spoke very little, and with humor. His tastes clearly bore him toward Western Europe. Why did he remain strangely removed from debates in the West, even though the development of his thought (history of mentalities, phenomenology) tallied with what was taking place in the West? Why did he who followed the same path as the historians of the *Annals* not maintain direct contacts with them? This absence of direct dialogue by someone whose intellectual evolution was so close is surprising.

But at the same time, what attached him so profoundly to the real Russia, communist or not? The first condition of his existence seems to have been integrity and continuity in the spiritual process he participated in within the scope of the nation. Once his material conditions disappeared because of exile, his intellectual existence became if not impossible, at least extremely disturbed, and participation in the Eurasian movement, in spite of sympathies with its other participants that were not very significant, seems to have been a means of survival. If he belonged to Russia, he who stated that his soul "was first of all a citizen of the world" (letter to Kojève, Dec. 18, 1927), paradoxically, it is without doubt through the Silver Age, itself nourished on the multiple sources of Western culture.

His place in the Eurasian movement is paradoxical and his actual participation rather limited, since it lasted only three years. In 1924, he was contacted by Souvtchinski, and in 1926 the only congress he participated in took place. Starting in 1928, other obligations required all his strength. Within the space of these few years, however, the movement provided him with the main part of his intellectual framework.

Passage through the Eurasian movement is revealing of Karsavin's attitude with regard to Russia, which was expressed openly only during those years and through the perspective of this movement. However, the movement remained engraved in him for the rest of his life and was a determining factor in his decisive choices, including no doubt his settling down in Lithuania and especially his refusal to leave Soviet Russia, followed by his death in the north of Siberia.

BIBLIOGRAPHY

Berdiaev, Nikolai A. 1918. *Sud'ba Rossii.* Moscow.

——. 1955. *Istoki i smysl russkogo kommunizma.* Paris.

——. 1972. *O rabstve i svobode cheloveka.* Paris.

Danilevskii, Nikolai. 1867. *Rossiia i Evropa.* St. Petersburg, 1992.

Gerassimov, Ju. K. 1996. "Xristianstvo i Evrazija." Colloque Karsavin, Saint Petersburg, 18–20 December.

Hauchard, Claire. 1996. "L. P. Karsavin et le mouvement eurasien." *Revue des Etudes Slaves* 68, 3.

Karsavin, Lev P. 1912a. *Ocherki religioznoi zhizni v Itali XII–XIII vekov.* St. Petersburg.

——. 1912b. *Osnovy srednevekovoi religioznosti v XII–XIII veka.* St. Petersburg.

——. 1912c. *Monashestvo v srednie veka.* Moscow.

——. 1918a. *Kul'tura srednikh vekov.* Petrograd.

——. 1918b. *Katolichestvo.* Petrograd.

——. 1922. *Vostok, zapad i russkaia ideia.* Petrograd.

——. 1923a. *Filosofia istorii.* Berlin.

——. 1923b. "Evropa i Evraziia." *Sovremennie Zapiski* 15, 2.

——. 1924. *O suscnosti pravoslaviia.* Berlin.

——. 1925a. *O somnenii, nauke i vere.* Berlin.

——. 1925b. *Uroki otrechennii very.* Berlin.

——. 1926. *Evrazijstvo (opyt sistematicheskogo izlozeniia).* Paris.

——. 1926. *Fenomenologiia revolutsii.* Berlin. Reprint Tver 1992.

——. 1927. "Osnovy politiki." *Evraziiskii vremennik* 5. Reprint Tver 1992.

——. 1928. *K poznaniiu russkoi revolutsii.* Reprint Tver, 1992.

——. 1934. "Valstybe ir demokratijos krize." *Zidinys* 5/6.

——. 1939. "Didzioji Prancuzu revoliucija i vakaru Europa." *Naujoii Romuva* 37.

——. 1991. "Apie Tobulybe." *Baltos Lankos* 1.

Kluchnikov, Sergei. 1997. *Russkii uzel evraziistva.* Moscow.

Lietuvos Ypatingasis Archivas (L.Y.A.). varied years.

Osorgin, Mikhail Andreevich. 1942. *Povest' o pustiakakh.* New York.

IV. Absolutism and Authority in Eurasian Ideology: Karsavin and Alekseev

Ryszard Paradowski

In 1923, there appeared in the orbit of the Eurasian movement Lev Karsavin, at the beginning its severe critic and interrogator. His rigid criticism, however, did not refer to the essence of Eurasian theories. What he found missing in the movement was philosophical background to support it. The main weakness of Eurasian ideas was, for him, poor theoretical thought. He argued that Eurasians' problems could be explained through philosophy and metaphysics only, and he wished they would develop this aspect of justification (Karsavin 1923a). It did not take long before he developed the theories to provide it. Moreover, his answers to some specific questions were so decisive and final that he contributed to the break of the Eurasian movement as an intellectual formation. Because of him the Revolution began to be evaluated in a different way and perceived either as a specific phase in the nation's existence when something new appears and the future of the nation is being shaped, or as a folk and creative phenomenon. Moreover, the leaders of the Revolution began to be perceived not as a personification of evil, but rather as not fully aware of their role as a tool of the people's revolution, or even as the best possible tool of the Revolution. "Bolshevism is a personification of some elemental aspirations of 'Russian nation,'" Karsavin wrote. "They are the best of all forms of the authority possible in Russia nowadays" (1923b: 329, 325).

KARSAVIN'S PHILOSOPHY

Karsavin was quite a distinctive thinker among the personnages of the Eurasian movement. Some crucial points in the history of the movement are associated with his name, not only the break and fall mentioned above. His access to the movement was accompanied by the intrigues that heavily affected the future shape of Eurasian ideology.[1] However,

---

[1] About P. Suwczyński's manipulations that brought about G. V. Florovskii's departure, and about preventing I. A. Ilin from joining the movement, see Sobolev (1992: 56).

neither the intrigues within the movement nor the person of the philosopher himself were most important. It was his philosophy of history and his opinions about the political system of Russia which was to emerge after the communist ideology withered and the Soviet system collapsed that influenced the movement most.

Karsavin's philosophical concepts belong to the major stream of Russian religious philosophy called the philosophy of whole-unity. The category (*vceedinstvo*) is as old as philosophy itself and can be traced back to Heraclitus, who pursued the idea of unity, relation, and mutual relationship between everything that exists. "Everything is unity, and unity is God," said Xenophanes. According to Anaxagoras, "there is part of everything in everything." However, they were Neo-Platonists who accepted this idea as an element of an orderly ontological system. Plotinus defined whole-unity as an internal structure of existence—an ideal world (perceived mentally) that emanated from Absolute-Unity.

In patristic theories, whole-unity was "self-defined" as a religious notion, and the church understood whole-unity as the mystical body of Christ and his person. Whole-unity came to be perceived as a set of archetypes of all things (paradigms) included in God-Unity, "primeval plans" of God for the world.

The next step in the development of the whole-unity concept was made by Nicholas of Cusa, who followed the opinion that, although the Absolute is beyond cognition, there are nevertheless a series of dialectical categories that may help understand it. Among other ontological principles such as, for example, the folding and unfolding of the Absolute, or the folded, concentrated, contracted existence of the Absolute in its moment, the principle of whole-unity always comes first, since it shows the internal structure of the Absolute. Karsavin drew on Nicholas of Cusa in his philosophy of whole-unity.

Karsavin was neither the first nor the most prominent representative of whole-unity philosophy in Russia. The most outstanding was Vladimir Soloviev, who based his system not only on the early ancient philosophers and Neo-Platonists but also on the late medieval mystics and Hegel. His philosophy was also deeply rooted in Russian tradition. "The ideological and theoretical basis of the whole-unity concept," writes V. N. Akulinin, "was a religious and philosophical branch in Russian social thoughts that started to emerge in the 1830s within an academic community of the Orthodox Church" (Akulinin (1990: 12). It was a reaction to the "dogmatic ambiguity" of the canons of the Orthodox Church, the inertia of Orthodox theology, and the long-held belief that Christianity does not need philosophical reflection on religious questions. Apart from theological communities, this new tendency was reflected in early

Slavophilism. The archetype of a philosophical category of whole-unity developed by Solovev and his descendants was a Slavophilic notion of *sobornost'* that denoted a free unity and excluded both individualistic law-lessness and external pressure to constrain it.[2] *Sobornost'* is "a Russian community, brotherhood, a choral principle, unity of love and freedom that lacks any external guarantees" (Berdiaev 1990: 87). Emphasized by Nikolai Berdiaev, this lack of external guarantees makes the philosophy of whole-unity an ideological justification of coercion in the thought of Karsavin.[3] As such it will be a philosophical justification and theoretical basis for Eurasian theories.

The starting point for Karsavin's philosophy of whole-unity, as noted above, was a "paradigm of Nicholas of Cusa," the image of whole-unity as a hierarchy of different types of whole-unity ("moments"), which are comprised of concentrated, "folded" forms of whole-unity, and in their folded forms are included in higher levels of whole-unity. The notion of triple-unity introduced by Karsavin himself (Chorużyj 1989: 84) is an important supplement to this image of total whole-unity, where the moments of lower types are deprived of any autonomy and are used only to actualize lower-level whole-unity. The notion of triple-unity denotes an indispensable phase in the development of any process that consists of pre-unity, self-division, and self-union again. Whereas whole-unity refers to the structure of existence, triple-unity means its dynamics. In this way, Karsavin's metaphysics changes into a philosophy of history. Of course, the above occurs in its complete form only in Absolute ideal existence. However, it can also be used to explain imperfect, worldly existence. A direct intermediate link between an ideal divine whole-unity and imperfect historical world is a notion of the Person. Since God is a Person, and an imperfect existence, even though imperfect, is similar to an ideal existence, then all existence must be a personal existence.

The three basic ontological elements of Karsavin's philosophy are God, Triple-Unity, and Person. A personal element of created existence is only a reflection of Absolute divine personal existence, but it is present in each moment and element of imperfect existence. The "image of worldly existence as a hierarchy of (imperfect) forms of whole-unity, because of the link between each whole-unity and triple-unity, occurs as a hierarchy of (imperfect) forms of triple-unity, and thus as a hierarchy of imperfect

---

[2] On collectivity (*sobornost'*) in early Slavophilism, see Walicki (1973: 146).

[3] "The science of the symphonic person means metaphysical justification for human slavery" (Berdiaev 1972: 30). S. S. Chorużyj suggested that Karsavin's version of the philosophy of the whole-unity is closer to the conservatism of J. De Maistre than to Chomiak's idea of "collectivity" (Chorużyj 1989: 91).

persons" (Chorużyj 1989: 84). Here, Karsavin's theory offers a concept of human communities understood as new separate persons, defined as "symphonic" or "collective" persons. They are "higher persons" when compared to the smaller groups and individual persons that are included in them (in a traditional sense of this notion). Smaller groups and particular persons are "moments" of "symphonic persons" that are present in them in their folded form. For Karsavin, such symphonic persons denote cultures, nations, layers and classes, and humanity as a whole (about a nation as a person, see also Trubetskoi 1994: 501). Contrary to Trubetskoi, Karsavin argues that humanity is a "real," "true" whole-unity. Humanity is a "whole-united . . . whole-timed and whole-spaced, developing subject," and even an "ideal whole-unity," within the relative imperfection of created worldly existence (Karsavin (1923b: 87).[4] Specific perfection is also represented by a social group understood as a historical collective individuality (not as a collection of atomized individuals); then a "notion of group . . . appears to be a notion of whole-unity," and this group can be perceived as "a certain whole, as an organism" (1923b: 92).[5]

Hence Karsavin's belief that the notion of group is not of a positive and thus not of a scientific nature, because a group is not determined by the spatial or time sphere of its members' activity, or by its size, or, especially by the individuals that compose the given group. A group "is first of all constituted and determined from inside, by its specific social interaction" (1923b: 89). This mutual interaction among individuals that constitute a group could make a starting point to show an immanent character of thedriving force of social dynamics. However, Karsavin is far from doing so, because then the concept of whole-unity hierarchy that culminates in created world—in humanity—and in the divine sphere

---

[4] This "philosophical service of metaphysical justification for the unity in humanity" was not accepted by Eurasians, or by Trubetskoi or Gumilev in particular. They also rejected the interpretation of this unity by Spengler, who argued that cultures are totally obscure to one another even though they are the creation of the same "primeval soul," the only primeval substance. Only disillusionment with the evolution of movement made Trubetskoi confess: "I think that there is nothing better than . . . work for the whole-European culture that is supposed to be the whole-humanity culture." Trubetskoi, "Pis'mo P. Savitskomu z 8–10.XII.1930 r," quoted in Kazin (1992: 86). This claim was far from the belief of Eurasians: "Humanity—unity of itself in imperfection, improvement and perfection. It is both becoming perfect and is perfect already."

[5] Perceiving a nation as an organism and attributing to it "soul" and the status of "person" was characteristic of the whole perspective of so-called "religious philosophy." "Each social whole, nation, state," wrote N. O. Losskii, "is a person of a higher rank: its basis is a soul that organises a social whole in such a way that people who are included in it serve the whole as particular organs." Losskii (1957: 3), quoted in Troitskii (1992: 12).

of the Absolute, would be pointless. So he claims that "no [social] relation and mutual interaction between two or more individuals can be explained without accepting [the existence] of a higher subject embodied in it." The existence of such a higher subject (whole-unity) is a precondition for both social ideals and the effectiveness of simple cognitive actions. Therefore there must exist a subject that includes these individuals in itself and that "goes beyond their spatial and time atomization." Otherwise, the common (in a given group or nation) perceptions of the world, similar orientations to the external world, common approaches, opinions, and aspirations, common ideologies that constitute a group would not be possible without accepting the priority of "general," without accepting as real everything that is concordant with "general" embodied in whole-unity of a higher rank, in a group that is attributed an ontological status.

From here, for Karsavin, there is only a small step to formulating a political ideal. Before he takes this step, though, he puts forward a philosophical justification for a (his and that of the late Eurasian movement as a whole) broad interpretation of a widely spread (also among Russian emigrants) opinion about Bolsheviks' contribution to the rescue of Russian statehood. What was on communism and Bolsheviks in the late 1920s, in the magazine *Evraziia* in particular ("what they do is necessary and important"; 1929), was far from ambiguous when accompanied by continuous attacks against the culture of the West and the deficiencies of its democracy.

THEORY OF THE STATE

This fascination with Bolshevism, which became more open in time, resulted from a "futuristic" approach, common to all Eurasians, and the tendency to contrast the "old" and "new." This approach even brought them the label of "Slavophiles of futurism epoch" (Stepun 1926: 445; see also Chorużyj 1989: 82). This approach made them reject "old" political-systemic solutions, both monarchist and liberal-democratic, and seek answers that seemed original at the time.

The methodology of Karsavin's philosophy of history represented still another opposition: an external layer of historical process and an internal invisible stream that in fact is its essence. According to this opposition (akin to Hegel's concept of a cunning Reason of History), the Revolution as a "healthy" historical process could be contrasted with the "criminal," as Karsavin called it, political practice of the Bolshevik regime. It also made it possible to tell the difference between a primitive, based on lie, false in its core communist ideology, i.e., between this that Bolsheviks think they do (for example they think they build communism) and their objective function of an unaware tool of internal revival of Russian nation. However, this methodology of "double measure" was not enough to reject communism totally. At least for some Eurasians, the previous ambivalence gave place to unrestrained apology for the Soviet regime.[6] But it did not refer to Karsavin himself, even though his philosophy stimulated a pro-Soviet intellectual trend in the Eurasian movement. His "balancing on the edge of a precipice" did not seem to be a gate left open to return to the country—at least, labeling Bolsheviks "criminals" was not the best way to make this return secure. "Bolsheviks were merciless and pointlessly cruel," he wrote, "but it may have been because of them that total extermination of cultural classes of Russian society did not take place; they may have weakened the power of the impetuous rather than strengthened it" (1923b: 327). Anyone who fails to see an image of a human that is emerging here is prone to choose an easier explanation: pro-Bolshevism of the philosopher. His indisputable anti-democratic orientation seems to make this explanation more probable.

It may seem that the rescue—intellectual and moral in this case—served as a means to overcome the lie. Karsavin, fascinated, like all Eurasians, with the impetus of Bolshevism, was not able to suppress this feeling. But if we accept that the image of society Karsavin saw beneath the thick layer of Bolshevik evil was true, it should be admitted that sometimes truth requires moral control, too. And it was the revolutionary truth, not the Bolsheviks' lie, that Eurasians failed to control morally. The evidence of this failure is their intellectual search in the area of another totalitarianism. The field of search had to be restricted in this way because, according to Eurasian philosophy, "a lower person is free only because it exists only in a higher person that individualises in it and is individualised by it" (1923b: 337) and because conscience of a "lower" person, i.e., a person through which such a control could be performed, is deposited in a historical collective subject. If we were to stick to notions of religious philosophy, we (unlike Karsavin) could say that God deposits freedom in "lower" persons, and he does not demand it to be returned. And this is what a political offer of Karsavin looks like. "Perfect freedom is possible," according to him, "only in perfect whole-unity," for example, in a state.

The key point for Karsavin's idea of the state and democracy is (he does not reject this notion but wants it to be understood more broadly) his clearly anti-individualistic declaration. It was so important that it

---

[6] "Having joined the Eurasian movement, [Karsavin] destroyed this movement with a trashy apology of Stalinian nationalism and cynical acceptance of the soviet activity as a 'common affair'" (Gessen 1979: 310).

should be mentioned together with another "positive aspect" of socialism and Marxism. For Karsavin, "socialists and Marxists defended universalism and fought against the idea of democratic individualism"
(Karsavin 1991: 190). They shared this opinion with Fascists, who, even
though they "understood the nature of social group no better than
Marxists," gave up the individual for the sake of a group. Karsavin, who
personally rejected Fascism (because it was exaggerated in its anti-individualistic approach and supposed "an individual to be an obedient tool
in hand of leaders and ideologists"), but found it to be "rather innocent
when compared to extreme, selfish individualism that negates society [he
probably means nihilism and anarchy here] and even to individualism
of democratic theories." On the other hand, it appears that Marxists
and Fascists are in a specific way more individualistic than democrats
(since they "strive for total equality of individuals," or because they
"replace a cult of society with a cult of a leader" 191).[7] Thus it is necessary, and fortunately possible, to accept an entirely different approach
to the relation between universalism and individualism that escapes Fascist
and communist extremity. This approach can be traced in the other category of philosophical system developed by Karsavin—the category of
multi-unity.

Unexpectedly enough, in his theory of a state Karsavin accepted a
positivistic assumption—he claimed that a state consists of a territory,
an authority, and population—but he equipped these elements with the
contents far from positivistic ones. As for the territory, he emphasizes
its unique and individual character and an organic relation (multi-unity)
among particular elements of the landscape ("a definite and alive country"). The nation that lives in a given territory is an organism too. As
an organism it influences its body and "the bodies of all fellow-citizens."
At the same time, the nation is in an organic relation with the territory
it lives in: "the body of the nation cannot be separated from the air
and earth that are common to us"; the earth consists of bodies of our
deceased ancestors.

Also, authority is connected with the country and nation. Without
authority, "neither will of the nation nor its self-consciousness can be
expressed. Although the nation is shaped by its home territory, common
origin, language, culture, and history, authority shapes it most effectively.
These natural bonds between country, nation, and authority cannot be
explained, according to Karsavin, by any individualistic theories—Marxist
theory of power, other theories of social agreement, or dogmatic theocratic
theory. Concepts based on a social agreement are, for the philosopher,

---

[7] However, Karsavin does not reject the notion of "leader."

ideologically false; the concepts and systems they legitimize are not even democratic, because in so-called democratic countries neither the nation that chooses from among the candidates offered, nor the representatives of the nation really rule. Who in fact rules in a democratic country? "Some power belongs to a cabinet of ministers," but in fact "the only stable element of authority" is bureaucracy and the army. These claims are not criticized by Karsavin. A democratic country is "alive thanks to its nondemocratic elements." Thus, on the one hand, a democratic theory distorts reality; on the other, any consistent attempts to put life into it would inevitably end up as anarchy. Crisis of a democratic country means that consistent democracy changes into anarchy, the blind fetus of individualism (188).

Surprisingly enough, this smashing criticism of democracy is followed by a pro-democratic declaration. "I think," Karsavin claimed, "that each country is alive and healthy to such extent to which it is democratic," and followed it by the still firmer claim that "a democratic system is an ideal of a state." And, "a so-called democratic state is only one of the state forms," very far from this ideal. Since a "democratic state" was for Karsavin a contradiction to a "democratic ideal," so he must have meant some other type of democracy. To understand it properly, we have to go back to some more general assumptions made by Karsavin.

First of all, it is not true that an individual "self" of man is the only reality. And the reality learnt by him is not only creation of his mind but it exists objectively. And if so, the philosopher concludes, then cognition, and even an opportunity to learn an objective reality proves that "self" and an object of cognition are "the two symptoms or moments" of the same multi-unity. Consequently, my "self" is less individual than it seems, and the unity between my "self" and an object of cognition is "self" as well (even higher "self" is higher than my individual "self"). When for example, we meet another human, I only individualize our potential unity. Together, we actualize a social person, multi-unity, that is "something more than my individual person." The organic, natural, primeval nature of this relationship is proved by the fact that I can learn other humans' thoughts "in the same way as I can learn my own thoughts, and their feelings—as my own feelings."

Karsavin, who accused Fascists of rejection "of all positive moments of individualism" claimed clearly that "true reality does not exist in a form of an individual consciousness of an individual person" (189); true reality is a social person. It exists only through individual persons, but "an individual person is only a moment . . ., only individualization of a social person." When mother rescues a child, it is not an act of her individual "self," and similarly, to defend my country against an aggressor is not an act of my individual "self." In both cases we have to do with an act of actualization and individualization of the nation itself, and the nation is a subject of both these actions. Thus it is the self-consciousness of the nation and its will that really exist. However, the internal content of the nation's spirit and will cannot be expressed efficiently in voting; to do so "we have to appeal to great national writers, poets, philosophers and geniuses."

Yet, because these geniuses cannot express their opinion directly since most of them have already ceased to exist, there is a problem how to interpret their opinions. Who is entitled to do it? Karsavin did not answer this question. Perhaps this was a secondary methodological problem for him. An important fact is that "to express its philosophy of life, the nation gives birth to geniuses." But how to use their teachings is unknown because "it is only God that is able to decide about all aspects of individual and national philosophy of life, and to learn whole-unity" (190). On the other hand, a proper selection is also a question of time. Karsavin knew, however, that life had its own needs, and the nation could not wait for either God (who, as we know, is not prompt to decide) or history. The will of the nation had to be expressed without delay. And it is the authority that is capable of doing this. "The authority is a form of self-consciousness and will of the nation." The state is also a form of self-consciousness and will of the nation. And the state must be understood as the multi-unity, too.

A group is the subject of social life and historical process. Its will is expressed in common, agreed activity of individuals. When such activity becomes necessary, then an initiator appears who will tell "what should be done and how it should be done," and who will shape a group's aspirations. The initiator "appears" or "emerges"—one is sure he is not going to be "chosen." There will appear or merge a whole leading team. The relationship between it and members of the group is not rationalized, because everybody "feels instinctively that leaders express and perform the will of all"; finally, even when a member of a group is forced to act, we can be sure that the authority "made him fulfil his own will." To prove this, Karsavin argues that when the authority (elite) goes beyond certain limits it will cause active resistance of the nation, and this will be prevented for the sake of the elite itself. When, however, the elite is already degenerate and the nation is healthy, then revolution develops. Far from a tendency to idealize a relationship between the elite and nation, Karsavin claims that there is a constant struggle between them. "That is why the forms of the state should be sought which will soothe sharpness of this struggle." However, neither a despotic state (with revolution and coups d'état against the rulers included in its mechanisms), nor a democratic state (because parties represent the interests of the elite not of the nation) performs this function properly. In fact there is not much difference between these two forms of the state.

The problem is to have a healthy ruling class because it is a necessary and sufficient condition to create a people's and really democratic state "through this class." If this class emerged from the nation, if it takes care of its needs and if it cooperates with it then "a nation is able to self-govern through this class" (190). Karsavin does not believe in an ideal state and he defines the conditions a state close to this ideal should meet. The best organized state is the one that: (1) helps the ruling class emerge naturally from the nation; (2) helps this class to cooperate with the nation, and the nation provides this class with "fresh blood"; (3) this coopera-tion not only prevents the ruling class from degeneration, but (4) gives it power and efficiency of action and (5) agrees upon "the influence of the ruling class, and of the nation itself through power and initiatives of the real authority."

In this way the question of the state system in a literary sense (as an organization of a "real authority") loses its direct importance for the sake of the elite and cooperation with a nation. However, to make this coop-eration efficient and keep the elite healthy, the nation must be well orga-nized, too.[8]

Like Jacobins in the past, Communists and Fascists wanted to trans-form society according to some rational plan, whereas, because of the irrational nature of national life, (193), the nation could organize itself only by itself. Thus, instead of building the state from the top down according to a rational plan, we should base it on a "natural process of self-organization," on "live social groups," not a "herd of voters." As a basis for this organization "a practical self-government" or "vocational and agricultural associations" should be set up. Also in this "not demo-cratic" country we have to do with specific representation, even though it is unlike parliamentary representation, because "every social group represents the nation in a specific way for itself."

---

[8] In its early phase the Eurasian movement tried to contrast a democratic state with its multi-party system to a political system based on one-party rule, a party that reminds us of Lenin's "party of a new type." "Thinking about a new party as an ascendant of a Bolshevik party—we give an entirely different meaning to this party, the meaning which makes it absolutely different from political parties in Europe. This is a special party, a party that rules and does not share its power with anybody else, and even excludes the possibility for any other identical party to exist. It is a state-ideological asso-ciation not identical with a state apparatus" (Ławrow 1993: 11). Karsavin rejected both multi-party and one-party systems as despotic.

Contacts among groups, indispensable to integrate the nation (and for multi-unity to become real), are made in such a way that a leader of every group, as a person known to all members and elected and "accepted" by this group (through perhaps an emotional response), can replace a group (let us use term replacement instead of representation here) and take part in the meetings (together with other natural executives) of the districts understood as organic territorial units. The executives are able (but Karsavin does not explain why they are able; perhaps emotional relationship will guarantee this) to solve common problems in total consent with the will of groups. Also called plenipotentiaries, they can nominate their own deputies for the councils of a higher rank.

Such a system has at least two very important advantages: "this kind of hierarchical order of social groups makes it possible to put in order the whole nation," and at the same time it guarantees natural generation of a ruling class. And what is most essential, an organic adhesion between the nation and state takes place (and this is what we meant—an effective removal of this controversy): "the nation-state" grows by itself. It is difficult to say whether such Hegelian adhesion between the nation and state can guarantee true democracy, free of violence and ideological deceit. Karsavin assures us that it can, provided the nation is "let to grow by itself." It seems, however, that this condition is difficult to fulfill, particularly when followers of a "rational" organization of the state, according to some particular interests that can be found both inside and outside the nation, are in power. This is so even though if we do not assume (and this is possible) that the nation consists only of such interests.

Advocates of the nation being left to "grow by itself," according to Karsavin, are representatives of rightist thinking in Russia. The precondition of this "self-growth" is a political mechanism that creates legal framing for self-organization at the cost of spontaneity, but one that guarantees stability and recurrence of "down-top democracy." The system of territorial self-government can assure this. Alexander Solzhenitzyn drew on this idea in his "Letter to the Leaders of the USSR," in which he demanded such districts be created as a sphere of freedom for the nation, and claimed the district that would not pose any threat for the central authority. Today, like the Eurasians he refers to, Solzhenitzyn promotes so-called *zemstva*—a unique Russian form of territorial self-government elected according to class and corporate principles.[9] He also follows the Eurasian idea of real people's authority and revival of Russian nation.

Certainly, suggestions of Eurasians, and Solzhenitzyn of course, can be understood as a version of local self-government that could compensate

---

[9] Interview by A. Solzhenitzyn for the TV program *Wzgliad*, 20 December 1994.

to some extent for the lack of parliamentary democracy and additionally hinder alienation of the political elite. However, creating opposition between this form of top-down democracy and parliamentary democracy excludes mechanisms that could prevent totalitarian system solutions.

ALEKSEEV AND THE EURASIANS

Eurasians, N. N. Alekseev in particular, say openly that their solutions have something in common with totalitarian ones. While Karsavin suggested organic, top-down democracy as the best solution for Russia, Alekseev went even farther. For him, Eurasian movement was the only acceptable solution.

First of all, Eurasians did not want to become a political party in its liberal-democratic and parliamentary sense,[10] because they did not want to be one of many other parties. Moreover, Eurasians rejected pluralism along with all the other "democratic cheat." They wanted to be compared to such movements as Freemasons, Catholic orders or the Catholic Church as such, or to a traditionally Russian movement of "the old across the Volga River" (Alekseev 1935: 33). Eurasians called themselves a "specific eastern order." They admitted that under certain circumstances they might be forced to act as a political party but it would be camouflage only, and the "Eurasian movement would keep its non-party character" (34). It is just a question of tactics.

These tactics would also decide whether, during the struggle, the Eurasian movement would become extremely leftist or extremely rightist, or whether it would gather even democratic powers to fight against Fascism. But a far-reaching Eurasian strategy might also include concealed actions, first of all in order to penetrate into successive regimes. "Eurasians must do everything to become the brain of this new regime." And what is most essential, they have to provide it with ideology; the regime is not able to generate itself.

If, however, coup d'état was carried out by a power close to the Eurasian movement, or was organized by Eurasians themselves, then the problem of tactics would arise. "Then we will face the instant necessity of building the state according to our own plan" (35). On the one hand, Eurasians rejected the accusation that after the takeover they would "ban" all other political parties, but on the other, they said openly that there would no longer be a need for political parties in Russia. It would be a people's "demotic" state, then, not "populist" because this term carries negative

---

[10] It can be suggested by the name of its main organ, "Politburo"—the same as organs of the CPSU and similar parties. See Kliementiev (1933: 100).

connotations. The problem was how the will of people would be expressed, since according to Eurasians voting was in itself the egocentric voice of "a voting corps of adult citizens." It was the voice of a "loose mass of the current population over age 18–21," not the voice of a real nation. Parliamentary democracy was for them an oligarchy of an adult generation that ruled the whole nation, not only those who did not have the right to vote at the moment, but also previous and future generations. Perhaps there exists such power, such a subject or mechanism that is able to express the will of a real, not democratically mutilated nation. Thus Eurasians would not just forbid the activity of political parties. What had to be banned was the system of representation as such. This system of "mechanical representation" had to be replaced by an "organic" system.

Eurasians did not seek far for this system. The idea that is a foundation for the system of councils ("Not in the Soviet Union form, of course," added Alekseev) solved the problem of organic "representation" quite efficiently (37). The model Alekseev referred to was fully concordant with Karsavin's concept of the hierarchy of symphonic persons. This model does not include either an individual or an "artificial union of people"; it is built up of an "organic territorial part of the whole" a council, a district or a city (even though it is not clear what their "organic" nature denotes and how an individual misses this organic element), a vocational association within these territorial units (since a vocational association is not an artificial union) and "national parts of the state." The Eurasian state intended to take over this whole structure, to strengthen it, to develop it and to improve it. Let us not forget about another two additional; but the most important elements of this structure. The first one is a scientifically proved Eurasian idea that was to replace a changeable and manipulated public opinion. Another one was the ruling elite, a vehicle of the state idea. This was to be performed not by the whole Eurasian order, but by its party emanation. Moreover, an organic balance between stability and dynamics would be kept through a proper proportion in the councils of the representatives from territorial units, national and vocational organizations and from the ruling elite (39). It was a Soviet system of a leading role of a party but corrected in three respects. First, it lacked a typical for "real socialism" parliamentary-democratic complex that made communists claim that "the party leads but not rules." Second, the principle of class-corporation replaced the principle of democratic centralism. And third, the leading party was reduced to one of equivalent elements of "organic" whole. But corrections referred to the party itself—not to the "order." Therefore, the third difference is an ambiguous one. In the communist party there were also revealed two layers—external and internal: the "order" and its tactical emanation. It should be remembered that the membership of councils in the soviet system was also influenced by a specific, even though not open, class-corporation principle: a "proper" representation of women, blue-collar workers, farmers, and working intelligentsia was carefully respected. Thus the Eurasians' offer differed from the communists' in two ways only: it was more sincere while showing real political mechanisms and used a different slogan to legitimize the idea of a Eurasian state. This slogan was the idea of Euro-Asian nations.

Eurasians intended to replace Bolshevism with the Eurasian idea itself. Bolsheviks did much to prevent this. But at the end of their rule they even gave up their own class idea and replaced it with a par excellance Eurasian idea of one soviet nation. They also relinquished the idea of proletarian internationalism for the sake of the whole-soviet patriotism. The latter one is a pale shadow of Eurasian nationalism.[11]

BIBLIOGRAPHY

Akulinin, V. N. 1990. *Fiłosofiia vceedinstva ot V. S. Sołoveva k P. A. Fłorenskomu*. Novosibirsk.
Alekseev, Nikolai N. 1927. "O Evraziiskom patriotizmie." *Evraziiskaia Khronika* 8.
——. 1935. "Evraziitsy i gosudarstvo." *Evraziiskaia Khronika* 11.
Berdiaev, Nikolai A. 1990. "Russkaia ideia." In Berdiaev, *O Rossii i russkoi fiłosofskij kulture: Fiłosofi posleoktiabr'skogo zarubezh'ia*. Moscow.
Chorużyj, S. S. 1989. "Karsawin i de Mestr." *Woprosy fiłosofii* 3.
Gessen, I. W. 1979. "Dieła emigrantskije." *Kontinent* 19.
Karsavin, Lev. P. 1923a. "Evropa i Evraziia." *Sovremennie Zapiski* 15, 2.
——. 1923b. *Fiłosofiia istorii*. Berlin.
——. 1929. "Eszczo o demokratii, sotsializme i evrazijstve." *Evraziia* 19.
——. 1991. "Gosudarstvo i krizis demokratii." *Novii mir* 1.
Kazin, D. P. 1992. "D. P. Swiatopołk—Mirskij i jewrazijskoje dwiżenieje." *Naczała'* 4: 86.
Kliementiev, A. 1933. "Dzieła i dni Lwa Platonowicza Karsawina." *Vestnik Russkogo Khristianskogo Dvizheniia* (1967).
Ławrow, S. B. 1993. "L. N. Gumilow i jewrazijstwo." In L. N. Gumilev, *Ritmy Evrazii: epokhi i tsivilizatsii*. Moscow.
Losskii, Nikolai O. 1957. *Kharakter russkogo naroda*, vol. 1. Munich quoted in Troitskii (1992: 12).
Sobolev, A. B. 1992. "Swoja swoich nie poznasza." *Naczała* 4 (1992).
Stepun, F. A. 1926. "Ob Obszczestwienno-politiczeskich putiach 'Puti.'" *Sovremenne Zapiski* 29.
Troitskii, Evgenii S., ed. 1992. *Russkaia ideia i Sovremennost'*. Moscow.
Trubetskoi, Nikolai S. 1927. "Obshcheevraziiskii natsionalizm." *Evraziiskaia khronika* 9: 24–31.
——. 1994. "O turanskom elemente v russkoi kulture." In Gumilev, *Chernaia legenda*. Moscow.
Walicki, Adrzej. 1973. *Rosyjska fiłozofia i mysl społeczna od Oswiecenia do marksizmu*. Warsaw.

---

[11] "For the state to exist it is necessary to develop among its citizens the consciousness of organic unity that can be either ethnic unity or class unity and therefore . . . there are only two solutions: either a dictatorship of the proletariat, or the consciousness of unity and specificity of a multinational Eurasian nation and Eurasian nationalism" (Trubetskoi 1927: 31; see also Alekseev 1927).

V. From Rejection to Attempts at Reconciliation: Poles and the Interwar Eurasian Movement

Roman Bäcker

INTERWAR RUSSIAN EMIGRATION AND POLISH PUBLIC OPINION

During the interwar period, many Russians were located in European countries and in many countries of other continents. In 1929, between nine hundred thousand and one million Russians were living in Europe, China, and the Middle East, according to estimates and incomplete data of the Office of Emigration in Geneva. Three to four hundred thousand of these were in France, followed by one hundred thousand each in Germany and Poland and twenty-five thousand in Czechoslovakia (*Ruch Slowiański* 1929: 295). Despite this, there has been a disproportionate amount of public and scientific interest in Russian immigrants both during the interwar period and now. A whole series of scientific publications has appeared in Prague, but only one article concerning Russian political immigrants in Poland has appeared in the Polish language (Czapski 1993). Equally rare are articles concerning how the matters of Russian immigrants were dealt with in Poland during the interwar period. The monthly *Ruch Slowiański (Slovian Movement)*, sporadically printed between 1928 and 1938 has only about ten mentions of Russian immigrants, despite an editorial staff of Tadeusz Lehr-Splawiński, Wladyslaw Tedeusz Wislocki, Henryk Batowski, and others who were not suspected of disliking Slovians. Most of these concern the number of Russian immigrants and only two comment on social and cultural issues of Russian immigrants in Poland.

INTEREST IN EURASIANISM IN POLAND

More surprising is the large interest in Polish journalists and outstanding Polish social scientists in a marginal area of Russian political thought termed "Eurasianism." In 1931, the leader and ideologist of Eurasianism, Petr Savitskii, counted that Poland appeared in nine press articles and four scientific papers about Eurasianism (by Marian Zdziechowski, Jan Kucharzewski, Marian Uzdowski, and S. L. Wojciechowski, a Russian immigrant) (Savitskii 1931). If we add to this Savitskii's extensive work on the history and views of Eurasianism in the *Przegląd Współczesny* (*Contemporary Review*), printed in two parts in 1933, and the interest revealed by the Polish secret service, it is clear to see the disproportional interest in Eurasianism from Polish intellectual elites.

This interest was undoubtedly caused by the originality of the Eurasianism concept itself. Eurasianism could not be classified as a monarchical or democratic trend, but was critical of the impacts of Western European culture on Russian life. Extreme anti-occidentalism led to the condemnation of the entire "European" part of the history of Russia (from Peter the Great to the Bolshevik Revolution). Eurasianism could not be treated as a typical Bolshevik trend or as one subordinated by them, for example, "poputchiks" or "smenovechovoksi." The self-identification of the Eurasianism movement was also different. Eurasianists thought of Russia as a separate continent between Europe and Asia, possessing a specific culture and able to develop independently. Eurasianist ideologists such as Nikolai Trubetskoi were scientists from well-known Russian intellectual families, and as such sparked lively responses to issues of Russian emigration. This may partially explain the interest from Polish intellectuals.

Among the articles mentioned by Savitskii (1931), we may identify only a few that contain concrete data and events. Most are descriptive and factographic in character. These articles were possibly inspired and even written by Russian emigrants in Warsaw. This is partially evident by the printing of the same unauthorized article on "New Russian Mental Trends" in both the nationalist-democrat *Gazeta Warszawska Poranna* (*Warsaw Morning Newspaper*) and *Kurier Warszawski* (*Warsaw Courier*) within two days (*Kurier Warszawski*, 28 Sept. 1927: 2; *Gazeta Warszawska Poranna*, 30 Sept. 1927: 9). This short article devoted to the taking over of the serious magazine *Russkij Vojennyj Viestnik* by a Eurasian group was a reliable description of the political ideology of this group of sympathizers.

KAZIMIERZ CZAPIŃSKI

The first, edited in Poland in January 1922 by outstanding socialist journalist Kazimierz Czapiński, had a totally different character and was characteristic of Eurasianism. The first ever non-Russian reaction was in the 1921 Sofia manifesto of Eurasianism titled *Iskhod k Vostoku* (Savitskii 1921; *Exodus to the East*). Czapiński was the author of many pamphlets and articles in the socialist press, devoted mainly to socialist ideology, the social role of religion, and international and especially Bolshevik issues. Czapiński's authority in this last issue was unquestionably socialist In an article titled "Eurazyjczycy: Z rosyjskich prądów współczesnych" ("Eurasianists: From Contemporary Russian Trends") (*Robotnik*, 26 Feb. 1922: 2), disrespect connected with his interest is clear. He writes about "the small conception of fevered thought of Russian emigration," a very strange form of reference to Orthodoxy, nationalism, and their masks. The joke is in this case understandable as a concept, idea, and gentle allusion about the intellectual abilities of the creators of Eurasianism. Czapiński's interest in the manifesto of Eurasianists stems from his observation of characteristic features of the Russian evolution of social thought. Czapiński rightly notices a new kind of Slavophile, based on an Orthodox and specific meaning of nationalism.

However, there is no reason to agree with Czapiński that treating the Russian village community (*obszczina*) as an economically outdated institution and accepting a creative means of sovereign personality in the economic area will lead to the bourgeois system and capitalistic individualism. Personality (*licznost'*) and symphonic personality were treated by Eurasianists as a feature less of individuals than of the cultural and historical community (e.g., Eurasia) or the nation. Czapiński's thesis about the imperialistic character of Eurasianism is also doubtful, due to the imprecise translation of Russia taking a central place in between Eurasian nations (Savitskii 1921: 7). The authors of the almanac wrote about the community of life, culture, and relativeness of soul that creates one Eurasian community. However, it is only after the analysis of subsequent Eurasian publications (which Czapiński surely could not know in 1922) that we are able to talk about cultural imperialism.

According to Czapiński, Eurasians were the creators of a new national bourgeois awareness in contemporary Russia, designing capitalism, Orthodoxy, and the fight against socialism, nationalism, and imperialism. The characteristics of an original ideological stream on the basis of an imprecise reading of an introduction of a first manifesto, led to the rise of an inaccurate interpretation with little connection to reality. This is reflective of the typical thinking of socialist journalists of the time, who were capitalist or remained under bourgeois influences.

MARIAN ZDZIECHOWSKI

Marian Zdziechowski largely avoided these traps, and in March 1922 gave a speech on Russian Eurasianism in Vilnius. A philosopher, expert on the Orthodox church, Russian messianistic thinker (see Zdziechowski 1922), and friend of many Russian intellectuals such as Sergei Trubetskoi, father of Nikolai (Hryniewicz 1995), he was probably the most predisposed in Poland to the ideals of Eurasianism.

Zdziechowski's analysis used the method of associations, rather than searching for general explanatory models or finding a place for this new phenomenon in established schemes. He compared known facts and intellectual phenomena with the contents of the first programming almanac of Eurasians and arrived at a set of accurate observations. He noticed that the reasons for rejecting European culture lay in the experiences of the First World War as well as in methods of running colonial wars (Waldersee's expedition to China in 1900). He noticed similar trends in Wlodzimierz Solowiow's poem "Panmongolism."

Zdziechowski's point of view is accurate about Petr Savitskii's ideology, expressed in *Iskhod k Vostoku*, that the protest against Bolshevism changes to a hymn to Bolshevism (Zdziechowski 1923: 278). Zdziechowski looked for an excuse for discouragement toward the West. He ascertained that "the view of a man fully insane from pain and in unconscious ecstasy kissing the hand of the executioner wakes a feeling of disgust" (278). However, he ends with this comment and does not search for Russian reasons. Zdziechowski does not see in Savitskii's revelations the imagery of the unique Russian soul, excusing the disgusting act, does not try to generalize it and doesn't look for comfortable stereotypes.

Zdziechowski explores Savitskii's ideology on the migration of civilized communities from the South to the North, emphasizing his carefulness in applying conclusions for the future that emerge from the analysis of historical phenomena. Zdziechowski states the theory that formation of new civilizations in towns with an average temperature of 5°C is only a presumption. Yet, for Savitskii, this presumption was one of the most important arguments for limited possibilities in his determination that the center of civilization will always be in the West's culture. Zdziechowski does not notice that the "climatic" hypothesis which negates the "civilizational" stereotype becomes a stereotype in itself.

We have no hesitation in the lack of reliability of the introductory theory in two articles of Trubetskoi placed in *Iskhod k Vostoku*. Trubetskoi was barely thirty years old, the son of a well-known philosopher and chancellor of the University of Moscow. The resistance of Zdziechowski led Nikolai to explore the prime of new, strong life in the Orthodox church caused by a revolution. Zdziechowski remembers Russification, the "police" function of the Orthodox church entirely subordinated to the Tsar, and gives examples of how the Russia delegate of patriarch Tichon-Eulogiusz functioned abroad. He goes on to list testimonies that prove the creation of martyrian Church experienced in faith and the rebirth of elementary human dignity (286–88). While he shows arguments for both views, he doesn't indicate which opinion he favors. We can only suppose (with regard to the speech construction) that in 1922 he favored Trubetskoi's view.

The friendly and reliable treatment of Eurasian views by Zdziechowski was not the result of personal relationships. Rather, Trubetskoi's ideas were presented according to articles in the almanac, and the result of political conditions and his negative opinion of Bolshevism. Zdziechowski took Zeneida Hippius' (Dmitry Merezhkovskii's wife) definition of Bolshevism, as "triumphant 'nothing.'" Furthermore, all anti-Bolshevik Russian political ideology seemed to be an ally of Poland for Zdziechowski, and he found similarities with Eurasianism which was non-imperialistic, not pro-tsarist, and directed inward toward the consolidation of Russia (289). Zdziechowski suggests the question of borders between Russia and Poland was not as important an agenda for Eurasians as it was for monarchists and Bolsheviks.

Zdziechowski finished his speech (printed a year later) with a rebuttal to an anonymous founder of Eurasianism, about his dislike for questioning the right of Poland to have Eastern border lands. The general opinion of Eurasianism defended them from the question of borders. The bigger the chances to guarantee any group of Russian emigrants the then borders, the bigger the approval from the Polish side.

MARIAN UZDOWSKI

This relationship is visible also in a brochure published at the beginning of 1928 by Marian Uzdowski, and connected with the pro-Pilsudski political camp publishing house Droga (The Way) (Broader 1975). The two last sentences of his thirty-five-page brochure are "With relation to Poland, the Eurasian movement took a hostile position from the very beginning, clearly stressing its aspiration towards connecting to Russia Eastern Polish borderland and Eastern Galicia. Under this position should be assessed" (Uzdowski 1928: 35).

Uzdowski proves this opinion with adequate quotes from an anonymous book written by Trubetskoi (of which Usdowski was unaware), about the legacy of Genghis Khan (Trubetskoi 1925: 3–5, 41). Uzdowski doesn't hide his negative attitude toward this ideological direction, but he refrains from forming accusations about imperialism, expansionism, or possessiveness.

This highly valued pro-Pilsudski journalist generally refrains from giving opinions, and about 40 percent of his brochure takes quotes from the most prominent texts of this time. The trend of the time was to take about ninety percent of all texts with descriptions of other parts of Eurasian views. Although Uzdowski doesn't quote texts published before 1927, or those of philosopher Lev Karsavin or historians Georgii Vernadskii and Mstislav Szachmatov, he also avoids criticizing the general ideas of Eurasianism.

The pro-Pilsudski journalist gave his brochure the title *Euroazjanizm*: "New idea in Russian anticommunist movement." However, in the text of this brochure Uzdowski proves the opposite to the thesis. He pays attention to the Eurasian idea of the soviet system (1928, 23), their opinion on Bolshevism as a system of not entirely implemented ideocracy, and the force fighting with capitalism for the realization of "true Russia" as the country of social justice (23–25).

If we remember the ideas of Eurasians concerning the need for creating an entirely ideocratic country and realizing the rules of social justice, then the conclusion about its placement in the more extreme position as Bolshevism seems logical. Eurasianism was an uncontaminated trend, more consequential than Bolshevism, and without Marxist covers that would come from the West. So on the program's conditions (in the square of supernational-state-totalitarian slogans) Eurasianism was a trend more radical than Bolshevism. This theory wasn't directly formed by Uzdowski, but is presented logically from him in quotes. One of the justifications for the subtitle is a community of a majority of Eurasians with other groups of Russian emigration, rejecting the idea of smienoviechostvo, recognition of Bolshevik power and return from exile. Marian Zdziechowski's analysis was both friendly, yet objective. As such, Uzdowski only collected material conducive to independent conclusions.

Uzdowski's brochure recalled a polemic written by S. L. Woyciechowski. This Russian journalist who lived in Poland was, together with N. S. Arseniew, an active and long-term activist of Eurasian organization. In May 1932, the period of the twilight of the organization's activity, he assisted its leader Savitskii in his efforts towards founding and activating Eurasian circles in Cracow, Vilnius, and Warsaw (GARF, 5911, 1, vol. 64, c. 13). From 1929, he was elected to the board of the Russian Literates and Journalists Society which had its headquarters in Warsaw (*Ruch Słowiański* 5, 7 (1929): 231).

Woyciechowski (in his article edited in *Droga* in February 1928) comments on the hostility of Eurasian movement toward Poland (Woyciechowski 1928: 156). He diminishes the importance of Trubetskoi's brochure (published under the pseudonym I. R.) treating it as an anonymous, demagogic propaganda brochure. It seems that even if Woyciechowski did know that under the pseudonym hid a founder and intellectual leader of Eurasianism, he would not have announced it.

Woyciechowski's critique that Eurasianism was hostile toward Poland was positive as well as critical. In opposition to Bolsheviks, Eurasians did not have the intention to subordinate Poland by treating it as a country that belonged to Romano-Germanic culture. The logical conclusion was that the border between Poland and Russia should run along the line of division of two cultures: Eurasian and European (1928: 168). This conclusion was made politically concrete through a thesis about the inviolability of borders defined in Riga's treaty (169). Woyciechowski goes beyond the classical law and international recognition of borders between the two states. He suggests to secure territorial autonomy for national minorities on eastern borderlands, the Poles in Russian give rights for the development of cultural life and in nation districts enable territorial autonomy (174).

Woyciechowski's propositions resulted from the will for friendly, peaceful, and full of reciprocal relations between "the two greatest nations—Polish and Russian" (174). However, he didn't admit the possibility of a Russia independent from the national existence of Ukraine and White Russia. In his opinion, both of these nations belonged to a Eurasian culture according to tradition. This base strongly limited the chances of Russian-Polish discourse.

Territorial autonomy was developed on many times by Polish left-wing parties, but was never formalized, due to growing Polish and Ukranian hostility and the capturing of White Russian organizations by communists (see Bäcker 1997: 397–408). Woyciechowski's article in one of the most influential Polish monthlies could not change this political situation. However, it became one of the important signals of the will to improve relations between Polish and Russian intellectual elites.

Andriej Surkov's article in *Jevrazijskije Tietrady* in 1935 had a similar character. This expert in Polish issues (see Surkov 1937: 77–84) thought it necessary to protect reciprocal polish and Russian intellectual relations from the attacks of traditional mistrust. It would become possible due to the normalization of economic and diplomatic relations between the Polish and Russian nations, and in particular relationships between youth.

The basis of this close up and reciprocal understanding is highlighted by both sides of Asian characters within the Russian culture. For Eurasians, it meant bringing out one of the important features of Eurasian culture, and for Poles, it meant the decrease of power of "pressure toward the West."

However, it is a community of ideology with different sights. As for Eurasians, the Asian features of Russian culture are essential parts of a cultural identity of superethnos. For Polish intellectuals, it only means the decrease of danger and a clear indicator of differences between Polish and Russian nations. It is a feature that allows a reciprocal separation and is axiologically neutral. Surkov rightly notices that Poles didn't idealize these features of Russia-Eurasia (Surkov 1935: 40).

Surkov criticizes the defining of Eurasianism as a form of pan-Asianism by Zdziechowski (1935: 39). According to Surkov, Zdziechowski (in his critical essay about the work of Prof. Jasinowski) is close to the false opinion that traditional Slavophily has changed to "Eurasian pan-Asianism." This is nothing else but Russian imperialism looking for an Asian base for itself. Surkov is correct in demanding indicating differences between pan-Asianism and Eurasianism. Asian features were for Eurasians only one of the components of identity of geographically and culturally comprehended Russia.

A more serious question is connected with the imperialism. From Woyciechowski's and Surkov's articles are the clear wills to create friendly Russian and Polish relations. There is room to accuse journalists and the Eurasian movement of anti-Polish sentiments and the will to include Polish land back it the borders of Russia. The words "collecting everlasting Russian lands" do not apply in this case. Although Eurasians apologized about the conquest of the Mongolian empire, and made an effort to create a multi-ethnic national culture of Eurasian continent, there was no way for Zdziechowski to forget it.

It is interesting that while Eurasian publications show with friendly declarations toward the Polish nation, they appear infrequently. It seems that differences are entrenched to such a large degree that trying to explain these differences may not be sensible.

PETR SAVITSKII AND *PRZEGLĄD WSPÓLCZESNY*

One is not able to detect the intention to improve Russian/Polish relations in an article by the leader of the Eurasian Organization, Petr Savitskii (Savitskii 1933a, b) in two issues of *Przegląd Wspólczesny*. This monthly was edited by Prof. Stanislaw Wędkiewicz and published by Stanislaw Badeni (Ph.D.). The political activity of the editors (both took part in the work of the Naczelny Komitet Narodowy (Head National Committee) did not have an influence on the monthly. It had universal ambitions and a strong pro-European character. Articles published usually had a high merit level.

Petr Savitskii's text on the history and main ideas of Eurasianism fulfilled all the formal criteria for publication in the monthly. However, the article was written by the leader of a Eurasian organization and as such had to have not only scientific character, but also propaganda. As such, we may suggest that the article was not analytical, but ideological.

In the article, Savitskii claims the characteristic feature of Eurasianism is its ability to distinguish Russia as Eurasia from other continents by the width and many-sided parts of a state in all areas. It also manifests life that enables the supremacy of the business of the whole over the profits of individuals (1933b: 100–101). Stratocratic anti-liberalism was connected with the critics of communism as an unfinished, unfulfilled system that was only the first step of Russian-Eurasian development towards Eurasian multi-ethnic integrity that forms a symphonical personality.

The Eurasian state was to be led by a national activities group, an elite that both believed in and wished to execute Eurasian ideas. Savitskii calls this ideocration (104). We may also add the idea of the Eurasian party as a new order (Alekseev 1927: 34). This is not mentioned in the Savitskii text, but is generally accepted in the Eurasian movement. This allows us to clearly see an outline of the totalitarian structure.

Savitskii, probably for the first and only time in *Przegląd Współczesny*, attempted to incorporate Marxism to the Eurasian theory. The acceptance of Marx's theory of Feuerbach ("Philosophers explained the world only by different ways but it is all to change it") reinforced the Eurasian belief that conception, identities and activities divide Russia from Europe, and converted it to a specific Eurasian world. Savitskii accepted the immanent laws of development and the rules of historical dialectics (1933b, 95). The rules of Hegelian dialectics are used for the etatism, saying that it is necessary to know opposites and realize borders. In practice, this meant the acceptance of the private sector—albeit rather small and subordinated to the state's centralized planned economy.

Savitskii did not accept the Enlightenment, and supported the Marxist theory of the development of human civilization. He neither treated proletariat nor broadly understood people as the powers behind social changes, rather arguing that belief and religion settle the new Eurasian system, together creating a complementary whole.

Savitskii's view does not represent ideas inspired by Vladimir Lenin. Rather, it is a dubious convergence of, from one side the official Marxism of the USSR, and from the other side the practical functioning of the state (reminding the idea of a party as a new order). These show similarities to the neoplatonic ideas of the French Jesuit Teilhard de Chardin (see Pomorski 1996: 354–55). Undoubtedly it placed it in the trend of believers of totalitarian solutions.

The editorial staff of *Przegląd Współczesny* had to be aware of the character of Savitskii's article as well as the ideas he believed in. The decision about publishing the article was surely justified because of the scholarly output of the professor or the Russian University in Prague. This is proved by a broad, two-page set of scientific publications of Savitskii's articles, printed as an annex to the first part of the article (Savitskii 1933a: 308–9). This decision induced the intellectual atmosphere that was in the fourth year of a huge economic crisis not only in Poland or Europe, but also in the United States. General acceptance of state control and authoritarian solutions lessened the resistance to allowing the columns of serious monthlies for propagating totalitarian thinking.

POLISH SECRET SERVICE:
NAIVE ILLUSIONS AND BRUTAL ASSESSMENTS

Public opinion was almost entirely uninterested in Russian emigration. As such the Polish secret service acted differently. It became a natural and quite safe agency for getting information about the USSR. As Polish officers of intelligence operating in Parisian environments as well as within Berlinian, Sophian, and Belgradian Russian emigrants, this marginal group of Eurasian intellectuals (scholars and writers) was not useful for the goals connected with the group. This does not mean there was a lack of interest in its operations.

The Polish secret service (particularly the East department of Second Unit Head of Quarter) closely cooperated with the GPU fictional conspiracy organizations that such as the Monarchic Union of Central Russia (MOCR) and the Monarchic Union of Russia (TRUST). In Poland, the delegates of TRUST kept in touch with Ignacy Daszyński and Roman Dmowski (Vojciechowski 1974; Michniewicz 1981: 222–23), and in 1926 at Pilsudski's demand they gave the Polish secret service the documents of the Soviet mobilization plan. Of course, these were false (Wraga 1949: 175). While there were many early warning signs, the real role of TRUST was not discovered until 1927.

Prior to 1927, Eurasians had good contacts with the delegates of TRUST, commenting they had influence among the Russian creators of culture and could affect the opinions leaning toward Eurasians within the highest circles of the Bolshevik party (see Woyciechowski 1928, 159). Special conspiracy procedures were created to maintain contacts with Russia, although their quality was limited (Russia was called Argentina and in correspondence were used terms and names that were to point the running of economic activities) (e.g., GARF 5783: 359–60). In the summer of 1926 there was even a "conspiratorial convention" near Moscow of the Eurasian Organization whereby Savitskii came as a delegate of Eurasians from abroad (Wraga 1949, 169). Savitskii's belief in the power of the Eurasian movement was impressive if Moscow was the place to print the first manifesto of Eurasians a year later (see Hryniewicz 1927).

More interesting than the ideological political illusions and manipulations of the secret service, is the perception of the exponents of the secret service. Ryszard Wraga (rightly Jerzy Niezbrzycki), an officer of the Second Department who did not have even a secondary education, treated the Eurasian organization as one that had scholarly goals. By accepting historical Russian imperialism and by appearing to use basic and idealistic anti-Marxist theories, Eurasians unintentionally misinterpreted historical materialism and consistently recognized Bolshevism as a necessary part of development of Eurasia. In his opinion these were pseudo-scientific conceptions (Wraga 1949: 169).

Savitskii and other ideologists of Eurasianism were educated enough to recognize the origin of their own opinions. A lot more attention has to be paid to the secret services' lack of respect for authorities. None of the numerous groups of scholars that were interested in Eurasianism (except probably Halperin 1985) wrote directly about a pseudo-scientific character of political thinking.

POLES AND EURASIANS, INTERESTS AND STEREOTYPES

The reasons for the interest of Polish interwar public opinion in the problem of Eurasianism were multiple. It was searching for possible cooperation with Russian political groups which guaranteed independence of the newborn Poland. The dominant part of the political scene of Russian emigration didn't allow for this possibility. Eurasians that separated from monarchists and Bolsheviks negated in their political program the possibility of expansion toward the West as potential partners.

Eurasianism was created and then propagated by scientists that sometimes had international esteem. It is worth mentioning linguist Nikolai Trubetskoi and historian Georgii Vernadskii. Because of their high social status, their opinions were tolerated, listened to, and more easily popularized in strange groups.

The basic criterion of the assessment of opinions of Russian emigrant groups by Polish public opinion was the relation to independence and the borders of the Republic of Poland. In special ways, this criterion concerned anti-occidental trends of thinking. It seems that the greatest awareness was formed in questions made by Jan Kucharzewski at the end of the chapter "The Legend of the Rotten West" in *Od Białego Caratu do Czerwonego (From the White to the Red Tsarate)*. He asked,

> Is the reaction against Bolshevism won't be a new period of Slavophile nationalism . . . against resurrected post of rotten west by the Vistula river? Russian Slavophilism always with mathematical precision was turning against Poland, among sighs and sorrows over its apostasy. Is this reaction against today's atrocities not going to come with their watchword of hate towards Europe, together with the lust of destroying everything what's western and with ascribing all misfortunes of Russia to the theories of rotten West? (Kucharzewski 1926: 316)

The criteria of independence and the borders of Poland were also classified by Eurasianists. What made the Eurasians different was the style of speech and a greater scale of pessimism-optimism towards finding Russian allies that would accept Polish rights. What is interesting is the greatest optimism in Eurasianism was from Marian Zdziechowski, while the socialist Czapiński knew the way of thinking of Russian activists and writers mainly from books. This last reason seems to be the most important variable that creates a difference between the two in the level of stereo-typing of not only Eurasianism, but of many other Russian trends and social ideas.

There is no way to agree with the opinions of Uzdowski or Czapiński of the imperialistic, hostility of Eurasianism toward Poland. The aspiration to regenerate or preserve the Russian empire in the natural geographical and cultural borders of Eurasia makes the declaration of Wojciechowski's about friendly relations of Eurasians towards Poland more realistic. It seems that one of the reasons for not finding cooperation between Eurasians and Polish political groups was (of course except for meaningful program's differences) cultural distance. Every negative opinion was treated as hostile and entirely misunderstood. However, the will to understand and to find allies wasn't able to overcome the stereotype.

BIBLIOGRAPHY

Alekseev, Nikolai N. 1927. "Evraziitsy i gosudarstvo." *Evraziiskaia Khronika* 9.

Bäcker, Roman. 1997. "Polska Partia Socjalistyczna wobec postulatu autonomii terytorialnej Galicji Wschodniej." In *Polska i Ukraina: Sojusz 1920 roku i jego następstwa*. Toruń. 397–408.

Czapski, Józef. 1993. "Mereżkowscy w Warszawie." *Puls* 1, 60: 9–17.

Halperin, Charles J. 1985. "Russia and the Steppe: George Vernadsky and Eurasianism." In *Forschungen zur Osteuropäischen Geschichte* 36, ed. Otto Harrasowitz. Wiesbaden. 55–194.

Hryniewicz, Wacław, OMI. 1927. *Jevraziistvo (Formulirovka 1927 g.)*. Moscow.

———. 1995. "Marian Zdziechowski o Rosji i prawosławiu." *Kresy Kwartalnik Literacki* 4, 24: 81–90.

Kucharzewski, Jan. 1926. *Od Białego Caratu do Czerwonego*. Vol. 1: *Epoka Mikołaja I*. Instytut Popierania Nauki, Kasa im. Mianowskiego, Warsaw.

Michniewicz, Władysław. 1981. "Sowiecka afera szpiegowska 'Trust.'" In *Niepodległość: Czasopismo poświęcone najnowszym dziejom Polski*, vol. 14. New York. 182–224.

Nałęcz, Daria. 1975. "'Droga' jako platforma kształtowania się ideologii piłsudczyków." *Przegląd Historyczny* 66: 589–608.

Pomorski, Adam. 1996. *Duchowy proletariusz: Przyczynek do dziejów lamarkizmu społecznego i rosyjskiego kosmizmu XIX–XX wieku (na marginesie antyutopii Andrieja Płatonowa)*. Warsaw.

Savitskii, Petr N. 1921. *Iskhod' k Vostoku: Predczustvija i sversženija: Utverždenije jevraziicev'*. Sofia.

———. 1931. "V bor'bie za Evraziistvo: Polemika vokrug Evraziistva v 1920-ych godakh." In *Tridcatyje gody: Utvierždenije Evraziichev*, Izd. Evraziichev, b.m.w., 1–52.

———. 1933a. "Eurazjanizm I. Ideje i drogi literatury eurazyjskiej." *Przegląd Współczesny* 12, 45 (April–June): 288–309.

———. 1933b. "Eurazjanizm II. Eurazjanizm jako intencja dziejowa." *Przegląd Współczesny* 12, 45 (July–September): 95–112.

Surkov, Andriej. 1935. "Jevrazija w priełomlienii polskoj mysli." *Jevrazijskije Tietrady* 5 (1935).

———. 1937. "Polsza kak sosied Jevrazii." *Jevrazijskaja chronika* 12.

Trubetskoi, Nikolai S. (pseudonym I. R.). 1925. *Nasledie Czingis-Chana: Vzgliad na russkiju istoriiu nie s Zapada a s Vostoka*. Berlin.

Uzdowski, Marjan. 1928. *Eurazianizm: Nova idea v rosyiskim rukhu przeciw-komunistytsznym*. Warsaw.

Woyciechowski, L. S. (rightly S. L.). 1928. "Polska a Eurazja." *Drog: Miesięcznik poświęcony sprawie życia polskiego* 2: 153–74.

Vojciechovski, S. L. 1974. *Trest: vospominanija i dokumenty*. London.

Wraga, Ryszard (Jerzy Niezbrzycki). 1949. "Trust." *Kultura* 4/5: 156–77.

Zdziechowski, Marian. 1912. *U opoki mesyanizmu*. Lwów.

———. 1923. *Europa, Rosja, Azja—Szkice polityczno—Literackie*. Wilno.

VI. Anti-Semitism in Eurasian Historiography: The Case of Lev Gumilev

Vadim Rossman

Lev Gumilev (1912–1992) is a prominent representative of Eurasian historiography and one of the most popular Russian historians of the post-Soviet era. In Russia he is often considered a philosopher of history of the rank of Herder, Oswald Spengler, and Arnold Toynbee. In spite of the fact that Eurasian visions were never articulated in his works of the Soviet period, his Eurasian sympathies have hardly been a secret. The central concepts of Gumilev are clearly Eurasian in their inspiration: the idea that the Tatar yoke was a military union of Russians and Tatars against their enemies; his admiration of Genghis Khan; his ideas about the congruity of the interests of nomads and Russians; his belief in the peaceful disposition of the nomadic people and the rebuttal of the "black myth" about their aggressive and wild temper.[1] It is remarkable that after *perestroika* Gumilev admitted the Eurasian presumptions of his works and discussed on many occasions his affiliation with the leaders of classical Eurasianism (e.g., his meetings and correspondence with founder of Eurasianism Petr Savitskii) (Gumilev 1991, 1993a).[2]

Gumilev's most important works were written in the Soviet period. However, his theories—specifically their anti-Semitic implications—acquired a considerable social significance only after glasnost when millions of copies of his books were published and when the avalanche of publications about his theories appeared in Russian periodicals. This late discovery of his books justifies the discussion of his theories in my study.

---

[1] The history of the ancient Turks and other nomads of Eurasia was a focus of his academic activity.

[2] Gumilev did not seriously influence Neo-Eurasianism, but many of his positions (specifically his interest in geopolitical distinctions) are very congenial to the ideas of Neo-Eurasians. Dugin is sympathetic to many of his concepts.

THE JEWS IN ETHNIC HISTORY

Ethnogenesis and the Biosphere of Earth is the book where Gumilev laid the foundations of his theory of ethnogenesis. The book could not be published before *perestroika* and was circulated in samizdat until 1989 (Gumilev 1989a).[3] My account of Gumilev's theory of ethnogenesis in this section is based for the most part on this early book. I complement this account several times by quotations from later works that better articulate the points that are important for the present study.

The subject of *Ethnogenesis* does not address the "Jewish question," only a few passing remarks are explicitly related to Jewish history. However, I shall argue that the invisible presence of the "Jewish question" is extremely important for understanding the logic of "ethnogenetic" theory and that the very edifice of Gumilev's theory promotes an anti-Semitic agenda. In the next section I shall explain how ethnogenesis affects the ideology of Gumilev's historical narratives.

The central insight of *Ethnogenesis* is the idea of the decisive influence of the landscape on the ethnicity. The course of ethnic history is determined by the relationship between the ethnicity and the landscape.

> Ethnicities are always linked to the natural environment through their economic activity. This connection is manifested in two different ways, in the adaptation to the terrain and in the adaptation of the terrain to the ethnicity. Gradually, the attachment to the landscape is formed. The denial of this type of connection amounts to the conclusion that people have no homeland. (1989a: 58)

Gumilev believes that ethnicity is a biological rather than a social phenomenon. Ethnicity is not simply influenced by geographical conditions; it is a part of the biosphere (41, 37). Particular ethnicities are attached to their areas in the same way animals are attached to their habitats. Loss of connection with the terrain is detrimental for both the "species" and the abandoned landscape.

The central characteristic of ethnicity, according to Gumilev, is the "stereotype of behavior." Ethnicity is not simply a racial phenomenon; it is manifested in deeds and interrelations of human beings. "The difference between the ethnicities is determined . . . only by the stereotype of behavior, which is the highest form of active adaption to the terrain" (42).

Gumilev does not explain the mechanisms which allow the landscape to shape the stereotypes of behavior. His accounts suggest that landscape

---

[3] The book was deposited in the All-Union Scientific Institute of Technical Information in 1979. The first six chapters are available in the English translation by Progress Publishing House.

determines economic occupation and economic occupation determines the moral code and the "stereotype of behavior." Some other contexts in his discussions suggest a much more profound mystical connection between the people and the terrain.

The concept of drive (*passionarnost'*) is another important component of the theory of ethnogenesis.[4] Drive can be identified with energetic potential or vitality. In the course of its development ethnicity exhibits some level of drive, high or low. The concept of drive has important moral implications. Gumilev believes that a high level of drive promotes sacrificial ethics. Members of the "driven community" are ready to sacrifice their lives for moral ideals that have nothing to do with their private interests. This sacrificial ethics enables communities with a high level of drive to win over communities with a low level. Moral goals are more valuable to such people than their own lives. These goals laid the foundations to the anti-egoistic ethics in which the interests of the collective prevail over the craving for life and concern for one's offspring. While drive is penetrating ethnicity, its development is creative. The degree of drive and number of "driven" individuals determine the rise and decline of ethnicities (1993b). The phases of ethnogenesis are the functions of the mystical waves of drive. The only evidence of the high level of drive is the prominence of individuals who demonstrate proclivity for the heroic ethics of self-immolation.

Heroic ethics is not only a historical stage in the development of one and the same ethnicity. In contradiction with his principle of historical development, Gumilev divides ethnicities into two groups, those with a special proclivity for heroic ethics and those who are unable to embrace its norms. He borrows the distinction between the nations of heroes and the nations of tradesmen from Werner Sombart. Romans, Saxons, and Franks are nations of heroes; Jews, Florentines, and Scots are nations of tradesmen. In opposition to the "nations of heroes," the "nations of tradesmen" are inclined to selfish and pragmatic utilitarian ethics.

The Jews are especially important in the list of "nations of tradesmen." Gumilev attributes to the Jews a change of course in the development European history. He argues that before the twelfth century the Romano-Germanic ethnicities lived in small communities and exhibited their original stereotypes of behavior. Members could effectively carry out communal goals and did not pursue individual satisfaction at the expense of the community. "'The craving for profit' was characteristic only for the Jews" (1989a: 406). In the twelfth and thirteenth centuries

---

[4] The translation of this term as *drive* was suggested by Gumilev himself. The Russian word is derived from the Latin *passio*, passion.

the drive tension of the Romano-Germanic super-ethnicity gradually dropped and the Jews could successfully impose on it their own commercial stereotype: "The spirit of capitalism is a result of the scarcity of the original creative tension, which arises during the period of increased drive. . . . The philistines are the by-products of the creative flight, from which they preserved only the "craving for profit" (408).

Gumilev describes this as a period of crisis. The European ethnicities lost their sense of morality and identity as a result of their engagement in dishonest commercial activity. The driven individuals" were displaced by "different types of tradesmen—money-changers, complaisant diplomats, intriguers, adventurers. These hucksters were complete strangers for the local ethnicities. They did not have any motherland. However, their lack of motherland satisfied the monarchs."

Gumilev calls the period of loss of the original drive the period of civilization. It is marked by vast waves of migration from their organic communities and natural environments to the urban centers. In the course of this development the immigrants seized power in the civilized countries and even instructed the native population. They "immigrants enter into a reverse relationship with the aboriginal population. They teach them and introduce technical improvements." These technological changes were often detrimental for both natives and environment. Gumilev explains the downfall of Babylon by the excessive melioration of the area introduced by the newly arrived Jewish advisers of the king (424, 415).

Gumilev does not believe that contact of different ethnicities necessarily leads to conflict, but he believes that only some contacts can be useful and beneficial. As an ideologist of Eurasianism, it is especially important for him to emphasize the natural (organic) character of the Russian-Turanian union. He distinguishes three types of ethnic contacts. "Xenia" is peaceful contact in which the "guest" feels at home in the landscape of the "host." The guest occupies his own ecological niche and does not try to influence the "stereotype of behavior" of the host. "Symbiosis" involves two ethnicities that occupy the same geographical region. "Chimera," the third type, is opposed to the first two. Here the guest suggests his own stereotype of behavior to the host. This type of ethnic contact is really "pernicious" for the host (143).

This account of ethnic contacts is further explained by the concept of "complementarity," which can be "neutral," "positive," or "negative" depending on the nature of the ethnicities in contact (1993b: 41). "Chimera" involves ethnicities with negative complementarity.

Gumilev argues that the "chimeric" type of contact occurs in the periods of influx of strangers, about whom he creates an entire demonology. Immigrants in very different parts of the world are described as the source of all evils. They treat the "country with its nature and people" as "a mere field for their actions," which are always "egoistic and selfish" (1989b: 371). Strangers are portrayed as devils who seduce the country into the commercial social order and take away the heroic ethics of the founders. Gumilev uses specific linguistic devices and metaphors to impress terror on the reader. The concentration of demonic metaphors in the description of strangers is really amazing. They are compared to "parasites," "vampires sucking human blood," a "cancerous tumor which devours the healthy cells" and "tapeworms in the stomach of the animal."

> The super-ethnic system . . . is closely connected with the nature of its region. Each of its constituent parts and subsystems finds an ecological niche for itself. . . . But if a new foreign ethnic entity invades this system and could not find a safe ecological niche for itself, it is forced to live at the expense of the inhabitants of the territory, not at the expense of the territory itself. This is not simply a neighborhood, and not a symbiosis, but a chimera, i.e., a combination of two different, incompatible systems into one entity. In zoology the combination of an animal and a tapeworm in the intestine is called a chimeral construction. . . . Living in his body the parasite takes part in his life cycle, dictating a heightened need for food and altering the organism's biochemistry by its own hormones, forcibly secreted into the blood or bile of the host or parasite carrier. . . . All the horrors of clashes at symbiotic level pale before the poison of a chimera at the level of a super-ethnicity. (1989b: 302)

The same idea is conveyed in a passage where strangers are compared to vampires:

> The parasitic ethnicity is like a vampire. It sucks out the drive from the ethnic environment and brakes the pulse of ethnogenesis. Chimera . . . receives all it needs from the ethnicities in the bodies of which it nestles. Thus, chimera has no motherland. It is an anti-ethnicity. Chimera arises on the border of several original super-ethnicities and opposes itself to all of them. It denies any tradition and replacing them with permanently renovated "novelty." (1993b: 41)

The stereotype of behavior of the strangers undermines the traditional moral codes, the ideas about good and bad, honest and dishonest, held by the culture. The "immigrants'" moral code is not very demanding because they have no stable tradition. It allows them to "adapt themselves very quickly to the changing circumstances" (42).

Strangers and immigrants are so dangerous that not even complete assimilation could save the country from potential chimeras. Gumilev claims they are not able to transform themselves in conformity with the stereotype of behavior of the host ethnicity.

> The subject of assimilation faces the following alternative. It needs to sacrifice his life or his conscience. It could avoid death by the price of repudiation of everything that was valuable to him and that converts

him/her into a second-class person. . . . The latter [the host culture] also gains little, since it acquires hypocritical and, as could be expected, inferior fellow-citizens. The motives of this behavior could never be controlled unlike its outward manifestations. (1989a: 86)

Jews are never mentioned in the discussion of types of ethnic contacts, but they are present even in their linguistic absence. The context and some particular remarks suggest that what is said about sinister "strangers" and "immigrants" could be said about Jews.

The next significant category of the theory of ethnogenesis is the concept of "anti-system." The ideology of "anti-system" is a mechanism by which the chimera realizes its destructive potential.[5] The specific ideological feature of "anti-systems" is a negative attitude to this world and to nature, opposed to a life-asserting attitude characteristic of the driven ethnicities. Moral relativism is an ingredient of anti-systems. The people who share in its ideology believe that any means are good enough in their struggle against the world of matter, betrayal, murder, and lie. They celebrate reason and logical arguments (460–61). Gumilev opposes this cold rationality to the healthy intuition characteristic of the life-asserting position. He characterizes intellectual movements such as Gnosticism, Manichaeanism, Ismailism, Catharism, and existentialism as anti-systems and points out that these ideologies are especially popular in cosmopolitan environments.

The ideologies of anti-systems can arise in two ways. First, they can be generated by the synthesis of two radically different cultures. Different ethnicities can have different "rhythms" and their joint efforts can produce a cultural "cacophony." Hellenism is an example of the "cacophonic" cultural development of heterogeneous entities.

Before the campaigns of Alexander the Great, Hellenes did not know about the Hebrews and Hebrews did not care about the Ionians. . . . Both ethnicities were talented and driven, but the contact of their ideologies gave birth to Gnosticism—a mighty anti-system. (458)

Second, the infiltration of the anti-systems can result from deliberate subversive efforts of strangers, "parasites" who often use the ideology in their political and ethnic struggle. Gumilev identifies these "parasitic ethnicities" with the "Little People" (*malii narod*), a euphemism for the Jews.[6]

---

[5] The term "anti-system" turned out to be one of the key-concepts of right-wing ideology. Some ideologists of nationalism identify anti-system with *perestroika*, cosmopolitanism, and Russophobia. See Kosarenko (1993).

[6] The concept of "Little People" as opposed to "Big People" was introduced by conservative historian Augustine Cochin and elaborated by Igor Shafarevich in his book *Russophobia*. Shafarevich used the concept as a euphemism for Jews who oppose themselves to the standards of the majority. For more details see my discussion of *Russophobia* in a chapter on Neo-Slavophilism. Gumilev uses the term in a broad sense; see (1989b: 249).

The Jews are painted as universal agents of anti-systems, which they supposedly use to eliminate original ethno-cultural stereotypes and pave the way for their own domination (1989b: 282). Gumilev points out that many founders of the ideologies of anti-system are Jewish. Ubedolaya, a founder of Ismailism, was a Jew. Jews created the Albigensian heresy and destroyed the original ideal of knighthood, and contributed to the development of Manicheanism (460). The theological decline of Europe is attributed to Jewish intellectual influence. Gumilev claims that in the ninth through eleventh centuries, the crucial period in the formation of the Western European theology, many Jews were invited to religious academies to teach various subjects because Europeans had no serious "scholastic tradition" or enough competent teachers. The Jewish professors took advantage of the situation and introduced Christian students to different ideologies of anti-system (256, 354). Gumilev exemplifies this by the intellectual biography of the well-known medieval theologian Scotus Erigena. Erigena was greatly influenced by the ideas of Carmat, introduced to him by Spanish and Provencal Jews in the theological academies. "They did not share Carmat's ideas, but they were glad to communicate these ideas to Christians in their own interpretation" (261). Gumilev claims that Jews did not believe in these ideas themselves and were perfectly aware of their destructive potential.

Judaists themselves were the antagonists of any anti-system. They loved in this world only themselves, their own deeds, and their offspring. They resorted to secrecy and lies, arms borrowed from their bitterest enemies, the Hellenic Gnostics, to bring their ethnicity to triumph. But they used these arms only against Gentiles and akums (idolaters). They knew perfectly well that Manicheanism subverts any positive system, and preferred to see Manicheans in other ethnicities, not among themselves (150).

I have already pointed out that the Jews are not mentioned explicitly in *Ethnogenesis*, though anti-Semitism is congenial to Gumilev's theory. Most of my quotations referring to Jews so far are taken from later works. However, it is interesting to note that he supports anti-Semitism even at the expense of his own logic. Some critics have noted that belief in ethnogenesis as a process and belief in stable and universal characteristics of some ethnicities are inconsistent. One can get an impression from his works that "the Jewish stereotype of behavior" is not susceptible to change. It is not clear from the narratives whether Jews ever could experience the rise of their drive and whether Jewish history could assume the heroic path of development.[7] Whatever the answer to this question,

---

[7] This contradiction between "the idea of ethnicity as a process and the belief in the invariable negative characteristics of some ethnicities" was noticed by Russian historian Igor Diakonov.

both his theory and his "stories" are anti-Semitic. In the next section we shall see how he employs his theory of ethnogenesis in explaining concrete history and how these biased theories shape the history of Eurasia he recounts.

JUDEO-KHAZARIA: "A DISASTER FOR THE ABORIGINALS OF EASTERN EUROPE"

Ancient Russia and the Great Steppe is the first book of Gumilev's where the "Jewish question" is thematized directly. The monograph focuses on the historical interaction between the Turkic nomads and the Slavs, between the Forest and the Steppe of Eurasia. The thrust of the book is congenial to his earlier works and is not very original. The "last Soviet Eurasian" repudiates the "black myths" of European historiography, those about the aggressive and barbaric character of the nomadic people and the Tatar Yoke. The observations and conclusions about the history of Khazaria go far beyond the short historical period and geographical location announced in the title. The common experience of life on the same terrain and economic and military cooperation have made the Russians and nomads perfectly "complementary." This "complementarity" of nomads and the Slavs is revealed against the background of their opposition to the Jews, specifically the Jews of Khazaria. The "stereotypes of behavior" of the nomads and the Slavs are similar, and was hard for both to find a common language with the Jews. This discussion of opposition to the "enemy" is the only new contribution of *Ancient Russia* to the story of Eurasia already known to his readers.

Khazaria was a medieval empire that occupied the southeast part of Russia from the Caspian and the Volga to the Dniepr. In the ninth century a large part of Khazars adopted the Jewish faith from Jews who fled the persecutions of Leo III of Byzantium. It is a locus communis in Khazaria scholarship to believe that it adopted Judaism to secure political independence, which was jeopardized by Muslim and Christian neighbors. The paucity of reliable data contributes to the popularity of the topic among nationalists and to fantastic speculations about Khazarian history.[8] Many nationalists credit Gumilev for the discovery of the Khazarian topic and its interpretation.

The academic credentials of Gumilev, specifically his expertise on Khazarian history, set him apart from most other nationalists. A student

---

[8] The myth of Khazaria is prominent outside Russia as well, partly due to lack of reliable information. Milorad Pavic's novel *Khazarian Diary*, where the myth takes a literary form, became an international bestseller; see Dunlop (1954) and Artamonov (1962).

of well-known historian of Khazaria Mikhail Artamonov, he has participated in archeological excavations of Khazar castles and has written
many academic studies on the subject (Gumilev 1966, 1967, 1974a, b, c).
However, his methods of historical inquiry and sweeping generaliza-
tions about very different historical epochs raise doubt about his claims.
Gumilev "reconstructs" the history of Khazaria on the basis of his theory of ethnogenesis. Most of his findings cannot be verified by conventional historical documents. He disparages written sources and chronicles
and sacrifices available data to make historical narrative fit his theory
of ethnogenesis. In addition, in spite of his claims about the apolitical
character of inquiries, he often projects contemporary realities to the old
days. His ideological purposes would be clear even to a person not very
well versed in the subtleties of medieval history of Russia and Eurasia.

JUDAISM IN RELATION TO
CHRISTIANITY AND ISLAM

Max Weber was interested in world religions because of their implications for the work ethic. Gumilev is interested in world religions because
they countenance certain "stereotypes of behavior." He believes that religion is a biological phenomenon, an important manifestation of the
unconscious and genetic memory of the ethnicity that reflects the phase
of ethnogenesis reached by the given ethnicity. Marx claimed that religious conflict is disguised class conflict. Gumilev believes it is essentially
ethnic conflict, a conflict of the stereotypes of behavior (1989b: 241,
104). The discussion of Judaism is based on these presumptions.

In his discussion of Judaism Gumilev exploits the centuries-old stereotypes of Christian anti-Semitism. He defines Judaism as a "genotheistic"
ethnic religion as opposed to monotheistic Christianity. He compiles a
list of the crimes of this ethnic God: he provoked the "persecutions of
innocent Egyptians, the cruel destruction of the original population of
Palestine, including children"; he "favored the pogrom [sic!] of the
Macedonians and other rivals of the Jews" (247: 96); he supported the
ideology of total destruction of the enemy. Talmudism, the modified
form of Judaism after the exile, assumed an even more aggressive and
cruel character. Gumilev believes that xenophobia is a specific element
of the Jewish stereotype of behavior and that Talmudism instructs the
Jews to tell lies to the Gentiles. It advocates the "teaching of predestination,
which takes away human responsibility for any crimes and misdeeds."
Finally, it propagates the extermination of the Christians. It articulates
the anti-Christian principles absent from the original Judaic doctrine
(Christianity is described as a "new young super-ethnicity") (96, 134).
Gumilev alleges that these cruel aspects of Talmud are not widely known

because it used to be a secret teaching of the rabbis (133, 141, 108–9).

He suggests that the Jews initiated the war against the Christians, described as a war of "stereotypes of behavior," and lists Jewish crimes against Christians. They denounced Christians in Rome; "the Judaic fanatics of Bar-Kokhba" initiated "brutal murders and pogroms against Christians"; they tortured and stoned members of Christian communities (98–99). In ancient Rome the Jews discredited Christians in the eyes of the Romans by their behavior. Due to ignorance about the difference between Jews and Christians, the Romans extended their negative attitude toward Jews to Christians (103). He also makes a ridiculous claim that Judaism was "disseminated in Rome through women, who have lost their traditional morals in the period of the Empire."

The dogmatic differences between Judaism and Christianity shed light on the difference between the stereotypes of behavior of the two "super-ethnicities." In particular, Gumilev contrasts the relations between God and Satan in Christianity and Judaism. While the Old Testament describes Satan as the associate of God, the New Testament describes him as an enemy of Jesus. This difference is due to the fact that Judaism is a monistic system: the compromise between God and Devil, good and bad, is necessary because they come from the same source (256). Gumilev cites Job, where God and Satan together "take an experiment over the helpless and innocent Job" to support his idea about the union of God and Devil in Judaism (106, 227). He identifies the Judaic Yahweh with the Devil and argues that the idea of the identity of Yahweh and the Devil is already present in the New Testament, specifically in the scene of fasting in the desert. Then he identifies the choice between the Old and the New Testament with the choice between Devil and God. The acceptance of the doctrine of Trinity by the Council of Nicaea did not allow the Christians to keep their allegiance to the Old Testament (248). This sharp line between Christianity and Judaism is reinforced by Gumilev's references to the early Christian teacher Marcion. He cites the philippics of Marcion against the Jews in spite of his hatred of Gnosticism. The way Gumilev articulates the difference between Judaic and Christian Gods reminds one of the ideas of Gnosticism (105–6).

It is very important for Gumilev to demonstrate the unity of the religious experiences of Eurasian ethnicities. It is not an accident that he draws many parallels between Christianity and Islam, their cultural traditions, customs, and social relations. He tries to show the serious conflicts between Orthodox-Muslim and Jewish cultures. He argues that "Jews were at odds with the Muslims more seriously than with Christians. They had conflicts with the Prophet himself" (116). He focuses on the subversive activities of the Jews within Muslim civilization. Abdulla Ibn-Saba, "a Judaist converted to Islam," introduced the ideas of Shi'ism and split Islam inside, creating the ideological basis for the civil wars that led to the disintegration and collapse of the Khalifat.

The theological principles of Orthodoxy and Islam have much in common. But they are opposite to the theological doctrines of Judaism.

> In the 10th century, the two Eastern religions, Orthodoxy and Islam, differed greatly in many of their tenets and ceremonies, but they were unanimous in that they contrasted God with the Devil and opposed their own positive principles to those of Judaism. It is not difficult to understand the difference. While Christians and Muslims prayed to one and the same God, although in a different way, the Judaists prayed to another God. This ruled out any confessional contacts with the Jews. Only business contacts with them remained possible. (248)

It is important to keep in mind that these assumptions about the relationship between the three religions underlies Gumilev's story of Khazaria and many of his other narratives.

JUDEO-KHAZARIA AND RUSSIA

In his story of Khazaria Gumilev sets out to demonstrate the negative role of Judaism and the Jewish stereotype of behavior in the medieval history of Eurasia. The message of this story in summary is that Judaism and the Jews have played extremely negative role in the history of both Russia and the Turks of Khazaria and are the historical enemies of Eurasian ethnicities. We shall see that the focus of his approach is the "stereotype of behavior" exhibited by the Jews in the course of their involvement in the Eurasian history. This stereotype of behavior turned to be incompatible with the heroic ethos of the original Eurasian ethnicities, the Russians and the nomads of the Great Steppe.

Gumilev considers the Khazars, one of the Turkic tribes between the Don and Volga Rivers, victims of the Jews. He believes that conversion to Judaism was the most crucial and tragic event in the whole of Khazar history. This conversion was facilitated by two waves of Jewish immigration to Khazaria. The first, relatively harmless wave (fifth and sixth centuries) came from Iran, where the Jews were persecuted for participation in the "socialist" Mazdakit movement. The Jews of the first wave did not bother the local population and took part in conventional economic activity. The second wave came from Byzantium in the ninth century. They fled from the persecutions of Leo III, who tried to convert them forcibly to Christianity (114–15, 117–18).[9] Just as in the seventeenth century the Jews persecuted in Spain found their shelter in Holland, in

---

[9] Gumilev justifies this persecution, claiming that the Jews always betrayed the Greeks in their wars with Persians and that they provoked social instability and iconoclasm.

the eighth century they enjoyed the hospitality of the Khazars and felt at home in the "Caspian Netherlands" (118).

The special training of the second wave of Jewish immigrants in Talmud and their orthodox adherence to the religious doctrines of Judaism made them especially dangerous for the native population of Khazaria. Gumilev emphasizes the difference between the two waves in their religious background. While the first wave was quite modest in its devotion to Judaism and confessed Karaism, the second wave was very well versed in the "misanthropic principles of Talmud." They treated the first wave with contempt in spite of the fact that the latter welcomed the Talmudists and helped them to get settled (124).

Gumilev points out that Khazaria attracted the Jews first of all as an important trade center situated in the center of the international caravan roads. A crucial role in the rise of Khazaria is attributed to the Jewish merchants, so-called "rakhdonites" (216). The "Jewish rakhdonites," he contends, "constituted a super-ethnicity which preserved a very high level of drive. The dispersion did not bother them, since they lived at the expense of the anthropogenic terrains, i.e., the towns" (216). He paints the rakhdonites as evil demons. He remarks that in the Middle Ages trade did not benefit the populace, since the economy of natural exchange provided everything they needed. Commercial activity was harmful for the population of both Khazaria and the world outside because of the specialization of the trade. It was incredibly profitable, because the rakhdonites dealt not in merchandise of wide consumption but in luxury goods. In twentieth-century categories, this trade is comparable only to foreign currency deals (*voliutnie operatsii*) and drug trafficking (127–28).

Gumilev also blames the rakhdonites for the underground trade that involved the purchase of stolen goods from the Northmen. Slave-dealing, in particular, involvement in the trade of Slavonian slaves, is the most serious charge logged by Gumilev against the Jewish rakhdonites. He claims that in the Middle Ages slave-dealing was the most profitable business. The Jewish merchants actively bought and resold this most profitable "merchandise." The Vikings and Hungarians supplied Khazaria with slaves and the merchants resold them to the Muslim countries in Baghdad, Cordova, and the Egyptian cities. Gumilev emphasizes that the pool of slaves were mostly Slavs, Russ, and Guzes, and that many were Christian. "Like Africa in the 17th–19th centuries, Slavic lands became the main source of the slaves for the Jews in the 9th and 10th centuries" (221). It seems that the main source of indignation for Gumilev is not slavery itself but the fact that the Jews purchased and resold Slavic and Christian slaves.[10] He points out that the Jews sold even Khazarian

---

[10] In the tenth century some Spanish Jews did owe their wealth to trade in Slavonian

idolaters, people who gave them a shelter in their hard days (130, 146, 153, 313). He cites this as evidence of lack of gratefulness in the Jewish stereotype of behavior.

I have already noted that Gumilev attributes racist and xenophobic attitudes to the Jewish "stereotype of behavior." "In order to replace the Turkic nobility the Jews decided to use love as their weapon" and started to marry Khazarian girls. The Jews . . . received children from the Khazarian ethnicity either as full-fledged Jews, or as bastards. By doing this they impoverished the Khazarian ethnicity and oversimplified the system" (139). "However, the Jews tried to promote only the sons of the Jewish mothers and treated the children from marriages of Khazarian women and Jewish men as aliens. They followed the centuries-old xenophobic Jewish tradition." These children, he remarks, were rejected by their former coreligionists and not allowed to study Talmud as full-fledged Jews. They were "hidden" in Crimea, where they professed Karaism (133).

There is a consensus among historians that Khazaria adopted Judaism to safeguard its political independence from its powerful Christian and Muslim neighbors. Gumilev does not accept this theory. He argues that Judaism was imposed in a religious upheaval (coup d'état). Obadia, an influential Jew, seized power, transformed the khan into a puppet, and introduced rabbinical Judaism as a state religion (136). The Jews occupied all the important positions in the state bureaucracy. Thus, the Jewish ethnicity was transformed into a social stratum of Khazaria. This "combination of the amorphous masses of subjects and the ruling class alien to the majority of the population by its blood and religion" paved the way for the formation of "chimera" (136). The accession of the new ruling elite marks the transformation of Khazaria to an "Empire of evil."

According to Gumilev, the period between the ninth and tenth centuries was a disaster for the aboriginals of Eastern Europe. It was the culmination of Judeo-Khazarian power, and aboriginals faced slavery or death (134). Many historians stress the religious tolerance of Khazaria, arguing that it was one of the few countries in the Middle Ages where Christians, Muslims, Judaists, and pagans could peacefully coexist. Gumilev instead paints the history of Khazaria as driven by Jewish religious intolerance and hostility toward Christianity and Islam. According to Gumilev, the Jewish political elite destroyed the Church organization, oppressed

---

slaves the Caliphs of Andalusia purchased for bodyguards. It is also true that some of these slaves were Christian. However, it is doubtful that rakhdonites took part in these deals, since the slaves were normally purchased in Bohemia. It is also remarkable that the Church did not mind slave-dealing by Jews and objected to Jews holding Christian slaves only out of fear of their conversion to Judaism. See Abrahams (1932: 114–15).

the Muslims, and practiced savage reprisals on religious dissenters. The religious intolerance and cruelty of Judaism was manifested in the military administration of Khazaria. Failure to carry out a military order was punished by death (143). The army was an army of mercenaries. "The chief of the Jewish community squeezed out the means from the Khazars for these mercenaries, which were supposed to suppress the same Khazars" (151).

Gumilev intimates that of the changes in the international politics of Khazaria after the adoption of Judaism also resulted from "Jewish stereotypes of behavior," specifically perfidity and lack of moral consideration for neighbors. International policy was determined by "considerations of profit and not by the considerations of faithfulness and prowess." Khazaria started to betray its former friends, the small nomadic ethnicities, and established friendly relations with the despotic medieval empires (Karolingians, Tan, Ottonians, Abbasids) (165, 167). The alliance of the Vikings and the Jews, he contends, was especially dangerous for the original Eurasian ethnicities as the "two plunderers" divided their gains (171). The alliance allowed the Vikings to seize English and French cities: the Jews helped them to acquire a navy and supposedly opened the gates of besieged cities from inside. In turn, the Vikings helped Jewish merchants control the credit operations of English kings and their vassals." They also helped them establish and maintain the world market of the Middle Ages.

Special emphasis is placed on the conflict between Khazaria and the Orthodox czardoms. Gumilev contends that Khazaria tried to instigate other countries against Byzantium and to avoid the open confrontation. The Varangian princedom of Kiev was a vassal of Khazaria. So the Jews had the opportunity to use Slavs in their campaigns against Byzantium and Muslim countries. The Slavic people paid "tribute by blood" to the khan of Khazaria. The Varangians "sent their subordinate Slavo-Russes to die for the trade roads of the rakhdonites" (187). It is striking that Gumilev blames the Jews for the atrocities committed by the Slavs in Byzantium. The Khazarian czar Joseph murdered some Christians and provoked a conflict with Khazaria. Then Pesakh, a military leader of Khazaria, came to Kiev and "urged Helga [prince Oleg] to fight against Byzantium for the triumph of the commercial Jewish community" (193). In the course of this war, Gumilev observes, Russian soldiers "committed the atrocities which were horrible and unusual even for this historical period."

> Many of the Russian soldiers were already converted into Orthodoxy. However, they crucified the captives, hammered the nails into the skulls, burned the churches and monasteries. . . . This war was very different from the wars typical of the 10th century. It seems that the Russian warriors had experienced and influential instructors [of warfare], and not only from Scandinavia. (195)

He intimates that only the Jews were capable of instructing the Russian warriors in this manner. The atrocities, he argues, were congenial to the principles of "total war" expounded in the Old Testament:

> The total war was an unusual novelty for the early medieval period. It used to be a common convention that after the resistance of the enemy is broken, the victor imposes the tribute and conscriptions. . . . But the total destruction of the population that did not take part in the military operations was a heritage of very ancient times. During the siege of Canaan by Joshua, son of Nun, it was prohibited to take captives and keep their lives. It was even prescribed to kill the domestic animals. . . . Obadiya, the ruler of Khazaria, revived this forgotten antiquity. (141)

After the campaign against Byzantium, the rulers of Khazaria sent soldiers to fight the Muslims. Gumilev alleges that the Russian soldiers not killed in the battles were slaughtered by the Jews. The reader can find the anti-Semitic sentiment of the "last Eurasian" in many passing remarks. He describes commercialism and money-centeredness as specifically Jewish traits of character. In one story he suggests that the peasants killed prince Oleg because of his "Jewish psychology," that is, his greediness in collection of tribute. Oleg decided to ignore all the contracts and agreements with his subjects. "This was a typical Jewish statement of a question, where the emotions of other party are not taken into consideration" (203). It is noteworthy that Gumilev exaggerates the tribute Russians were supposed to pay and even intimates the theory of Khazar Yoke in Russia. This theory was elaborated in more details by some of his students.

Prince Svyatoslav demolished Khazaria in the second part of the tenth century. Gumilev explains the collapse of the empire by the decline of Oriental trade and the rise of Orthodox Russia. He claims that for the Khazars and other local ethnicities it was emancipation from the alien power. What remained of the Jews, he claims, became relic ethnicities (Crimean Karaims and Caucasian Tats).

Gumilev laments that the destruction of Khazaria did not halt the subversive activity of the Jews against Russia. The Jewish community tried to monopolize commerce and craft in Kiev and incited Russian princes to wage wars against their neighbors. The wars created huge slave markets because the captives were enslaved. The trade brought fabulous fortunes to the Jewish slave-traders especially active in Kiev and Chersoneses (479, 314). Gumilev even adds new fuel to the ritual murder charges: "They starved the captives. Just as in ancient times when the Jews had bought Hellene and Christian slaves only to kill them. One monster of cruelty even crucified the monk of the Kiev-Pechersky Lavra on the cross" (315).

In Kiev these harmful activities eventually caused Jewish pogroms, which Gumilev explains as a response to the subversive activities of the Jews:

> The Jews could not carry on their destructive activity in Russia. They moved to Western Europe. The backbone of the Jews did not lose their will to victory. They found their shelter in Western Europe. . . . The descendants of Khazarian Jews forgot about the country where they lived and acted. It was only natural. The Lower Volga was not their motherland, but rather a stadium for their trial of strength. (212–14)

Therefore, they found a "new Khazaria" in Spain. Gumilev points out that in Spain the Jews had many privileges, including the right to settle in a ghetto where they could practice their own legislation. This privilege provided the real impunity for their crimes against Christians and for their deliberate propaganda of skepticism, which undermined Christian doctrines (354). He refers to the Jewish crimes—permanent betrayals, anti-Christian activity, feigned conversions into Christianity, dissemination of the doctrines of anti-system—to justify the atrocities perpetrated by the Spanish Inquisition (327).

THE JEWS AND THE NOMADS: THE KHAZAR ORIGINS OF THE EASTERN EUROPEAN JEWS

The hypothesis about the Khazarian origins of the Eastern European Jews was most recently advocated by English writer Arthur Koestler.[11] This theory was used by some radical Palestinian hardliners to delegitimize Jewish claims to the land of Israel.[12] Gumilev denounces the the-

---

[11] Renan (1883) was the first to suggest that Eastern European Jewry came from Khazaria. This hypothesis was supported by a number of Jewish and non-Jewish historians, in particular, Garkavi (1869), Gumpilovich (1903), von Kutchera (1909), Friedman (1954). More recently this hypothesis was elaborated by Koestler (1976).

[12] An interesting example of anti-Semitic use of the Khazarian hypothesis for Eastern European Jewry is Zhdanov (1993), "What Is Zionism in Action?" Zhdanov, vice-president of the International Slavic Academy of Education, Arts, and Culture, resorts to the popular rhetorical argument according to which Jews could not blame other people for anti-Semitism because they are descendants of nomads and have no connection with Semites. "Russophobes like to blame everybody and talk everywhere about anti-Semitism. . . . Anti-Semitism is a hostility toward Semitic peoples based exclusively on national features. . . . But is it really true that the Jews belong to the Semites? Of course, not. In reality Semitic peoples include only Arab nations and ethnicities. . . . Sefards did have some relation to the Semitic people, because of a few mixed marriages. . . . But the other wave of Jews came to Europe from Russia. It was so-called *ashkenazi*, inhabitants of steppe regions. They accepted Judaism as . . . a more profitable religion. They have nothing to do with the Semitic people. . . . Consequently, anti-Semitism is related only to the Arabs. . . . Unfortunately, this phenomenon exists and is exemplified by the Jews' hatred of Arabs. . . . Therefore, Israel is both a Zionist and anti-Semitic country." The chairman of the Palestinian government in exile, one of the most radical Palestinian organizations, Shaaban Khafez Shaaban, also advocates this theory. He insists that "the ethnic aspect of the 'Jewish question' has lost not only academic, but any possible sense

ory about the Khazarian origins of Eastern European Jewry, but he does not advocate the rights of the Jews to the land of Israel. In this section I will try to articulate the intellectual origins and cultural context of his position. Specifically, I will argue that his opposition to Khazarian origins of Eastern European Jews can be better understood against the background of the association between the nomads and the Jews in some trends of European culture.

The idea of the nomadic origins of the Eastern European Jews and about the nomadic essence of the Jewish mentality was prominent in Europe in the fin-de-siècle and interwar period. The idea about the surviving "nomadic instincts" and "nomadic nomos" of the Jews was expressed by French Hebraist Ernst Renan. René Guénon discussed the "perverse nomadism" of the Jews. Helena Blavatsky, founder of theosophy, suggested that the Jews have Turanian blood. She believed that the Jewish race is a mixture of Mongol-Turanians and Indo-Europeans (Blavatskaiia 1937: 1: 393). The symbols of the Russian Revolution represented by Jews and Mongols were quite prominent in the essays, poems, and fiction of some Russian poets and intellectuals of the Silver Age (e.g., Scythians). In the nineteenth century this idea was especially articulated by the notorious German anti-Semite Adolf Wahrmund in his work *The Nomadic Way of Life and the Modern Domination of the Jews* (1887). Wahrmund suggested that modernity is a modified type of nomadic life and that the ubiquity and success of the Jews in the modern period can be attributed to the nomadic instincts they have preserved and which are in demand in the modern societies. The nomadic conditions of modernity are natural and advantageous for the Jews but disturbing and inconvenient for the Aryans, whose origins are agricultural. Since agriculture does not play a part in the life of the nomads, Wahrmund describes their ethos as parasitic. He also talks about the sordid moral qualities of the nomads.[13]

---

because of the very recent appearance of Turko-Mongol 'ashkenazi'"; see Antonov and Shaaban (1993). The same line of argument can be found in an article by Robert David (1989), an Israeli journalist and member of the Communist party of Israel. He finds the theory of Khazarian origins of Russian Jews plausible. Jewish intellectuals, he claims, instigated a conspiracy of silence on all aspects of this theory because it deprives Zionists of the opportunity to accuse the argument of anti-Semitism.

[13] It is interesting that Wahrmund's ideas have been rediscovered by German philosopher Reinhold Oberlechter. In "The Farmers and the Nomads. The Anti-Neolithic Counter-Revolution as a Law of Modernity" (1995) he argues that "whatever the nomads call themselves, the Golden Horde or the Chosen People, their animality is obvious in all the spheres of life. . . . They transform everything into steppe and desert." His paper was translated and published by the Russian Fascist magazine *Ataka*.

The association of the Jews and the barbaric nomads was manifested not only in the works of the obscure intellectuals. Alfred Rosenberg and some other Nazi ideologists often described Bolshevik Revolution as a revolt of the barbaric nomadic elements under the leadership of the Jews. Rosenberg compared the Jewish Bolsheviks with the Huns, Tatars, and other nomadic invaders in Europe in ancient and medieval periods. He explained the popularity of Bolshevism in Russia by the overdose of Tatar blood in Russian veins.[14] Rosenberg was not alone in these beliefs; rather, he reproduced irrational fears that haunted European intellectual folklore and mythological constructions.

Gumilev's theory can be construed as a response to this persistent association of Jews with nomads. His goal is to save the nomads from the "canard" about their barbarianism and wild temper and to stigmatize the Jews. In many of his works he suggests that the similarity between the nomadism of the Jews and nomads is superficial. The attitudes of the nomads and Jews to the landscape are very different. While the nomads establish a special relation to the landscape, the Jews try to escape any attachment to the land. They use the landscapes but never get attached to them. The Jews use the terrain as parasites and consider it only in pragmatic terms. Their attitude is directly opposite to that of the nomads, who are not rootless (Gumilev 1994: 305).

In this sense Turanian nomads have much in common with traditional Russian farmers. The nomads have a "positive complementarity" with Russian ethnicity and Eurasian terrain. Farmers and nomads are perfectly compatible in their economic occupations and stereotypes of behavior. The Jews, on the other hand, could not peacefully cooperate and coexist with the aboriginal Eurasian ethnicities. This is the message of many stories recounted by Gumilev. He discounts the "black legend" of European historiography about the aggressive character and barbarism of the nomads. But he reinforces the black legend about the parasitic Jews, which has even deeper roots in European historiography than the legend about the barbaric nomad hordes.

I would like to distinguish the following theses in the corpus of Gumilev's writings to summarize our discussion:

(i) The history of the Jewish ethnicity has had an abnormal course of development due to the Jews' detachment from the natural terrain. They could not consume energy from their own terrain. Therefore, they turned into a parasitic ethnicity that exploits other terrains and the people occupying them.

---

[14] These ideas were especially articulated in Rosenberg's *Plague in Russia* (1922); see Laqueur (1991: 112). I quote the Russian edition of this book.

(ii) The Jewish "stereotype of behavior" includes disregard for the sacred norms of morality and tradition, selfish in-group morality, feelings of ethnic superiority and exclusivity, and willingness to betray. In his stories the Jews appear miserly, secretive, unscrupulous, mendacious, and perfidious and exhibit the most abominable features of character. They are greedy and mercenary by instinct; they slip easily into crime; they engage in immoral pursuit of wealth; they easily betray people who have helped them; they are hypocritical, secretive, and cruel. This perverse moral code makes them alien and hostile to other Eurasian ethnicities and explains the latter's hatred toward them.

(iii) The state of the Western world is a result of the invasion of the Jewish "stereotype of behavior." It is important to observe that for Gumilev the encounter of Russia with Khazaria is not a local episode but part of the global historical narrative. The history of the confrontation with the Jews shapes the national myth of the role of Russia in the world historical process. The Eurasian identity of Russia was shaped by its opposition to Khazaria. The Jewish "stereotype of behavior," the huckster, turned into the negative model of Russian identity ("Judean propaganda played the role of catalyst in the conversion of the Slavs into Orthodoxy" 283). Gumilev's "narratives" have a Nietzschean flavor. They praise people who can commit and get away with violent actions and provoke contempt for hucksters and "nations of tradesmen" without disposition for violent actions.

It would be interesting to identify the sources of Gumilev's anti-Semitic position. I would suggest that it was influenced, at least in part, by his teacher Mikhail Artamonov. I believe that the ideas of Artamonov, an expert in Khazarian history, were an important source of his inspiration. Artamonov's works are much more solid by conventional academic standards. But the *History of Khazaria*, his magnum opus, contains many controversial and biased characterizations of Judaism. Some controversial ideas of Gumilev's *Ancient Russia and the Great Steppe* can be found in Artamonov: exaggeration of the role of Khazaria in Russian history; explanation of the fall of Khazaria by reference to conversion to Judaism; an extremely negative attitude toward commerce and trade (described as parasitic occupations); accusations of the Jewish ruling elite of mismanagement and alienation from the main body of the citizens (1994: 334–36).[15] The two scholars use the same denigrating and abusive language when they talk about Judaism and Jews.

---

[15] Artamonov also influenced other Soviet historians of Khazaria. Svetlana Pletneva (see 1986: 70–71), whose account is much better balanced, also blames Khazaria for "speculative resale of goods," "commercial parasitism," and domination of Jewish commercial capital over the common people.

DISCUSSION OF GUMILEV'S THEORY BY RUSSIAN NATIONALISTS

Gumilev's ideas received a lot of publicity in debates on historical and social issues in Russian periodicals. Liberal critics were unanimous. They criticized him for disparagement of historical documents, for pseudo-scientific jargon, and for racist and anti-Semitic streaks. Many historians complained about his "fabrication" of data and arbitrary interpretations of documents (see Mirovich 1991; "Etika etnogenetiki" 1992; Yanov 1992).

The works provoked surprisingly mixed reactions in the circles of Russian nationalists. Fascination was common (see Kozhinov 1992, 1993; Ioann 1993). Many nationalist leaders and ideologists used his theories to legitimate their political agenda, using the categories of ethnogenesis and even incorporating his pseudo-scientific language into political programs. Others dismissed his theories and found "Zionist leanings" in them.

The history of Khazaria received special attention from nationalists. Some considered the political experience of Khazaria a metaphor and symbolic anticipation of Jewish rule in the early Soviet period. They describe early Soviet Khazaria as imposing its Jewish Bolshevik faith on the whole country and oppressing indigenous political expression. For instance, Yury Sedykh-Bondarenko juxtaposes the Khazar, Tatar-Mongol, Nazi, and Judeo-Bolshevik yokes of Russia. In the face of these foreign attacks, he argues, Russians were forced to choose totalitarian methods of ruling (Sedych-Bondarenko 1993).

Other nationalist leaders go farther in their admiration of Gumilev. *The History of Russia and Russian Literature* by Vadim Kozhinov, a well-known literary critic, is an elaboration and complement to the anti-Semitic insights of his teacher, in which the history of Khazaria occupies a very important place. He claims that in the Soviet period the Jews tried to impose a conspiracy of silence on the study of Khazaria. They allegedly persecuted Russian historians engaged in the study of Khazaria, through the Central Control Committee (TsKK) and the State Political Administration (GPU), where they held powerful positions (Kozhina 1992: 167–69). The history of Khazaria was so dangerous and shameful for the Jews that they tried to conceal its details by all possible means. He credits Gumilev and other Soviet historians of Khazaria who had enough courage to study the subject. Kozhinov himself sets out to demonstrate the influence of the history of Khazar-Russian relations on the development of Russian literature. His discussion of Khazarian history, which follows Gumilev's outlines, is supposedly indispensable for understanding this particular stage in the development of Russian literature. However, many passages of this history look like an exercise in anti-Semitic hatred for the sake of the exercise.

Kozhinov's main thesis is that Russian resistance to the Khazarian invaders is the central theme of the epic stage in the development of Russian literature. The "Khazar Yoke" was supposedly much more devastating and significant than the Tatar yoke. He argues that the chronicles of the atrocities of the Tatars in fact could have described the atrocities of the Judeo-Khazars (167–69). The idea about the severe Khazar yoke in the epic stories is obviously an extrapolation of Gumilev's historical speculations on literature. Kozhinov repeatedly concentrates on "historical" episodes that demonstrate the cruelty and gratuitous and ritual sadism of the Jews. Jews supposedly bought Christian captives from Iran only for the purposes of sadistic pleasure of killing them (169).

Kozhinov revises some parts of the story of Khazaria as presented by Gumilev and adds some new "revolutionary" details. The Jews came to Khazaria, he claims, from the Muslim East (Iran and Khoresm), not from Byzantium. The Jewish community dominated in Khoresm and tried to seize political power in the country, directed by the "local intelligentsia" (*habres*).[16] Kozhinov identifies these members of the local intelligentsia with the scholars (rabbis). He goes on to argue that in Khoresm Judaists sustained the "ideology of a powerful, rebellious social movement" (173). He aligns the ideology of "Jewish intelligentsia" in Khoresm with Mazdakism, "a socialist and communist movement in its inspiration." The members of the movement "suggested the introduction of economic equality and socialization of property." In the eighth century the rulers of Khoresm called the Arabs to help in their struggle against the Jewish rebels. The Jews came to Khazaria after the suppression of their subversive activity in Kharesm. Kozhinov points out that the Jews did not believe in Mazdakism but used it as a subversive ideological instrument to undermine the power of the state. It was not an accident that they abandoned "communist ideology" as soon as they came to Khazaria.

Allusions to the political history of the twentieth century permeate Kozhinov's account of medieval Russian literature. He is even more interested than his mentor in historical reconstructions and extrapolations. He draws a number of parallels as he reads what he believes to be the political history of twentieth-century Russia into medieval history. He claims that Zionist ideology and practice "should help us to understand the distant historical realities of Khazar kaganate" and describes Mazdakites as rabid Bolsheviks and bigoted Zionists (176). He blames the medieval *habres* for treating other people as dust, the attitude exhibited by Zionists toward Gentiles and non-Zionist Jews.

---

[16] Kozhinov claims that, according to Bartold, an orientalist, the word *habr* is derived from Hebrew *haver*, identical to German *genosse* and Russian *tovarisch*. This *haber-tovarisch*, he contends, ran from the eighth to the twentieth century.

Kozhinov suggests that historians have neglected a very important stage in the development of Russian literature. The only piece of folklore he could find to substantiate this thesis is the *bylina* (epic story) *Ilya Murometz and the Yid*.[17] He intimates that Jewish literary critics have tried to conceal this masterpiece of Russian folklore from the public and dropped it from the collections published in the Soviet period. The *bylina* describes the fight of Ilya Murometz, the epic Russian hero (*bogatyr*), with a strong Khazarian warrior who is defeated after a long struggle. Kozhinov claims that the end of the *bylina* has a symbolic meaning. In the course of the battle the Jew (*Zhidovin*) pins Ilya Murometz to the ground, but the latter summons up new energy from the earth and overpowers the enemy. The "rootless cosmopolitan" of Khazaria is described as alien to Eurasian soil. Kozhinov's conclusion, which is congenial to the ideas of Gumilev, is the awareness of the inseparable unity of Ilya with his native land that is epitomized in this Russian *bylina*. This unity is opposed to the "rootlessness" of his enemy (172).

Paradoxically, some nationalist critics perceived Gumilev's theory of ethnogenesis as Zionist in inspiration. They found that the central thesis of the Gumilev's theory, the idea of the close connection to ethnicity, is congenial to the tenets of Zionism. The theory of ethnogenesis lends itself to this interpretation, although he could hardly have it in mind. Some Russian nationalists consider Zionism an ally in the struggle against the "inauthentic" Jews of Diaspora. In an article in the newspaper *Den'*, Sergei Kosarenko interprets ethnogenesis in the spirit of Zionism. He claims that the establishment of Israel and restoration of the lost connection with the native soil transformed the Jews who have moved to Palestine into the normal ethnicity. However, from now on all the Jews of the Diaspora fail the test on authenticity and should be condemned.

> In terms of ethnogenesis the Israelis constitute a normal ethnicity. However, the Jews of Diaspora during their two-thousand-year history turned into a unique group, which uses terrain already occupied by other ethnicities. With this, the Jews of the Diaspora regard the local population as . . . a certain kind of fauna. It is widely known, that the Jewish intelligentsia played a significant role in the formation of Russian revolutionary intelligentsia as the incubator and the backbone of anti-system. But . . . [without the Jews] this anti-system could not seriously affect the fate of Russia. . . . After the October upheaval the state officials refused to collaborate with the Bolsheviks, and the positions in state institutions were

---

[17] *Ilia Muromets i Zhidovin* in the original Russian. In colloquial Russian the word *Zhidovin* (*zhid*) has pronounced anti-Semitic implications (like English kike). In the old Slavonic languages it did not necessarily have the pejorative meaning. It is believed that the word *Zhidovin* refers to the Khazarian warrior.

occupied by the Jews from the Shtetles. This helped the government, but also gave birth to the ethnic chimera similar to the one in Judeo-Khazaria. (Kosarenko 1993)

It is not hard to guess that most other nationalists do not consider Zionism an ally. Apollon Kuzmin, a historian of Russia and a conspicuous representative of the ideology of National Bolshevism, condemns both Zionism and Gumilev. His paper on the subject can be divided into two parts (Kuzmin 1993). The first part challenges the Eurasian ingredients in the stories of Gumilev and the historical lapses derived from them. The second promotes his own political agenda. In his historical critique Kuzmin points out that both Gumilev and Kozhinov abuse and disparage the credible historical documents. He also clearly indicates that many "facts" in Gumilev's account are misrepresented. Kuzmin contends that Gumilev downplays the significance of the Tatar yoke and exaggerates the role of Khazaria in Russian and world history—the amount of the "Khazar tribute," Jewish presence in Khazaria, and role of Judaism in the religious life of the kingdom (Kuzmin claims that the Talmud was not familiar to Khazar Judaists, who confessed Karaism). He also points to obvious exaggerations of the level of technical development of Khazaria exhibited in the works of Gumilev. He points out that Eurasian sympathies blinded Gumilev to the effects and significance of many historical events.

In the ideological part of his critique Kuzmin detects Zionist ingredients in Gumilev's theories and exposes his secret Jewish sympathies. The academic arguments of the first part of his paper give way to the crazy style of the Nazi pamphlet. He claims that the discussions of Khazaria by Gumilev and Kozhinov are obviously Zionist. The clear indication of their Zionism are the fantastic exaggerations of the role of Khazaria and the importance of the Jews in world history found almost on every page. Kuzmin claims that this vision of the world history is beneficial only to Zionists. He argues that "Gumilev's description of Jews as the people. who have demonstrated the inexhaustible drive for two thousand years, fuels the pride of Zionist Nazis [*siono-natzisti*]." Kuzmin even resorts to argument ad hominem. He claims that Gumilev himself must have Jewish blood because his mother's real last name was Arens and that Anna Akhmatova grew up in the Jewish milieu (235–36). Kuzmin has his own explanation of the origins of Gumilev's anti-Semitism.

Where did [Gumilev's] unexpected and unusual anti-Semitism come from? Abrupt changes of attitude are very typical for people of mixed origins. It was perfectly demonstrated by Grigorii Klimov, when he described "Hitler's Political Bureau," in which everybody was either of mixed origins, or converted to Christianity, or had Jewish wives. But in our case anti-Semitism is intentional and overt. . . . Apparently, the author is trying to catch on this "bait" potential critics from the anti-Zionist camp. The leaders of Zionism have proved more than once that anti-Semitism serves the purposes of Zionism. (251–52)

Kuzmin further explains the popularity and media attention of Gumilev's theories by their Zionist leanings. He argues that the concept of ethnicity—specifically in terms of the stereotype of behavior—supposedly exposes the congeniality of his theories to the doctrine of Zionism, and that Theodor Herzl's definition of nationhood is identical to Gumilev's. Kuzmin tries to disavow the very idea of Jewish ethnicity.

Gumilev's concept of ethnicity can refer both to the nation and to the pseudo-ethnic mafia. Then, in conformity with this theory one is entitled to call the relation between the two international conflict. Then one can start to advocate the "Little People" and their right to have their own way of being (*samobytnost'*) and develop their culture against that of the Big People (251).

In closing, I would like to make some observations about the link between neo-Eurasianism and the theories of Lev Gumilev. It should be acknowledged that he never addresses geopolitics explicitly and does not employ conventional geopolitical distinctions, like the distinction between Atlanticism and Eurasianism that figures so prominently in the articles of Aleksandr Dugin. Except for some passing remarks about the Varangians, the sea and maritime civilizations do not occupy any place in his works. In many respects his discourse is close to the paradigm of classical Eurasianism. He opposes Eurasia to the Romano-Germanic world and does not pay much attention to the United States. However, the anti-Semitic component of his theories makes his discussions very congenial to contemporary neo-Eurasianism and to the ideological position of the false friends of Eurasianism described by Trubetskoi in *Racism*.

Just like the false friends of Eurasian movement of the 1920s, Gumilev believes that the cosmopolitan Jews with their socially menacing stereotype of behavior are the real enemies of Eurasia. His account of history suggests that peaceful and mutually beneficial coexistence of Russians and nomads with Jews is hardly possible. The relationship will always produce "chimeras" and never get close to the productive "symbiosis" characteristic of the organic relations of cooperation. In contrast to classical Eurasians, Gumilev considers Jews an ex-territorial ethnic entity. He disqualifies the Jews from membership in the grand Eurasian family of ethnicities due to their negative "complementarity" and parasitic and perfidious habits. The Jews used the space of Eurasia as a "mere field of action" and their stereotype of behavior evoked the special social odium of the indigenous Eurasians. Gumilev does not appeal directly to racial criteria. However, many of his discussions about the racial composition of Eurasia and "harmless" and "dangerous" ethnic contacts easily lend themselves to interpretations in the spirit of racist doctrines.

Gumilev's conclusions about the relations between Eurasian ethnicities are hardly convincing. What strikes the reader is not the Jewish stereotype of behavior but the anti-Semitic stereotypes of Gumilev's thinking, camouflaged in pseudo-scientific terminology and quasi-academic tone. In fact, his "enlightened" position reinforces the most primitive anti-Semitic stereotypes.

The Eurasian identity of Gumilev's discourse does not mean that its significance is confined to one trend in the nationalist ideology. The impact of his historical speculations, in particular his images of the malicious Khazarian Jews, on many other trends of Russian nationalism cannot be overestimated. The references to his terms and ideas in the next chapters further illustrate the scope of his influence.

NEO-EURASIANISM:
LEVIATHAN, BEHEMOTH, AND THE JEWS

The Eurasian perspective on the "Jewish question" is an important component of contemporary Russian anti-Semitic ideology. Before embarking on an analysis of the specific problematization of the "Jewish question" in neo-Eurasianism, it behooves us to introduce some historical background and to articulate the political contexts, which promoted the development of Eurasianism and neo-Eurasianism.

Eurasianism is a school of social thought and cultural criticism that began in 1921 in Sofia as a Russian émigré movement advocating a "turn to the East." It was founded by a group of Russian intellectuals and scholars, Prince Nikolai Trubetskoi, a linguist, Georgii Florovskii, a theologian and philosopher, Pierre Souvtchinski, an art critic, and Petr Savitskii, a geographer and economist. Eurasianism greatly influenced trends in historiography (Georgii Vernadskii, Gumilev), linguistics (Trubetskoi, Roman Jakobson, Viacheslav Ivanov), music (Igor Stravinsky), and cultural studies. Many prominent Russian émigré intellectuals sympathized with Eurasianism and contributed to Eurasian periodicals. A remarkable example is Alexandre Kojève (Alexander Kozhevnikov), the prophet of the "end of history" and teacher of many French post-modernists.

Originally Eurasians were primarily concerned with denouncing European elements in Russian history and culture and vitriolic rejection of the "tyrannical yoke" of Romano-Germanic civilization. They especially focused on innate cultural, linguistic, and religious ties with Russia's Asian brothers. By the late 1920s and early 1930s the emphasis shifted toward the geopolitical construction of a future Russian-Eurasian state.

What linked Eurasian theoreticians together was the conviction that Russia, as a unique cultural area, was to remain separate from and even in opposition to Western Europe. Most Eurasians felt that communist control was a necessary evil that would eventually be replaced by a more suitable form of power (for this reason, some supported the Bolsheviks). As a group, Eurasians gradually fragmented to the point of complete disintegration by 1935.[18]

The advent of *perestroika* awoke Eurasianism from its slumber and led to a flood of interest among Russia's post-Soviet intelligentsia. Its ideas became extremely popular and pervasive in the political language of the leaders of different movements of the *perestroika* period. The collapse of the USSR contributed to the popularity of Eurasian concepts and terminology in political debates and intensified academic discussions. My analysis of the revival of this ideology is confined to one group of neo-Eurasians.

This group of Russian nationalist intellectuals is united around the newspaper *Den'* (Day) and the journal *Elementi*. They develop the arguments of early Eurasianism and reshape them for present-day political debates and the needs of those shaken by Russia's loss of status as a world superpower. The special section "Eurasia" in *Den'* became an intellectual forum for the discussions of different Eurasian projects and concepts. Aleksandr Prokhanov, editor-in-chief of *Zavtra*, Aleksandr Dugin, Shamil Sultanov, Vadim Shtepa, and Anatolii Glivakovskii became the most prolific authors who identified their ideological stance with the Eurasian ideology. They have denounced the attempts of "cosmopolitan forces" to integrate the doctrines of Eurasianism into their discourse, counting themselves the only legitimate successors of classical Eurasianism in contemporary Russia (Dugin 1993a).

The adoption of the Eurasian perspective marks a new stage in the development of nationalistic discourse. It offers a number of advantages to the nationalists. First of all, it helps them abandon the anti-communist posture of the mainstream nationalistic discourse of the *perestroika* period. Thus, it allows the reconciliation of different ideological attitudes to the Soviet period, to consolidate the diverse nationalistic trends and shape a common language for the anti-liberal opposition to the govern-

---

[18] The most recent studies of Eurasianism include Isaev (1992, 1993); Luks (1986, 1993); *Evrasiia: Istoricheskie vsgliadi russkikh emigrantov* (Moscow, 1992); *Rossiia mezhdu evropoi i Asiei: evrasiiskii soblasn* (Moscow, 1993); *Mir Rossii—Evrasiia* (Moscow, 1995). Presumably, the paucity of research on Eurasianism in Western languages is due to its relatively insignificant role in Russian political ideology of the Soviet era. Eurasianism was perceived by Western scholars for the most part as a trend that characterized the peculiarities of the intellectual life of Russian emigrants.

ment. In particular, the Eurasian paradigm provides ideological justification for the alliance of Left-Right forces in their opposition to liberalism and Western-style democracy. Another important advantage of this ideology is its appeal to both Russian and other national minorities of the former Soviet Union. The Eurasian perspective underpins resistance to local separatist tendencies and permits escape from accusations of parochial Russian chauvinism. So the shift of emphasis from *Blut* to *Erde* permits extending the sphere of influence of nationalist ideology, both ethnically and socially.

At the same time, and perhaps most important, Eurasian ideology offers a consolation and provides a new identity to the numerous people who experienced a crisis of identity and fragmentation of lifeworld due to the collapse of the USSR. The Eurasian ideology is not only nostalgic but also forward-looking, since its members insist that in historical perspective the future belongs to the young Eurasian civilization, the pivotal area of history and the heartland of the world.[19]

It is important to observe that the ideology of neo-Eurasianism is significantly different from original Eurasianism in spite of the declarations of movement representatives. Whereas classical Eurasianism set Russia in opposition to Western Europe and Romano-Germanic civilization, many neo-Eurasians have altered the original concept of "Eurasia," embracing not only Asia and Russia but Europe as well in their theoretical formation of one united continental power that will stand against the foreign infiltration of the Atlantic, or American states. The new concept of a Eurasian empire from Dublin to Vladivostok was elaborated by the late Jean Thiriart, a Belgian geopolitician and leader of the movement Jeune Europa. Thiriart visited Moscow in 1992 and established friendly relations with the editorial staff of *Den'*. His most eccentric idea is to surrender Western Europe to the Soviet Army to deliver it from "American occupation" and political service to Israel (Thiriart 1992a, b; Thiriart and Ligacheov 1992; Dugin 1993b). This radically new geopolitical concept of Europe was accepted by at least some Russian neo-Eurasians.

While the original Eurasians feared Europeanization and the infiltration of Catholicism, "enemy number one" for the neo-Eurasians is now Americanization and Judeo-Protestantism, including their offshoots liberalism and market economy. We shall see in due course that the anti-American thrust of the argument is especially important for understanding

---

[19] The neo-Eurasians borrow "pivot state of Euro-Asia" and "Heartland" from Halford Mackinder, a British geopolitician, in his short lecture "The Geographical Pivot of History," read in 1904 to the Royal Geographical Society of London.

the neo-Eurasian perspective on the "Jewish question." Neo-Eurasians coined the term Atlanticism, which refers to maritime or oceanic civilizations (so-called "thalassocracies") as opposed to continental Eurasian civilizations ("tellucracies").[20] Atlanticist civilization is represented by Great Britain and the United States; Russia and Germany are typical Eurasian land civilizations. The Atlanticist civilizations are market-oriented. Because of their geographical location they are better equipped to promote trade. Their concern with individual freedom and human rights is an outcome of their commercialism. The Eurasian states are agricultural, authoritarian, and military oriented. Strong state power and civil religion designed to conform to the needs of the state are their major concerns. The wars of two kinds of civilization, Leviathan and Behemoth,[21] are natural, and the preservation and acquisition of living space—the Great Space of the Soviet Empire—are essential for the survival and normal functioning of great powers (Dugin (1992a, 1993a: 92–94). These ideas are heavily indebted to the theories of Western European geopoliticians Friedrich Ratzel, Rudolf Kjellen, Halford John Mackinder, and Karl Haushofer.[22]

Whereas the early Eurasians spoke of spiritual ties with their "Turanian brothers," neo-Eurasians consider the Arab and the traditional Muslim world, especially Islamic fundamentalism, as Russia's natural allies in resistance to the sinister anti-continental powers Americanism and Zionism.

---

[20] The terms "thalassocracy" and "tellucracy," introduced by Schmitt (1950), are derived from Greek *thalassa* (sea) and Latin *telluris* (earth). See Dugin (1994a: 63).

[21] Leviathan and Behemoth are monsters mentioned in Job (41: 33–34), later interpreted as apocalyptic animals. Thomas Hobbes was the first philosopher to employ the two images in a political sense, Leviathan for the strong peacekeeping state and Behemoth for rebellion and civil war. Hence the title of his book on the English civil war, where the rebellious forces of Behemoth are identified with the clergy and other centrifugal forces. Neo-Eurasians reinterpret the symbolism in terms of geopolitics and reevaluate the status of the two monsters, Behemoth as a symbol of the continental powers and Leviathan of maritime civilizations. Dugin (1996a: 26). Schmitt drew on the biblical source, where Behemoth is apparently a giant ox, hippopotamus, or elephant and Leviathan a sea beast, "king over all children of pride," whom Yahweh alone can control. The Jews in this context are associated with Leviathan. Schmitt could have in mind the original Jewish sources. In the Talmud Leviathan is called the favorite fish of God (Baba Bathra, fol. 74, a–b). It is interesting that Norman Habel (1985: 557–58), a contemporary commentator on Job, distinguishes a special meaning of Behemoth as "symbol of the mighty historical enemies of Israel." We shall see how the champions of neo-Eurasianism understand the connection between Leviathan and the Jews and use it in their political discussions.

[22] The theories of Karl Haushofer are especially important for neo-Eurasians, since he insisted on the necessity of the geopolitical unity of Russia and Germany. The Haushofer school formulated a theory of "great expanses," which resulted in the 1939 Molotov-Ribbentrop German-Soviet pact.

In contrast to classical Eurasianism, some neo-Eurasians believe the conflict of the geopolitical powers, Atlanticism and Eurasianism, goes back to the ancient world where the two kinds of civilization already confronted each other. In neo-Eurasian discourse the distinction between Atlanticism and Eurasianism becomes pervasive to the point of obsession. It is used for political history and history of literature, art, and philosophy (e.g., Thales is obviously an Atlanticist, while Heraclitus is a Eurasian).

Last but not least, whereas in classical Eurasianism the "Jewish question" was marginal and mainstream Eurasianists tried to condemn anti-Semitism, anti-Semitic statements and concepts are indispensable ingredients in the discourse of neo-Eurasians. I argue that neo-Eurasian anti-Semitism is not just an eclectic construction, a mixture of anti-Semitic arguments. Neo-Eurasianism shaped a new justification for anti-Semitism which should not be confused with that of other nationalist trends and was not familiar to the founders of classical Eurasianism. In the following two sections I will juxtapose and contrast two different interpretations of the Jewish question enunciated by early and contemporary Eurasians. The examination of the real texts of classical and neo-Eurasians demonstrate a discontinuity in the attitude to this problem.

THE "JEWISH QUESTION"
IN CLASSICAL EURASIANISM

Although some members of the movement have directly addressed the "Jewish question," only a few of them tried to answer this question in terms and categories of Eurasianism. In this section I will examine the discussion of the "Jewish question" by four representatives of the Eurasian movement. The first discussion is an essay "Racism" (1935) by Nikolai Trubetskoi, one of the founders of Eurasianism. The second is the essay "Russia and the Jews" (1928) by Lev Karsavin, the prominent leader of the left wing Eurasians. The third is an article "The Jews" (1929) by "Red Prince" Dmitrii Sviatopolk-Mirsky, another leader of the Left Eurasians. The last is the paper "Jewish Easternism in the Past and in the Future" (1931) by Yakov Bromberg, a minor figure in the movement.[23] All four essays are very important for understanding the early Eurasian perspective on Judaism and Jews. Bromberg's paper is especially valuable as an example of the perception of Eurasianism by a Jewish member of the

---

[23] The term "Easternism" (*vostochnichestvo*) was coined by Bromberg as the opposite of "Westernism" (*zapadnichestvo*). Bromberg deconstructs the conventional distinction between "Slavophilism" and "Westernism"; Slavophilism is only a type of "Easternism."

group, pondering on the peculiarities of the specific Russian Jewish identity and experience and trying to advocate a new perspective of Russian Jewish history suggested by Eurasian discourse. This essay could probably shed light on the personal hopes and expectations of the Russian Jewish intellectuals who were involved in the movement or sympathized with it in different periods of post-October history (e.g., Sergei Efron, Artur Lurie, Roman Jakobson, Semeon Frank, Lev Shestov). The ideas of Lev Karsavin can help to get a better grasp of the implications of the "Jewish question" for the religious project which was advocated by some members of the Eurasian movement. Trubetskoi's essay was written in 1935 when the Nazis already had come to power in Germany. The Eurasian movement was already at low ebb. Trubetskoi denounces the rising Nazism and condemns Russian nationalists who chose to collaborate with Nazi Germany. The focal point of his paper is an attempt to dissociate the Eurasian movement from anti-Semitic undercurrents.

Trubetskoi starts his paper with a discussion of the attempts of some Russian émigré anti-Semites to inveigle the Eurasianist movement into their cause and employ Eurasian ideas and concepts as a justification for their anti-Semitic instigations. Trubetskoi expounds their argument. The indigenous population of the USSR consists of representatives of three races: Eastern European, Turanian, and Tungidian (according to the classification of von Eikstedt). The three are very close to each other due to mixed marriages and common cultural and psychological features. The Jews do not belong to any of these races and, consequently, their cultural and psychological features are alien to those of the natives of Russia-Eurasia. The Jewish presence in Eurasia exerts a corrupting influence on the native population. Marriages with Jews, the argument goes, should be prevented, because racial features never completely disappear, and the Jewish genes affect the racial hybrids.

Trubetskoi disavows this "anthropological materialism" and condemns the misuse of Eurasian concepts by Russian anti-Semites. He does not deny the existence of the laws of heredity, but inheritance determines only features that are morally neutral, e.g., mental activity, aptitude for music, mathematics, humor and some other talents. In the case of the Jews, Trubetskoi argues, one can talk about their inherited "quickness of wit, combinatorial talents ('pushiness,' 'resourcefulness') and passionate temper," that is, features which can be beneficial for the host people (1935: 261).

Trubetskoi believes that the corrupting influence of the Jews is not a mere fancy of the anti-Semites. This influence can be explained, not by reference to racial features. but as a result of complex socio-psychological circumstances. The key to the "Jewish question" is a specific psychology of immigrants that does not depend on racial features. The Jews are "immigrants with a stable immigrant tradition of two thousand years." Trubetskoi contends that observation of the peculiarities of life of Russian immigrants in Western Europe and their moral standards could facilitate a proper understanding of the Jewish syndrome. Such phenomena as solidarity when confronted by strangers, cliquishness and cronyism, and double standards of morality are very characteristic for communities of Russian immigrants in Western Europe. In this respect Russian immigrants of the first generation had much in common with Shtetl Jews. The concept of identity and attitudes to the host culture of the young generation of Russian immigrants is more complex and ambiguous. On the one hand, they feel strong attraction to the host culture and wish to become like others. Sometimes they are even ashamed of their Russianness. On the other hand, they try to dissociate themselves from the host culture and even despise it. The psychological complexes of the young generation of Russian immigrants remind Trubetskoi of the attitude of intelligent Jews to Russian culture. The major indicator of this "immigrant psychology" is the immigrants' objective approach to national values and ideals.

> The young immigrant who adopted the culture of the host people and is a native speaker of its language does not share the patriotic enthusiasm of this people and tends to look at everything dear to this people coldly, from the "objective point of view." This objective point of view exposes the absurdity and theatricality of everything strange which is not experienced from inside as one's own. . . .
>   And this necessarily induces the irony, the vitriolic and corrupting irony which is so characteristic of the Jews. This irony is a revenge for the fact that "they" (foreigners, gentiles) have their own national enthusiasm and their own concrete sacred notion, the motherland. . . . This irony also functions as a mechanism of self-defence, since in the absence of this irony the immigrant would lose his identity and would be absorbed by the strange people. . . . The most typical Jews really enjoy the dismantling of all the ideals of the strangers and their substitution by the cynical and cold calculation of benefits. These Jews like to find vile motives behind the sublime and to express themselves in pure negation. (260–61)

Trubetskoi admits that in many cases the negativism and skepticism could be counted as a productive step in the creative evolutionary process, but he remarks that in most cases Jewish irony goes far beyond constructive criticism and is not conducive to good results. Their corruptive activity is detrimental not only to the host people but also to the Jews themselves. It exposes a special neurosis that requires special treatment.

Trubetskoi does not propose any project of possible treatment but he makes clear that the racists' policies and their proposed limitation of rights would not help eliminate the problem, and remarks that the civil emancipation of the Jews should be promoted and mixed marriages encouraged. He claims that the aloofness and particularism of the Jews are facilitated by their religious separation and by the persecutions, but he does not expatiate on these subjects. He deliberately avoids discussion of the religious problems, since for him Eurasianism is a purely scientific doctrine. It does not take into consideration racial factors and does not presuppose any commitment to a particular creed and religious ideals. Nor does he address question of concrete ways to integrate the Jews into the Eurasian community, although he apparently favors a policy of assimilation.

The religious dimension of Eurasianism and the concrete policies of the future Eurasian state toward the Jews are especially important for Lev Karsavin, a student of Western religious history by training. Karsavin distinguishes three "ideal types" of the Jews on the basis of their different behavioral patterns and possible influence on the rest of the Eurasian community. The first is "religious-cultural Jewry," the natural ally of Russians and other Eurasian people in the struggle against the destructive influences of the West on the original Eurasian culture. The second is represented by Jews completely assimilated into Russian culture.

"Jews at the cross-roads" constitute the third type, which is really dangerous both for the Eurasian community and for authentic Jews themselves. They represent the assimilating "periphery of the Jewish people in the state of decay," Jews who could accept neither the host culture nor the cultural and religious tradition in which they were born. The perverse way of assimilation of this third type, Karsavin argues, is determined by the specific universalism of Judaism and the reluctance of assimilating Jews to exchange their chosenness for a "mess of pottage." These Jews do not accept any organic culture because of its particularity and believe in some international and abstract culture of all humanity. Their ideas are cosmopolitan, abstract, and lifeless. It is not surprising that these denationalized Jews are especially susceptible to the destructive ideas of Marxism and other revolutionary international doctrines. The danger comes not from the skepticism, nihilism, and irony of the assimilated Jews, as Trubetskoi suggests, but from the universalist and cosmopolitan ideals and aspirations of modernity they have adopted.

These "Jews at the cross-roads" greatly contributed to the Europeanization of Eurasia and the realization of the Bolshevik project, although Karsavin admits that the communist revolution could not be explained only by reference to their subversive influence. The Bolshevik coup was primarily a result of the decay of Russian culture and the Jews only facilitated the destructive processes in Russian society. Karsavin argues that the new Eurasian state needs to support a healthy and organic

Jewish culture in its struggle against the "periphery of assimilating Jews." These "non-Jewish Jews," to use the term coined by Isaac Deutscher (1968), a biographer of Trotsky, are dangerous and harmful, both for the truly Jewish and truly Russian social life and culture.

Karsavin believes that the Jewish community should enjoy all the rights of other Eurasian people and become an "equal member of the Eurasian federation." The Jews do not need a territory within Russia-Eurasia, since they are united not by territory but by religious and cultural tradition, especially their "Law." The question about Jewish communal life outside Eurasia is especially challenging. He resolves it by reference to different possible "incarnations" (*individuatsii*) or realizations of each culture.

The Jewish people are a united and organic whole. But organic wholes are not homogeneous and are divided into united particular wholes. Jewry is not an exception, but its peculiarity and role in human history is that it is divided according to the internal propinquity of its parts to certain cultures. One part is naturally kindred to the Romanic culture, the other to German or Eurasian-Russian culture. Therefore, Russian Jewry, the incarnation of Jewry, is also the incarnation of Eurasian culture. The "correlation" and double-nature of Russian Jewry could be determined empirically (1928: 428–29). Karsavin insists that the Eurasian "incarnation" of Jewry does not presuppose the complete absorbtion and assimilation of the Jewish people. Jewish religious tradition and particularity should be kept intact.

Support of "religious-cultural Jewry," however, does not imply that Eurasians are indifferent to the centuries-long argument between Judaism and Christianity. In a response to his Christian critics, Karsavin maintains that Orthodoxy is not compromised by Eurasian ideology. In particular, the Eurasian project, hopefully, will help accomplish the task of the religious conversion of the Jews. Support of the idiosyncratic features and locality of Jewry would facilitate the conversion of the Jewish people as a whole, as opposed to painful individual conversions. It should be observed that Karsavin believes in a special non-universal Christianity and claims that the famous words of Paul ("There is neither Greek nor Jew. . . . But Christ is all, and in all"; Colossians 3:11) are often misinterpreted as an expression of Christian cosmopolitanism. Christianity does not presuppose cosmopolitanism and, consequently, conversion does not imply complete assimilation. Jews should enter the Orthodox Church as Jews, as a specific Jewish congregation and not simply as individual cosmopolitans. The Eurasian project could naturally lead to the voluntary baptism of the Jews into the Orthodox Church.

It is not surprising, Karsavin argues, that Western Christianity was not able to convert the Jews. Russian Orthodoxy is better equipped to cope with this problem, because Russians and Jews, Orthodoxy and Judaism, have much in common in spite of the incompatibility of many Christian and Judaic doctrines. In contrast to universalistic Catholicism, Orthodoxy preserves the ethnicity of its converts and is not aloof to national ideals and concerns. This is especially attractive for the Jews, who are concerned about their national particularity. Neither Judaism nor Orthodoxy is interested in proselytizing activity and imposing its creed on other people. Social ideals and moral concerns are especially important for both. The idea of a special historical mission permeates the historical consciousness of both Russians and Jews. Russian religious philosophy has much in common with Kabbalah and Chasidism. It is not a coincidence that Russians and Jews often encounter each other in history and that Russian history is interwoven with Jewish history from its very first days (423–24).

The "Red Prince," Sviatopolk-Mirsky, was a friend of Karsavin. He was an ideologist of the extreme Left wing of the Eurasian movement and a member of the editorial staff of the newspaper *Evraziia*, published in Paris for only two years (1928–1929). It is remarkable that his article was published in a series of essays entitled *The Ethnicities of the USSR*. In contrast to Karsavin and many other Eurasians, Dmitrii Sviatopolk-Mirsky is not concerned with Jewish activity in the Russian Revolution, the subject which preoccupied many other members of the Russian intelligentsia at the time. His central concern was the integration of Jewish "extraterritorial ethnicity" into the Eurasian cultural zone. He does not believe that Zionism can resolve the problem of "extraterritoriality" and condemns this movement as the "most harmful type of retrospective romanticism." Zionism has implicated small groups of Jews into the imperialist politics of Great Britain and the exploitation of the Palestinian Arabs (1929). Sviatopolk-Mirsky believes that the best way of integration for the Jews is their peasantification. He remarks that "there are more Jewish peasants in the USSR than Jewish colonists in the Palestine." "The peasantification of the Jews of Russia is not merely a demographic enterprise. The approximation of the class structure of Jewry to the normal structure of the neighbouring ethnicities could help more than anything else to extirpate the real plague of Russian life, the endemic anti-Semitism. It is going to be an effective means, since it has been already determined that in the areas of the old Jewish agricultural communities anti-Semitism is negligible." "Anti-Semitism is a very serious plague," he goes on to argue. "It is one of the first obligations of any conscientious Russian person and, in particular, of any Eurasian to fight against it." According to Sviatopolk-Mirsky, the prominence of the Jewish leaders in the Revolution and the construction of the USSR is an important contribution to the Eurasian cause, not a crime against Eurasia.

The Jews were instrumental in the preservation of the unity of the political and economic organism and the overcoming of Russian chauvinism. The centrifugal aspirations of the Jews who have emancipated themselves both from provincial nationalism and chauvinism have greatly contributed to the establishment of the present supernational unity of the Soviet country. The "Jewish preponderance" is a compensation for the centuries in which the Jews were not admitted to the state and social construction.

The historical and spiritual propinquity of Russian Jews to Eurasia is a focus of Yakov Blomberg's paper which seems to be very much informed by Karsavin's account. In his paper Bromberg attacks the Jewish Westernizers, the proponents of Enlightenment and Bildung. The fruition of their project failed to provide the promised security and prosperity to the Jewish community. Emancipation in Western Europe did not bring about a blending of cultures, and was accompanied by the growth and intensification of nationalistic hostility and racist ideology. In Russia the destructive Bolshevik Revolution caused a "territorial and economic defeat of the main ethnic base of Judaism, that is, the Eastern Jewish people of Russia." The Westernized Jews themselves contributed to this defeat and to the collapse of the Russian-Eurasian state which shaped their identity and sustained spiritually their cultural and religious development. The "Jewish Westernizers" broke off from the Eastern Jewish tradition. Their intellectual development, namely, the contamination of Jewish religious enthusiasm with the alien form of destructive Western ideas, exemplifies the phenomenon which was called "pseudomorphosis" by Oswald Spengler.[24] The Jewish Westernizers are opposed to the lower strata of the Jewish population which have preserved the Eastern Jewish traditions and the wisdom of generations which lived in the great space of Eurasia. The crisis of Eastern Jewry and the persecution of Jewish religious and cultural life in Soviet Russia by the "Jewish section" of the Bolshevik party marks the spiritual bankruptcy of the "cause of Moses Mendelssohn" and the concomitant crisis of the "peripheral false culture" of Berlin Enlightenment which was produced by him: "We witness the downfall of all the hopes of fanatic Jewish Westernism. We don't know yet whether the kingdom of reason and justice exist on the earth or have to come from somewhere else" (Bromberg 1931: 201).

---

[24] Spengler borrowed the term "pseudomorphosis" from geology. A pseudomorph is a mineral that has replaced, or appears in crystal forms foreign to, its original formation. By the same token, some cultural forms, e.g., the religious enthusiasm of Jewish revolutionaries and Westernizers in Bromberg's example, are foreign to their original formation. Russian culture for Spengler is also pseudomorphic, since it adopts the foreign form of Byzantine Orthodoxy. The "pseudomorphic" origin makes the crystal fragile. Spengler discusses this concept in the second volume of *Decline of the West*.

Bromberg believes that the "Eastern Jewish people (*vostoevreiskii narod*)" are a separate entity, the product of Eurasian "place-development" (*mestorazvitie*).[25] It is noteworthy that he disregards the word "European" in the standard Russian expression "Eastern European Jewry." His "Eastern Jewish people" is a Russian translation of German "Ostjude." Bromberg suggests that Eurasian Jews need to look back and take seriously the "Oriental and Asian legacy of their culture," which "became a bugaboo for its enemies" (Bromberg 1931: 203). The Jews should be proud that they are "the only real Asiatics in Europe." The Eurasian project, sustained by "Jewish Easternism," should help Eastern Jews to denounce the myths of Europocentric historiography and maintain their Oriental identity just as Eurasianism helps Russians discover their cultural Asiatic roots.

The discourse of Westernism and Enlightenment made the Eastern Jews blind to the congruity of Russian-Eurasian and Eastern Jewish cultures. This congruity and propinquity were especially articulated by Oswald Spengler, who introduced the concept of a specific "Magian Culture" that encompasses Islam, Judaism, and Eastern Orthodoxy.

It is a time for the Eastern Jews to stop asking for equivocal compliments and half-recognitions from the enlightened West. They need to interpret their historical experience, especially the starting point of this experience in Asia, in the Middle Eastern *oikumen* in a new light. The recognition of this fundamental fact immediately generates a sense of religious and cultural unity with the "host people." This "host people" also entered the circle of Asian cultures after its reception of Byzantine Orthodoxy. Whatever our assessment of the differences between Orthodoxy and Judaism, they belong to one and the same Asian Magian culture, for the description of which we need to give credit to Spengler (203).

The original congruity of two "Magian" cultures explains a number of congenial phenomena and development parallelisms in Eastern Jewish and Russian-Eurasian social and spiritual history. These phenomena are downplayed or completely ignored by the discourse of Westernism adopted by the Jewish "pseudo-intelligentsia." Westernist discourse is tendentiously preoccupied with Russian-Jewish confrontations and pogroms. The clichés and stereotypes of Westernized historiography do not permit understanding Jewish-Russian constructive and creative interaction in history and the symbiotic relation between the two people. An adequate historical account of Russian-Jewish relations requires the assumptions of Jewish Easternism that Bromberg tries to spell out.

---

[25] The term "place-development," coined by Petr Savitskii, is a specific cultural center closely connected with geographical location.

price Bromberg had to pay for his loyalty to the Eurasian perspective on Russian history.

Bromberg's account of Eastern Jewish history can be better understood against the background of some undercurrents in the tradition of Jewish German Enlightenment. Eastern European Jews were stigmatized in this tradition as the archetypal "bad Jews" who failed to fit the Enlightenment ideals of individualism and rationality. For both the Germans and the German-Jewish partisans of Enlightenment the East was a source of anxiety and corruption. The Talmudic discourse of the superstitious and irrational *Ostjude* was opposed to the civilized rational language of the assimilated and enlightened Western Jew. In the language of Haskalah, Eastern Jewry symbolized Asiatic, primitive, even barbaric culture (Bauman 1988: 77). It is interesting to note that for Arthur Koestler, a German-Hungarian Jew writing in English, Soviet Russia with its cruelty and Gulags was associated with the activity of Eastern Jews, the descendants of Asiatic Khazars, the converted tribe of Oriental nomads (see Gilman 1986: 333). Bromberg is reacting against this stereotype of the Eastern Jew and tries to reverse it. The Jewish Westernizers and the tradition of Haskalah with its excess rationality and universality are responsible for the Russian Revolution and for all its extremes. The "Asiatic" and "primitive" culture of Eastern Jews is a victim rather than a source of social and cultural disaster. Its "irrationality" and "mysticism" are the virtues of this culture rather than its drawbacks. The real perverts and victims of the process of "pseudo-morphosis" are the Jews of the West who betrayed the Magian essence of the "Asian" Jewish culture. It is interesting that Bromberg's twist in evaluation is congenial to the ideas of the German renewer of Chasidism, Martin Buber, and some other German-Jewish writers of the first part of the century (Arnold Zweig, Hans Kohn, Bruno Bettelheim) who opposed the idealized healthy, culturally integrated Eastern Jews to the rootless, disassociated, fragmented Jews of the West (see Buber 1911: 9–48; Gilman 1986: 273–305).

Bromberg's perspective on Jewish-Russian-Eurasian congruity is not just a curious episode in the intellectual history of Russian emigration before the Second World War. One can find a continuity in the early Eurasian quest for Russian-Jewish integration and the attempts of some contemporary authors to juxtapose the experiences of Jews and Russians. Some authors articulate ideas about a special similarity and spiritual

---

reincarnation of the vile, dark, grovelling, greediness, infamy, filthiness, the embodiment of human vices in general and the specific ethnic vices in particular (usury, spy, traitor)." Bromberg refers to the writings of Nikolai Gogol, Feodor Dostoevskii, and Vasily Rosanov, among others. For a discussion of the anti-Semitic ideas of these writers, see Dreizin (1990); Goldstein (1981); Khanin (forthcoming).

propinquity of Russians and Jews today. Two examples will suffice. In a 1991 paper, Vladimir Toporov, a well-known Russian linguist, focuses on the positive experience of Russian-Jewish interaction. It is interesting that, unfamiliar with Bromberg as he seems to be, he focuses on same episodes of Russian-Jewish history as Bromberg did (Toporov 1991). His ideas about the special propinquity of Russian and Jewish mentalities and outlook are also congenial to Lev Anninskii, a well-known literary critic and a champion of neo-Eurasianism (Anninskii 1993). These authors do not necessarily articulate the Eurasian aspects of the congruities in the historical and spiritual experiences of the two peoples but one can easily notice a continuity between Bromberg and the writings of these authors.

The discussions of the "Jewish question" by four representatives of the Eurasian movement suggest different perspectives on the appropriate "Jewish" policies of the future Eurasian state. Trubetskoi points out that the suggestion to incorporate racism and anti-Semitism in Eurasian ideology came from outside. But one can suppose that the fact of these suggestions is not mere coincidence. In the 1930s Eurasianism was associated in the minds of many contemporaries with the ideologies of the growing Fascist movements because of a number of similarities in their programs. Anti-Westernism, anti-liberalism, emphasis on economic autarchy, ideocracy, organic democracy, and preoccupation with geopolitics made Eurasian programs sound very similar to those of the Fascist parties (Luks 1996).

It is in itself remarkable that some sympathizers tried to smuggle racist ideas into the movement and that some people believed Eurasianism was perfectly compatible with anti-Semitism. However, as follows from the discussion of the "Jewish question" by Trubetskoi, Karsavin, Sviatopolk-Mirsky, and Bromberg, mainstream Eurasians did not share the racist assumptions of radical Russian chauvinism and adamantly condemned anti-Semitic rhetoric.[29] The anti-Semitic tendencies in the original Eurasian movement were at worst marginal. None of the classical Eurasian authors questioned the Eurasian identity of Russian Jews and all at least recognized the possibility of their successful integration into the Eurasian cultural zone.

It is also interesting to observe that none of the four Eurasian theoreticians found the Zionist project of settlement in Palestine and restoring the bonds with the old territory promising or politically feasible. This is especially surprising given their strong belief in the special bond between ethnicity and territory. Moreover, one has the impression that they con-

---

[29] Some publications in Eurasian periodicals explicitly condemned anti-Semitism. See, e.g., "The Emigrant Antisemitism," signed by the pen-name Evrasietz (Eurasian), *Evrasiia* 31 (1929).

sidered Zionism a rival for potential Jewish friends of the Eurasian movement. According to classical Eurasian authors, Zionists overlooked or ignored the attachment of Eastern Jews to Eurasian "place-development" and the reluctance of Jews to embrace the idea of their own independent state and autonomous territory (Karsavin 1928: 428; Bromberg 1931: 202).

Thus, all four theoreticians believed that nothing could preclude the inclusion of the Jews into the "Eurasian brotherhood." Even if the Jews in general or some particular groups tended to fall prey to emigrant psychological complexes, extreme particularism, the temptations of Zionism, and the ideology of Westernism, they were still full-fledged members of the Eurasian cultural and geographical landscape, and the Eurasian state of the future should be concerned with their absorption and full accommodation. We shall see in the next section that many neo-Eurasians abandoned almost all the assumptions of classical Eurasianism regarding the "Jewish question." Moreover, their version of geopolitical nationalism has created a new geopolitical justification of anti-Semitism.

THE JEWS IN NEO-EURASIANISM

It is expedient to preface an analysis of the reevaluation of the "Jewish question" in neo-Eurasianism by introducing one of the most prominent theoreticians of the movement, who has shaped its conceptual language and outlined the new context of the discussion of the "Jewish question." Aleksandr Dugin is the most prolific writer among the neo-Eurasians of contemporary Russia. A former member of Pamyat, he left this organization in the late 1980s to set up his own group. Dugin introduces himself as a "metaphysician, conspirologist and an expert in sacred geography." He is editor-in-chief of three journals, *Milii Angel, Giperboreia,* and *Elementi.* The paradigm the "Jewish question" in Dugin's works is determined to a great extent by the theoretical sources of his position. He believes that Eurasianism is a trend which exemplifies the ideology of an international movement of Conservative Revolutionaries to which he feels allegiance.

This ideology is interpreted in a very broad sense,[30] as a revolt against the predominant values of modern civilization corrupted by rationalism,

---

[30] Some scholars emphasize the Russian roots of the movement. Göran Dahl remarks that "the concept of 'conservative revolution' first appeared in the Berlin paper *Die Volksstimme* in 1848. . . . The first more frequent and serious use of the term, however, appeared among Russian writers, among them Dostoyevsky, as a metaphor for what was to be done in the world where God had died. . . . However, it was Hugo von Hoffmansthal a speech in 1927 . . .—who brought the concept wider attention. Von Hoffmansthal was expressing the widespread discontent with the Weimar Republic, arising from a tension between a modernizing society and a culture not ready to accept parliamentary democracy and industrial capitalism as an adequate environment" (Dahl 1996: 26–27).

liberal democracy, and materialism. The Conservative Revolution is a trend of the Counter-Enlightenment which supposedly transcends the conventional distinction between right and left, due to its combination of the conservative values of the Right and the revolutionary methods and spirit of political experimentation of the Left. The political movements of Italian Fascists, German National Socialists, Romanian Iron Guardists, and Spanish Falangists tried to realize some aspects of the project. The best formulations of the ideology can be found in the theories of German "Young Conservatives" (Carl Schmitt, Arthur Moeller van den Bruck, Oswald Spengler, Ernst Jünger, Ludwig Klages, Martin Heidegger, Werner Sombart) (see Mohler 1989; von Klemperer 1968; Sontheimer 1962; Breuer 1993; Pflüger 1994), and National Bolshevism (Henrich Laufenbach and Ernst Niekisch).

Dugin contends that almost all Conservative Revolutionaries were Russophiles in different degrees. The ideology of Conservative Revolution found its expression in many other authors as well. Dugin draws inspiration from German Aryosophes (Guido von List, Jörg Lanz von Liebenfels, Herman Wirth), baron Julius Evola, a late Italian Fascist, the poems of Ezra Pound, and the sociological insights of Vilfredo Pareto, Ferdinand Töennise, and Max Weber. He is fascinated by the concepts of the analytic psychology of Jung and the theories of French conspirologists. Dugin also appeals to the Russian historiosophes and philosophers of culture Konstantin Leontiev and Nikolai Danilevskii.[31] His criticism of modernity draws on the theories of some French post-modernists (Jean Baudrillard, Georges Battaille, Giles Deleuze). But his major authority is undoubtedly René Guénon, French Orientalist, metaphysician, and religious thinker.[32] Dugin has personal contacts with the representatives of

---

[31] Danilevskii's *Russia and Europe* (1871) is a prophecy about the Russian people's destiny to lead Europe out of social and spiritual anarchy by a genuinely organic unity of religion, culture, politics, and social organization, the four main elements of civilization. Danilevskii anticipated some concepts of Spengler (in particular, "cultural types" and the cyclical pattern of their history).

[32] René Guénon (1886–1951) was a French metaphysician and historian of religions. His works were devoted for the most part to criticism of the modern world and discussion of the significance of Eastern religious traditions in the rediscovery of tradition in the West. His writings include *Orient et occident* (1924), *La crise du monde moderne* (1927), and *La regne de la quantité et les signes des temps* (1945). Guénon emphasized the unity of truth and of traditional forms of religion, united in opposition to the modern world, which is based on forgetting the principles of tradition. He believed spiritual realization is impossible outside tradition and orthodox forms of religion. He embraced Islam and moved to Cairo in 1930, where he spent the rest of his life. His ideas influenced not only his direct students and successors but many intellectuals, artists, and politicians of Europe as well (in particular, world-renowned historian of religion Mircea Eliade, Jacques Dumezil, founder of the surrealist movement André Breton, novelist André Gide, and ideologists of fascism Charles Maurras and Julius Evola).

the French *nouvelle droite* (Alain de Benoist is an editor and contributor to *Elementi*) and other leaders of the radical nationalist parties and movements of Western and Eastern Europe.[33] These contacts allow him to keep Russian nationalists informed about recent developments of Western European nationalism, to facilitate the intellectual exchange between different groups of nationalists, and to coordinate their activity. Dugin's theories were lambasted by almost every group of Russian nationalists, mostly for their provocative apology for some Nazi leaders and heir "contamination" of the authentic Russian movement by Fascist and Germanophilic ideas (Kurginian 1993; Kazintsev 1993; Bulichev 1993; Golovin 1992).[34] However, many of his concepts greatly influenced Russian nationalist doctrines and the political language of the Russian anti-liberal opposition.

AMICUS AND *HOSTIS*: *PAX EUROASIATICA* AND ITS MYSTICAL ANTIPODE

The attitude to the "Jewish question" in neo-Eurasianism is determined by the specific concept of Russian nationalism and a concomitant national myth. Following Carl Schmitt, Dugin claims that every political group or movement needs to define itself by the choice of friends (*amicus*) and enemies (*hostis*).[35] The enunciation of the fundamental principles and orientations of Russian nationalism allows it to distinguish the Jews as a serious political and spiritual enemy of Russia. In his paper "Apology for Nationalism," Dugin is trying to define the idiosyncratic features of Russian nationalist consciousness as opposed to nationalisms of other nations and ethnicities Dugin (1994b). For the American, nationalism is associated with pride in the achievements of liberal civilization and market economy. French nationalism is concerned with the cultural identity and loyalty to France. German nationalism is ethnic and racist, while the nationalism of Serbs and Romanians is Orthodox. Jewish nationalism is religious and messianic.

In contrast to all other types of nationalism, Russian nationalism has four distinctive features. It is (1) religious and messianic, (2) geopolitical,

---

[33] The following Western European journals are relevant for his concepts: *Géopolitique* (France), *Krisis* (France), *Nouvelle Ecole* (France), *Orion* (Italy), *Perspectives* (Britain), *Politica Hermetica* (France), *Vouloir* (Belgium).

[34] Kurginian believes the phenomenon of Dugin testifies to the infiltration of Fascist ideas into the Russian patriotic movement. The infiltration discredits the movement and therefore is especially beneficial to liberals. Other critics emphasize the anti-Christian connotations of his position and their misgivings about his attitude to the Muslim East.

[35] Carl Schmitt introduced the friend-and-enemy distinction as a specific political criterion. See Schmitt (1976: 26–27).

(3) imperial, and (4) communal (141–43). Dugin does not rank these features. Nevertheless, one can infer from his account that he privileges one aspect of nationalism over others. The religious, messianic, imperial, and communal facets of Russian nationalism can never be properly understood without reference to its geopolitical foundation, its most important and original feature. The religious and messianic aspects of Russian nationalism do not determine its peculiarities. The phenomenon of Russian nationalism should be interpreted in the context of a specifically Russian concept of living space.

> Russian nationalism is inseparably linked with space. Russians distinguish themselves not by blood, ethnicity, phenotype or culture. They are more sensitive to space than any other people. . . . It is difficult to understand the origins of this "national intoxication" with Russian space. Perhaps, this unprecedented phenomenon and the religious metaphors of Russia—the "Last Kingdom," the "country as the world," the "Ark of Salvation"— can be explained by the combination of Slavic sensitivity and the nomadic instincts of the Turks in the steppe. . . . Russians regard space as sacred. Their attitude to space is anti-utilitarian. They never tried to exploit their land or to derive profits from it. They are guardians of space, initiated into its mysteries, rather than its colonizers. . . . Therefore, in many cases Russians prefer non-Slavic people affiliated with Russian space to other Slavs. (142)

The geopolitical foundations of Russian nationalism are reflected in the ideology of the Russian Orthodox Church. Politically, the special geopolitical status of Russia and the specific Russian sensitivity to space require the form of Eurasian empire.

The religious ideology is closely connected with the geopolitical identity of Russians. It legitimates this identity. For Russians, Orthodoxy is neither "a branch of Christianity" (as Protestantism) nor the universal Catholic Church. After the fall of Constantinople, Orthodox Russia became "the last shelter of Christ's truth in a world of apostasy" and "the last unspoiled bulwark of faith and sacredness in a world of evil." The doctrine of "Moscow—the Third Rome" of the monk Philotheus, Dugin argues, presupposes that Russia is the Fourth Empire and the "Restraining Force," "the catechon" of the second Epistle of Paul to the Thessalonians ("For the mystery of iniquity doth already work: only he who now letteth will let, until he be taken out of the way" II Thessalonians 2:7). Russians are the eschatologically chosen people entrusted with the "mystery of grace" and empowered to prevent the appearance of the Man of Sin.[36]

---

[36] Dugin refers to the theory of the Old Believers, schismatics who split from the Orthodox Church in the late seventeenth century. They believed and still believe that the Antichrist has already come and often identified him with one of the Russian emperors.

The form of the empire is a condition sine qua non for the survival and preservation of Russian space. Russians are "Eurasian Romans" who unite all other people and languages by their special religio-spatial *Weltanschauung.* The imperial consciousness is tolerant to different ethnicities and creeds insofar as they keep loyalty to Eurasian space and do not encroach upon the construction of the empire.

The communal character of Russian nationalism presupposes that all social projects need to appeal to the communal subjects. The individuals could not be dissociated from the nation even in theory.

> A person of Russian of origin who is detached from other Russians is erased from the sphere of interests of Russian nationalism. It is not surprising that a Russian Diaspora never existed in history. . . . Falling out of the social field of Russian people, a Russian ceases to be a bearer of Russian spirit. (142)

Russian Jews do not belong to those non-Slavic people, allegiance to whom can "override the other Slavs," although they live on the same territory. Jewry is opposed to Russian nationalism in all possible respects. Their aspirations, attitudes, and allegiances expose them as the major enemies (hostis) of the Russian-Eurasian project.

For Russian nationalists a Jew is not only one stranger among others but the mystical antipode of their own nationalism. Their national self-consciousness stresses aspects that are directly opposite to those of Russian nationalism.

(1) Jewish messianism and religious nationalism are opposed to the very foundations of Russian nationalism, which is based on Byzantine Orthodoxy. The basic assumptions of Jewish eschatological messianism did not allow them to see Byzantium as the "millennial kingdom." The same assumptions did not allow them to recognize Russia as the "Restraining Force" (catechon) and the successor of Byzantium.[37] The Jews link the "millennial kingdom" with the future, with the coming of Messiah. Conversely, the "millennial kingdom" of Byzantium, came to be associated in Jewish consciousness with the worst period of the Diaspora, with humiliation, suffering and wandering among people who did not recognize their election and their mission.

---

[37] It is important to emphasize Dugin's appeal to the replacement theology suggested by the seventeenth-century schismatics and abandoned by the Orthodox Church (the idea of realization of "millenarism" in Byzantium). Dugin believes the schismatics preserved the most authentic aspects of Orthodox tradition. Russia had been bequeathed the "divine presence" from Byzantium.

(2) The Jews deny the sacredness of space because they did not accept the Coming of the Son and, consequently, did not accept the idea of the redemption of the earth.

For two thousand years the Jews did not have their own land, their national space. This fact has affected their ethnic psychology. They used to regard the environment as something strange, foreign, that is, purely functional, lifeless and decorative. The Jews don't understand and don't like space. They considered all the kingdoms in which they have lived "tref," that is, desacralized, corrupted and impure. It is only natural that Russians, being aware of this Jewish mentality, opposed it to their own concept of space and nature. In Russian consciousness the natural objects are the full-fledged living "citizens" of Russian nation, the "baptized elements," which are permeated with the transforming force of Orthodox kingdom. It was a fundamental feeling of Russians that the redemptive sacrifice of the Son "rectified" the world of being (148).

(3) The concept of empire also exposes the incompatibility of Russian and Jewish mentalities. The destruction of the second Temple marked a new period in Jewish history, the period of the Diaspora, and the deprivation of their statehood. In Jewish consciousness the coming of Messiah is associated with the restoration of the Temple and Israel. In contrast to this, Russians associate the Temple with the Body of Jesus Christ and, in a broader sense, with the Orthodox Church, hence, the contradictions in their perceptions. Whereas Russians felt the presence of the Temple, the Jews experienced the absence of their third Temple. Consequently, the Jews identify the "Eurasian Romans" with the "blasphemous usurpers of their own national tradition" (148–49).

(4) In terms of the communal aspect of Russian nationalism, Russians are opposed to the particularism of the Jews. The Jews have their own "mystical self-identification." They feel isolation and aloofness to the life and values of the people with whom they temporarily lived. The Russians disappear in the absence of the communal (*sobornii*) unity. The Jewish "ego," on the other hand, is fostered by the absence of the kingdom and lack of involvement in a communal unity with other nations.

It is important to observe that Dugin's definition of Russian nationalism is normative rather than descriptive. He is trying to construct a new normative concept of Russian nationalism which would be able to encompass and integrate different trends of Russian nationalism. His special concern is pragmatic, to consolidate religious, socialist, and Slavophilic trends and blur the differences between heterogeneous nationalistic discourses. However, one should not be confused about the real nature of this synthesis. Dugin does not admit that his list presupposes a hierarchy of the features of Russian nationalism. But it is not difficult to observe that the basis for this integration is the doctrine of Eurasianism. The geopolitical aspect of Russian nationalism enjoys superiority over all other aspects. Furthermore, all other aspects make sense only by reference to and in the context of geopolitical Eurasian axis of the whole construction. Geopolitical language is a master-language constantly used for formulating the central religious and social problems. It is used as a mediator which unifies and combines different "ideolects" of Russian nationalism.

One can clearly see that Dugin translates different problems into geopolitical language. Russian Orthodoxy is only a religious justification of old Russian geopolitical ambitions.[38] Russian communitarianism is only a function of the Russian geopolitical essence. Needless to say, his accounts of Orthodoxy and Russian communitarianism (*sobornost* and *obschinnost*) are substantially different from both Russian Orthodox Church doctrine and the conventional Slavophilic notion of community. Ultimately, he is concerned with geopolitics, geoculture, georeligion, geotradition, and geocommunity.

Given the prominence of the geopolitical argument, the explanation of the animus against the Jews is not difficult to understand. The supposed Jewish distaste for space is a key to understanding the opposition of Russians and all other Eurasian or Indo-European ethnicities. The difference between the Eurasian and Jewish spiritual "styles" is an outcome of their difference in the perceptions of space. One can observe that Dugin's concept of the relation between the Jews and the original population of Eurasia is reminiscent of the position of the false friends of the Eurasian movement dismissed by Trubetskoi as misinterpreting and misapplying of Eurasian doctrine.

EURASIANISM VERSUS ATLANTICISM

I have observed that the political thinking of neo-Eurasians is governed by the distinction between *amicus* and *hostis*. In this section we shall see that the Jews have their own allies, the maritime Atlanticist civilization and mondialism, the understanding of which can clarify the sources of the Eurasian animus against the Jews.

---

[38] Dugin believes the ancient Aryan cults had the same ritual and symbolic paradigm as Christianity. In this Aryan consciousness Russia-Eurasia was already associated with the "Residence of the Gods," the "Great Sweden," the "white country of light," the motherland of the most ancient Aryans, the ancestors of the Hindus. Dugin condemns the moralistic and sentimental ingredients of Christianity that came from Protestantism, Masonry, and the intelligentsia (1991a: 52–53; 1991b: 148–49).

The term "mondialism" (from French *monde*—"world") was borrowed by Russian neo-Eurasians from French right-wing intellectuals. It does not necessarily refer to maritime civilizations but emphasizes the unifying and totalizing tendencies of the contemporary world which have reached their climax at the present stage. Dugin defines mondialism as "the concept of integration of the planet under the rule of the West and laying the foundation for a World State ruled by one World Government in the future" (Dugin 1996b: 40). Trying to transform the world into a global "melting pot," the cosmopolitan and anti-national mondialistic civilization appeals to the "universal values" common to all mankind and tries to instill these values in the national consciousness of all ethnicities. The mondialist philosophy pretends to be universal and conceals its partiality. The ideas of "new world order" and Pax Americana are the clear expressions of these global ambitions of the mondialists. The Jews greatly contributed to the propaganda of "universal values" and human rights.[39] Dugin points to the affiliation of the Jews with the subversive Left movements, the "fifth column" of mondialism. The Jews introduce the mondialistic tendencies into every movement in which they participate. In the communist movement the mondialistic tendency is exemplified by the ideology of Leo Trotsky. He was preoccupied with the idea of the universal "permanent revolution" and considered Russia a springboard of the messianic communist revolution. The Eurasian communists had quite different social visions. Lenin believed in the establishment of socialism in "one separate country," while Stalin believed in a "Eurasian Empire" of Soviet nations (Dugin 1993c: 99).

The identity of the goals of Atlanticism and the Jews is another important consideration which urges linking the two enemies of Eurasia. It is not a coincidence, they claim, that the expulsion of the Jews from Spain in 1492 coincided with the discovery of America. The ships of Columbus

---

[39] Valerii Zakharov defends the old-fashioned version of Eurasianism. But his ideas about the congruity of Europocentism and ancient Judeo-centrism are on the mark, since he spells out the neo-Eurasian reasoning. Zakharov contends that the Jewish philosophy of history is the prototype and model for the Europocentric one. It is the first attempt to describe the history of all humanity and discover one pattern in human development. "Universal human history has only one providential meaning, that is, the triumph of one people, Israel, over all mankind. It was the major point of their concept of world history." Although the Europocentric philosophy of history is rational and cosmopolitan, and the Jewish one is theocratic and nationalistic, they have much in common. European "universal values" are no more universal than Jewish "universal history." Europocentric standards are only a product of the Romano-Germanic ethnicities and should not be imposed on Eurasian historical development (1992: 166–69).

took to America carried many Jews whose "pernicious influence was unbearable to Catholic Spain" (Prussakov 1994; see also Putilov 1993).[40] The activity and ideology of many well-known Jewish leaders is governed and informed by the ideology of Atlanticism. The fact that the Jews wield political power in the U.S. and shape its foreign policies is often cited as evidence of their adherence to Atlanticism; he specifically talks about Armand Hammer, Henry Kissinger, and the Jewish advisers of Bill Clinton (Okhotin (Dugin) 1993d).

The origins of the spiritual bond between Atlanticism and the Jews can be found in the continuity in their historical experience. The spiritual tradition of both Americans and Jews is Western in origin. Both Jews and Americans are the heirs of the mythical civilization of Atlantis. Dugin also contends that the commercial maritime civilizations of Atlanticism only continue and enrich the nomadic tradition of the Semites: "Maritime existence is the extreme development of nomadism which acquires a new quality at the moment of transition from land nomadism to floating in the continental seas and finally to the decisive moment of entry into the open Ocean" (1997a: 56).

Dugin builds a symbolic opposition between nomadism, Water, West, Sea, iconoclasm, the Semites, and the Ship, on the one hand, and Fire, East, Land, sedentary life, iconodulism, and the House. The symbolic link between all these elements is quite sophisticated but need not occupy us in this study.

Dugin also observes that many American founding fathers and presidents directly identified America with a new incarnation of Israel. He contends that the idea of special congruity between America and the Jews was also shared by some prominent Jews (he refers to the works of Edmond Wiseman, Simon Wiesenthal, and the projects of some early Zionists to found Israel in America) (1996c: 41–49).

Both Americans and Jews have a special proclivity for commercial activity. Historically, the maritime civilizations concentrated on the commercial spheres and were associated with some specific branches of the Semitic race (Phoenicians, Carthaginians, and Jews). The paradigmatic encounter of maritime Semites and continental Aryans in human history is the Punic war between Rome and Carthage, the incarnations of Behemoth and Leviathan. The proclivity for trade is completely alien to the very spirit of Eurasian (Indo-European) culture. Dugin draws on the

---

[40] Some historians believe Columbus and some crew members were Jewish and that the ultimate goal of the expedition was to find a new place for the Jews. From the beginning, Columbus never planned to go to India. See Amler (1993).

oeuvre of Georges Dumezil, in which he argues that the caste of hucksters was not familiar to traditional Aryan society. Dugin believes that it is a fact of far reaching political significance.

> Within the Indo-European civilization the traders (*torgovtsi*) as a special caste or class emerged only at the late stages of development as foreign and racially alien components. In the Greek-Latin and in the Mediterranean area, the 'Semites' and other representatives of the Levant were the bearers of the trade order... Thus, capitalists and traders are the social 'saboteurs,' the social 'strangers' (*inorodtsi*) within the economic systems of Indo-European white people.... Their civilization had introduced special laws which curtailed trade and debarred usury. It was the socio-economic manifestation of the white race and its social ethics.... Capitalism introduced not only economic but also racial and ethnic alienation. (1995a: 23)[41]

This idea is included in the political program of Dugin's National Bolshevik party. Dugin believes that the Punic war has never ended. It resumes again and again. In the course of the cold war the eternal Carthage of maritime civilizations has retaliated against the eternal Rome. Dugin believes that the Jews contributed to the defeat of the Behemoth of Soviet Eurasia.

TRADITION AND COUNTER-TRADITION

The war of the continents, however, is only a projection of a more important and fateful conflict of two different metaphysical forces in history, the forces of Tradition and counter-Tradition, Initiation and counter-Initiation. The geopolitical encounter and the role of the Jews in the confrontation of two continents have to be explained in the context of the general neo-Eurasian philosophy of history. This philosophy of history is heavily indebted to the theories of René Guénon.

According to Guénon, human history has a cyclical pattern. The current period of history is associated with the extreme degradation of the Primordial Tradition, the Tradition which was universal before it split into a number of particular secondary religious traditions in the post-Babylonian period. Today the anti-traditional profane values ("the kingdom of quantity") have displaced even the traces of the Single Truth which were preserved in the secondary traditional forms. Two ideas are especially important with regard to the preservation of the Primordial Tradition.

(1) Different secondary traditions preserve the Truth of Primordial Tradition in different degrees. Orthodoxy and Islam are the most tra-

---

[41] According to Dumezil, traditional Indo-European society was composed of three castes: priests (spiritual), warriors (kings, rulers, administrators), and producers (peasants, craftsmen).

ditionalist religions, while Catholicism and especially Protestantism have lost the original insights of the Tradition. The humanistic and moralist values of mondialist civilization poisoned these traditions. Russia-Eurasia has a universal mission to denounce the anti-traditional forces.

(2) In spite of the sharp conflicts between exoteric secondary traditions, the esoteric traditions of the same religions (Hermetism and Gnosticism in Catholicism, Hesychasm in Orthodoxy, Sufism in Islam) have much in common and reproduce the logic of the Primordial Tradition. The orthodox forms of religion are better than its modernized and consequently corrupted forms.

René Guénon believed that kabbalah, the esoteric trend in Judaism, should be associated with the Primordial Tradition like other esoteric traditions and that the negative and corrupting influences come from the distorted versions of Judaism and from some secularized groups of the Jews, who foster the forces of anti-Tradition and counter-Initiation. Dugin disagrees with Guénon. He argues that the examination of the Jewish *kabbalah* exposes the incompatibility of the basic principles of this teaching with the principles of other esoteric traditions. Dugin believes that the source of subversion is not the "secularized" and "profane" Jews, but rather the "most orthodox nucleus" of Jewry. He contends that "the Jews are the bearers of the religious culture, which is profoundly different from all historical manifestations of Indo-European spirituality, from the ancient Aryan pagan cults to Hinduism and Christianity. . . . In the Indo-European civilization the Judaic community was always perceived as something strange and foreign to the Indo-European mind-set and culture" (1994c: 245). Two elements preclude the identification of Indo-European esoteric tradition with its Jewish counterpart.

First of all, in contrast to other esoteric doctrines the Jewish esoterism insists on the particularity and superiority of Israel over all other people. This principle is incompatible with the doctrine of the Integral Tradition. Dugin describes metaphysics of the *Zohar* as "a dreadful and radical xenophobic teaching."

> Judaic esoteric eschatology suggests that the end of time is the upshot of the ancient struggle of the Jews against the gentiles. . . . In the eschatological situation, the Judaic religious impulse takes the form of an aggression against all forms of non-Jewish spirituality, which are identified with demonology. (1994d: 281)

Second, the incompatibility of the two traditions is determined by the specifically Judaic concept of cosmos, which does not have analogies in the religious concepts of other ethnicities.

The comparison of the Judaic metaphysics, on the one hand, and the diverse Indo-European traditions, which were united by one and the same "style," demonstrates that the interpretation of Cosmos constitutes a fundamental difference between the two. Judaism interprets the world as a Creation alienated from God. It sees the world as an exile, as a mechanical maze where the "chosen people" wander. The true mission of the "chosen people" is revealed not in the glorious victories of Joshua, the son of Nun, or the seer Ezdra, but rather in the tragic peripeteia of the Diaspora. The Diaspora correlates better than anything else with the spirit of classical Judaism which draws an insurmountable abyss between the Creator and the Creation. . . . The Cosmos of the Indo-Europeans is a living reality directly connected with God. . . . Even in the darkest periods of history . . . the nexus of the Creation and the Creator, the Cosmos and its inhabitants, with the Light of Original Cause is never broken. It continues either through the miracle of eucharistia . . . or through an heroic overcoming, or through a salutory, courageous asceticism. Indo-European consciousness is the consciousness of the autochthons *par excellance.* This consciousness is bound up with the soil, not with the Diaspora, with possession rather than loss, with connection, not with the gap in connection. . . . The orthodox Jews consider the Indo-Europeans 'naive and infantile optimists' who have no idea about the dreadful mystery of the Abyss, about the theological drama of the cosmic Diaspora. The Indo-Europeans, on the other hand, believe that Jewish religious pessimism distorts the proportions of the sacred cosmos, deprives it of its solitary energies, de-sacralizes earth, space, time, and the unique fate of the autochthonous people. (1994c: 245–46)

Dugin believes that the kabbalistic metaphysics of Rabbi Isaac ben Solomon Luria of Safed and his successors could provide a key for understanding both the Jewish concept of cosmos and the metaphysical essence of Jewry. The comparison of this "most clear and most authentic Jewish doctrine" with Indo-European traditions exposes the incompatibility of the most esoteric forms of Judaism with the grand Primordial Tradition. Whereas the neo-Platonic philosophy described the process of creation as the emanation of the Principle into the exterior world and propounded the gradual incarnation of divine essences into sensible forms, the Lurianic *kabbalah* describes the process of creation as the contraction (*tsimtsum*) of the divine essence and as exile from the original plentitude of divine potentialities. God withdrew into himself and concentrated his essence. The interpretation and functions of the *sefirot* in the Lurianic *kabbalah* is also substantially different from the neo-Platonic concept of emanation.

The primordial man, Adam Kadmon, first and highest of the *sefirot* and an emanation of the creator aspect of God, poured light into ten vessels. But the vessels that held these lights could not contain their power and shattered. As a result the *sefirot* broke into myriad pieces (some flowed back, others flowed into the void). Since that cataclysm, nothing in time, place, or order is where it is supposed to be. Dugin contends that the Jewish myth about the unsuccessful emanation stresses the incompatibility and incommensurability of Creator and creation in Judaism. The Jewish cosmos lacks harmony and cannot function properly, because of the insurmountable distance that separates it from God. This distance will never disappear, even in the period of Great Shabat after the coming of Messiah. Thus, in Judaic metaphysics cosmos is identified with a Diaspora abandoned by God. "The creation is only the tragic symbol of Vanity without any hope for redemption" (1994e: 253). The impossibility of theophany and the doctrine of absolute distance between Creator and creation "communicate to the Jewish religious consciousness a sceptical attitude towards cosmology, mythology and all other aspects of Tradition which articulate the immanence and the absolute unity of the Principle" (252). In sum, the Gnosis of Despair and absolute vanity of the universe are crucial elements of the kabbalistic and authentically Jewish worldview.

Dugin concedes that the Jewish tales about the Golem display the same logic as the myth of creation in Lurianic *kabbalah*. In medieval Jewish folklore the Golem is an artificially created human endowed with life by supernatural means. This Dugin contends, is the concept of "rough form animated by something essentially exterior to it."

> The Jew recognizes his own ego and his own people . . . in the grotesque image of the Golem, in the dismal human apparatus, which absorbs all the hopelessness of the abandoned world created once and forever. . . . The Jewish gnosis is the Gnosis of Despair, and therefore, the maxim of Ecclesiastes 'he that increaseth knowledge increaseth sorrow' is related first of all to the Jewish knowledge about God and to the knowledge of the Jews about themselves. (252)

This Jewish vision of the universe and man, Dugin contends, goes against the basic intuitions of Indo-European religions, specifically the concepts of Christianity. Christianity is characterized as a purely Indo-European religion. Dugin draws a line between historical Christianity and the "eternal (*nadvremennoe*) and pure" "superreligious Christianity." This "eternal Christianity" is a "primordial teaching" that "providentially appeals to the people of the North" and has a fundamentally anti-Judaic orientation (1990: 4).[42] Although historically speaking, the discussion of continuity

---

[42] Roughly speaking, the people of the North are identified with Aryans and the original population of Eurasia. Following German Aryosophes, Dugin believes that the Nordic people (*Sonnenmenschen*) are creative and spiritual, while the "people of the South" (*Mondmenschen*) are mean, materialistic, and externally oriented. He points out that the distinction is not purely geographical. The "Nordic spirit" can be found in southern parts of the globe, while the primitive spirit of the South is present in the far North. He explains this phenomenon by the migrations of the descendants of Hyperborea; see

between Christianity and Judaism makes sense, metaphysically the two religions have nothing in common. Dugin claims that "Judaism rejected not only the personality and mission of Jesus, but also the very principle of the immanent God" (1991c: 24). The Judeo-Christian Christianity is not the real "perennial Christianity" associated with the grand Tradition (1995a: 11).

Dugin claims that the difference between Judaism and Christianity is such that the basic concepts—eschatology, Messiah, demonology—have directly opposite meanings.

> In the Judaic consciousness the Messiah is not a Divine Hero who comes down from the Heaven of Principle to rectify the worn cosmos and to save the degraded human community, as it is for the Christians and for other non-Judaic eschatologies. The Messiah of the Judaic sources cannot be identified with the direct and triumphal revelation of the Transcendental.... Their Messiah will not bring anything new.... Judaists believe that both the saving and the saved are this-worldly and immanent. (1994e: 257–58)

Judaism does not have the soteriological element common in all other religions; the Messiah of Judaists does not bring any "good news" and does not promise the "return" to the original state. It is not surprising then that the Jewish Messiah is identified in "eternal Christianity" and other traditional religions with the Antichrist.

THE JEWS AND THE CRISIS OF THE MODERN WORLD

In the passage quoted Dugin claims that the orthodox and esoteric religious forms of Judaism constitute an opposition to Russian nationalism and Tradition. However, in the narratives of Aleksandr Dugin the "secularized" and assimilated Jews also function as agents of counter-Tradition. The "sorrowful and mysterious face of Judaism" is revealed not only in the Lurianic *kabbalah*, but also "in the novels of Kafka, the philosophy of Michelstaedter and in the scientific concepts of Einstein, a theoretician of the absolute Vanity of the material universe" (256–57). Moreover, sometimes assimilated Jews, specifically Arthur Koestler, Otto Weininger, Carlo Michelstaedter, and Martin Buber, "reveal to the gentiles (*goim*) the horrifying mysteries of the 'Judean war,' being ashamed of the dubious tactics of the Diaspora." Their writings demonstrate that the artificial cosmopolitan ideology would never be able to reconcile Jewish meta-

---

(1993e: 42–43). In sacred geography the West is the side of death, darkness, and decline, the East of life, bloom, and light. The West and the Jewish tradition are associated with Atlantis, the pure primordial tradition with Hyperborea. On the Atlantic origins of Jewish tradition, see Guénon (1991: 16–17).

physics with Indo-European, and that the "energies of our ethnicities, religions, theological and sacred instincts will inevitably burst through the old clothes of unnatural, unfounded and unrealistic doctrines" (1994c).

The accusations of the secularized Jews are based on Dugin's beliefs in the deep structures of the unconscious. He believes that the "racial and continental unconscious" of different ethnicities burst through the cosmopolitan structures and institutions of modernity. He accepts the ideas of Karl Gustav Jung about the collective Jewish and Aryan unconscious.[43] Furthermore, the collective national unconscious enjoys superiority over national consciousness, since the latter can fail to conceptualize the most profound intuitions and aspirations of the given ethnicity. Consciously or unconsciously, the Jews reproduce in their theories and other endeavors the ideas of Counter-Tradition and counter-initiation grounded in their esoteric tradition. Therefore, the logic and symbolism of *kabbalah* and the aspects of esoteric Jewish Weltanschauung are present in the theories of the most secularized Jews. Assimilated Jews are involved in the corrupting activities and enthusiastically participate in all subversive Atlanticist and mondialist projects of the contemporary world. It is not surprising that the major theoreticians of "contemporary intellectual perversity" and the advocates of destructive counter-traditional tendencies are Jewish.

Dugin identifies these theoreticians with the "children of darkness" and "saints of Satan" of Islamic tradition. The destructive influences of the modern world are associated primarily with mondialism, liberal democracy, materialism, atheism, neo-spiritualism, effeminization, and a bankocracy that supplants the conventional capitalism of the "third estate." All these tendencies can be understood as secularized forms of Jewish esoteric doctrines.

(1) Dugin contends that mondialism, especially the mondialistic concept of the "end of history," is only a secularized version of Jewish "kabbalistic eschatology," which lacks a soteriological dimension. The theory of

---

[43] Jung believed Freud's attribution of a negative value to the unconscious was a threat to German culture. The unconscious of "the youthful Germanic peoples" is a source of creativity and new cultural forms "that still lie dormant." Direct repression of the "Wotanic elements" of the German psyche can lead to the eruption of these elements in primitive and destructive ways. Jung regarded National Socialism as a destructive manifestation of the dark elements of the repressed German unconscious. The Jew has a wider area of psychological consciousness and it is less dangerous for him to put a negative value on his unconscious. Jung believed that the Jews use the unconscious of the host people. Therefore, they "have never yet created a cultural form of their own" Stevens (1994: 113–22).

the "end of history" predicts the death of ethnicities, religions, national states, isolated unique civilizations, and ideologies, that is, the major agents of history. Dugin claims that the most interesting and radical exponent of the theory is not Francis Fukuyama but Algerian Jew Jacques Attali, a director of the European Bank for Reconstruction and Development in London and special adviser to the French government and François Mitterand (since 1981). Dugin believes Attali has articulated the most important aspects of the concept of the end of history and spelled out all its Jewish implications. Attali is very well versed in *kabbalah* and Jewish esoteric tradition. His books, *1492* and *Lignes d'horizons*, the latter translated into English as *Millennium: Winners and Losers in the Coming World Order* (1991), perfectly illustrate the ideas of Guénon about the proclivity of assimilated Jews to anti-traditional activities and justify his misgivings about the special dangers coming from their "deflected nomadism" (*nomadism devié*). Attali opposes the new "Trade Order" ("Order of Money") to the "Order of the Sacred" ("religious order") and the "Order of Force" ("military order"), the old ways of controlling violence. Attali suggests that the new economic order is better equipped to prevent violence. First of all the new "Order of Money" is based on the new technologies of communication, which use the new "microchip-based gadgets," "nomadic objects" (microprocessor, cellular phone, personal computers, video disks, internet, etc). The pervasive employment of "nomadic objects" in social practices transforms contemporary culture into a new "nomadic civilization" and makes spatial and territorial aspects of human life less significant. Attali talks about the penetration of the nomadic tendencies into different social spheres (labor, citizenship, acquisition of professions) and describes the new nomadism as the "highest form of the Order of Money."

Neo-Eurasians associate the futurology of Attali with the forces of anti-Tradition. The "Trade Order" presupposes global unification; it cannot tolerate alternative forms of social organization. The neo-Eurasian champions of Tradition are afraid that the increased mobility in the material world, facilitated and countenanced by the "new Trade Order," will be inevitably accompanied by loss of connection with the spiritual dimensions of the universe and pave the way for the complete degeneration of human civilization. The universalism of mondialism is a parody of the true universalism of the Traditional civilization. Dugin believes the new deterritorialized "Trade Order" is a prelude to the coming of the Antichrist, the real master of this world (Dugin 1997b: 128–30; Levalois 1991: 3–8; Dugin 1996b: 40).

(2) The institution of liberal democracy is also Jewish. Dugin traces the roots of political ideologies back to religious or metaphysical doctrines.

It turns out that the structure of liberal democracy reproduces the Jewish paradigm of Diaspora and exile. In spite of the formal declarations of liberal democrats and rhetoric of human rights, the citizens of the liberal state are completely alienated from all forms of engagement in the process of decision-making and are deprived of full-fledged political expression. An anonymous secret political elite manipulates the consciousness of the people and presents its own decisions and policies as products of a collective process of decision-making. Liberal democracy is the "society of spectacle."[44] The citizens of liberal democracies turn to the alienated subjects, the Jews of Diaspora, the exiles from Paradise. The paradisical state is associated with organic democracy and the hierarchical social order, where the community is united around the same spiritual values and ideals and there is no gap between the individuals and the state (Dugin 1991d: 89).

Dugin describes the governing mondialistic cosmopolitan and anti-national elite ("the System") as Jewish. "The ideal pattern of the 'System' is described by Franz Kafka in his famous novel, *The Castle*, where the relations between the population of the village and the unapproachable Castle on the hill are grotesque, horrible and irrational." He goes on to argue that the interpretation of the novel by Max Brod, "the expert in Talmud and *kabbalah*," provides a new perspective for understanding the nature of the absolute and the irrational power of the contemporary political elite of the System.[45]

> On Brod's reading, the central point of the novel is the allegory of the specifically Jewish, Judaist and even kabbalist interpretation of the Law (Torah), which reveals itself to the orthodox believer as a sophisticated design incomprehensible and absolutely alienated from the individual. Hence, the Castle is not a metaphor for the society of alienation but rather the very symbol of the Jewish Weltanschauung, of the Talmudic vision of the structure of the universe. This universe is absurd and lifeless because of its distance from the Creator, who reveals himself to his people only through a set of strict and incomprehensible prescriptions, which constitute the paradoxical maze of the Law. . . . If we take the Castle as a literary and symbolic image of the System, we can better understand the worldview of those representatives of the hidden elite who not only take advantage of the undemocratic model of the System but also justify it by reference to theological arguments. . . . If the people is healthy and if its spiritual

---

[44] The term spectacle was introduced by Guy Debord (1979), a French neo-Marxist sociologist and severe critic of liberalism. It refers to the vast institutional and technical apparatus of late capitalism, all the means and methods power employs, besides direct force, to obscure the nature of power.

[45] Max Brod (1884–1968) was an Austrian writer and a member of the Zionist movement, and a lifelong friend of Franz Kafka. His interpretation of *The Castle* appeared in the introduction to the first German edition of the novel and later in *Franz Kafka: A Biography* (1947).

tradition is different from that trend of Judaism which theologically justifies the Castle, then the People's Revolution should become the natural response to the despotism of alienation. (1995b: 9–10)

Procedural democracy with its concomitant processes of alienation is opposed to the substantive democracy of traditional civilization.

(3) The desacralization of cosmos in Jewish esoteric tradition promotes materialism in modern science and philosophy. The "economic materialism" of Marx and the "psychiatric materialism" of Freud exemplify the contribution of Jewish "intellectual perversity" to the degradation of the modern world. Both theories explain the high and the superior by reference to the low and vile.

Dugin believes that Freud's psychoanalytical materialism is an important ingredient of liberal discourse and that it is very dangerous. Psychoanalysis allows the mondialists to profanize the expressions of high spirituality and values of traditional civilization and reduce them to mere psychological sexual complexes. Dugin follows the pattern of Nazi propaganda when he describes psychoanalysis as a Jewish science based on the intellectual constructions of Jews and the experience of Jewish patients. He contends that the counter-initiative nature of psychoanalysis suggests that the original source of this doctrine is the Jewish Masonic organization B'nai B'rith.

Dugin claims that Freud reduces sacred, superhuman symbols to terms of individual sexual experience, the primal and primitive drive for coitus, disparaging the wholeness of psychic life and the highest archetypes of the unconscious. In Freud's psychoanalysis, the world of the unconscious is identified with the demonic and infernal world inhabited by perverse and devilish images. He draws a parallel between psychoanalysis and the doctrines of *kabbalah*.

> The Jewish *kabbalah* describes these spheres of vice as the world of *klipot*, world of shells, where infernal entities violate all the religious proscriptions... Psychoanalysis opens the door for the development of the inferior underhuman forces.... Its contents have much in common with the dark rituals which are associated with worship of the devil. (Dugin/Okhotin 1995c: 50–51)

The practice of psychoanalysis is damaging for the unconscious of the patient.

(4) Freud's psychoanalysis is closely connected with another corrupting tendency of the modern world, effeminization. Dugin argues that Freud's Eros is not the full-fledged and all-embracing cosmic Eros of the Indo-European tradition, but an exclusively feminine Eros, the chaotic Eros

of the matriarchal cultures, not governed by high ideals and principles. This Eros does not have any particular organizing nomos; it is the blind libido of the kabbalistic demoness Lilith. "Freud insists that this Eros is supposedly oppressed by the patriarchal complex which is associated with consciousness and the ethical imperative. In other words, he simply does not recognize patriarchal and purely masculine sexuality, describing it in terms of 'oppression,' 'complex' and 'violence'." The highest expressions of masculine Eros—heroism, contemplation, sacrifice, abstention—are not recognized by Freud as manifestations of eroticism. In reality, only the masculine eros can sanctify and illuminate the great energies of love.[46]

Dugin believes this predominance of feminine Eros in psychoanalysis is due to the Jewish descent of its founding father. Otto Weininger equated Jews with women in the chapter of his *Sex and Character* (1903) entitled "Jewry." Following Weininger's concept of bisexuality, Dugin claims that the Jewish psyche is feminine and that heroism and religious faith—the highest expressions of masculine eroticism—are incomprehensible to the Jews, and in particular to Freud, who associated the ego and consciousness with Thanatos, the cosmic force directly opposite to Eros. Dugin believes that Jewish femininity is also expressed in a proclivity to masochism. In his review of the first Russian edition of Leopold Sacher-Masoch's novel, Dugin argues that whereas the characters of the Marquis de Sade could be construed as caricatures of the Indo-European (Aryan) type of "hero" or "master" who tries to destroy all obstacles in his way, the characters of Masoch are caricaturized Jewish types, ever-suffering people, who find special pleasure and excitement in their own pain and suffering.[47] The heroes of Masoch and de Sade, Dugin argues, are the horizontal projections of two types of eroticism, Jewish and Aryan (1995c: 64).

It is important to keep in mind that Dugin attributes significant political implications to processes of effeminization. Political problems and conflicts are imbued with sexual connotations. Tendencies to effeminization are manifested in the ideology of human rights, pacifism, ethics of non-violence, rise of feminism and homosexualism, and the all-absorbing liberal ideology of "soft" feminine oppression. In mondialism the totalizing

---

[46] Dugin's concept of eroticism is heavily indebted to the book of Giulio Evola (1889–1974), *Metaphysics of Sex* (*Metafisico del sesso*), originally published in 1958 by Atanor.

[47] Leopold von Sacher-Masoch (1836–1895) was an Austrian novelist many of whose main characters take pleasure in having pain inflicted on them. The term "masochism" is derived from his name. Freud in his essay "Dostoevsky and Parricide" discusses moral masochism as a phenomenon specifically typical of the Russian psyche.

reconciliation of all ideological and cultural movements is realized through the castration of the most important elements of all traditions, that is, at the expense of the essential aspects of all specific and authentic ideologies. The eclipse of heroic and masculine values, Dugin argues, is seen in the political and sexual orientation of post-communist politicians. "The abundance of effeminized types among post-*perestroika* politicians, coupled with their specific ethnic extraction exposes the process of denationalization and emasculation which accompanies the economic and political diversion of the West" (Dugin/Okhotin 1995c: 154). The Jews are trying to suppress the impulses and manifestations of Russian masculine sexuality evident in the construction of the Eurasian Empire (Dugin 1994f).

(5) The next destructive tendency of modern civilization is the rise of neo-spiritualistic movements and subversive Masonic organizations. This is also closely connected with the activity of the Jews. Dugin blames the Jewish activists of neo-spiritualistic and Masonic groups for their destructive influence on the world during the period of modernity. He mentions the Beddarid brothers, the founding fathers of the rite of Memfis-Mizraim, Max Teon, the Grand Master of "H.B. of L.," Samuel MacGregor Mathers, one of the founders of the Order of the Golden Dawn, Mira Alfassa, the "Mother" of Auroville, and French philosopher Henri Bergson (1993c: 51).[48] These neo-spiritualist trends are said to be even more dangerous than "pure profanism and agnosticism" because of their similarity to the doctrines of the Tradition. In fact they are only distortions and caricatures of authentic esoterism. All these groups adopt the concepts of progress and evolution that indicate and manifest the corruption of modern civilization.

---

[48] The rite of Mizraim is named from its claim of origin with the Egyptian king Menes, or Misraim. The foundations were laid at Milan in 1805 and introduced into France in 1814, but it was founded earlier by Count Cagliostro and Jews used to be its chief supporters. See Preuss (1924); Hackethorn (1897: vol. 2). "H.B. of L." probably stands for "Hermetic Brotherhood of Luxor" Luxor is an Egyptian town. The Golden Dawn was a famous occult organization founded at the beginning of the century. Mira Richards (Alfassa and "the Mother") embraced the philosophy of Hindu mystic Sri Aurobindo and took the guidance of the ashram after his death in 1950. Auroville is a large religious city in India growing out of Sri Aurobindo's teaching. Henri Bergson is mentioned in this context because his theory of spiritual evolution and the concept of *élan vital* influenced many occultist movements. He also had connections with conspicuous members of occult establishments (in particular, Samuel Mathers was his brother-in-law). Guénon claimed Bergson "tried to de-rationalize the European consciousness and introduced into it some chaotic and infra-corporeal intuitions." Dugin (1993c: 104) suggests that all these organizations emphasized the horizontal materialist values typical of the Atlanticist organization.

In sum, the abominable conditions of modern civilization are associated with the "Judaization" of the world. The world of the "end of history," of mondialism and materialism, destitute of manlihood and spirit, emphasizes the provisional triumph of the Jewish principle. Dugin is trying to address the question of how the Jews can acquire such incredible power. Here a theory of Jewish conspiracy comes into the picture.

THE "ENLIGHTENED" SCIENCE OF CONSPIROLOGY

Dugin's discussion of theories of conspiracy employs again the concept of collective unconscious. He tries to keep his distance from vulgar Judophobic notions of conspiracy, but on a more sophisticated level he finds these theories "interesting and plausible." He distinguishes five different concepts of conspiracy: Masonic conspiracy, Jewish conspiracy, conspiracy of bankers, conspiracy of the poor, and conspiracy of heterodoxes. In his descriptions, all these theories have more or less pronounced anti-Semitic implications. Furthermore, the idea of Jewish conspiracy is discerned as a central and most basic one: "The idea of Jewish conspiracy, undoubtedly, corresponds to deep unconscious archetypes of very remote and diverse human communities. It is most likely that this theory is the activation of unconscious energies, which constitute the 'conspirological instinct' at its source" (Dugin 1993c: 20).

The importance of Jewish conspiracy in Dugin's theory may be fully appreciated in the context of his interpretation of the origins of the archetypes of the collective unconscious. For him the archetypes constitute not only a specific "psychic reality," but the "remnants of a sacred Weltanschauung that are partly obliterated from the genetic memory of mankind" (1993f). The theory of Jewish conspiracy, therefore, is a part of the sacred outlook embedded in the deepest layers of the unconscious and finds its realization in all anti-Semitic theories and ideologies. These anti-Semitic feelings and concepts are legitimated by the very structure of the sacred Weltanschauung. However ridiculous a particular concept of Jewish conspiracy may sound, it is justified because of the foundational "archetype" of which it is an imperfect and distorted copy. To paraphrase Hegel, everything unconscious for Dugin is real and everything real is unconscious.

> The idiosyncracies of life, and, speaking of the Jews, their specific appearance and even their historically revealed proclivity for the subversive and destructive forms of "gescheft," are only the excuses for expression of a much more deep, sacred, and well-grounded mystical and theological hostility of Russian nationalism to the Jewishness in all its manifestations. (1993a: 149)

NUREMBERG VERSUS AUSCHWITZ

Dugin does not suggest a concrete policy that should be adopted by the Eurasian Empire to handle the "Jewish question." Instead of concrete discussion, he resorts to very emotional and ambiguous language. At the end of one of his articles, Dugin talks about the inevitability of a "metaphysical battle" between Jews and Indo-Aryans and about the necessity to establish "chivalrous rules" for this battle that might prevent the transformation of such a "profound metaphysical conflict" into "total war" involving "blind hatred and gloomy violence." He argues that the difference between metaphysical war and physical is that "the first aims at the victory of a single Truth, while the second aims at the destruction of the enemy. . . . As it turned out, the German concentration camps could destroy Jews, but were unable to abolish Jewishness. By the same token, the Chasidic commissars were not able to slaughter the entire population of 'Russian tref kingdom' in bloody genocide" (1994c: 247–48).

Dugin tries to oppose the physical annihilation of the Jews and "metaphysical" anti-Semitism as two completely different and almost incompatible phenomena. In this manner, he blurs the obvious connection between Auschwitz and its ideological justification. Dugin emphasizes that many members of the SS, and specifically the intellectuals from a branch of Waffen-SS called Deutsches Ahnenerbe (German Ancestral Heritage),[49] did not share the Judeophobia of other National Socialists. He blames Hitler for the deflections from the classical ideology of Conservative Revolution in this question. Dugin opposes Ahnenerbe to mainstream Nazi ideology and claims that it bears comparison with a "medieval knightly order," with its high moral ideals. He describes this organization as an "intellectual oasis within the framework of National Socialism," which preserved and fostered the ideas of Conservative Revolution in their purity" (1994g: 25). Dugin believes that the ideas of Ahnenerbe could be effectively utilized by Russian nationalists.[50]

---

[49] Ahnenerbe was founded in 1935 as a private institute of learning with Himmler as curator. By 1939 it turned into a branch of Waffen-SS and part of Himmler's personal staff. Its functions were financing and publishing Germanic research on ancient Aryan symbols, language, runes, mythological archeology, and folklore. The projects were initiated and inspired by the ideas of Hermann Wirth, a German-Flemish specialist in prehistory. The pseudo-academic researches of Ahnenerbe were framed to supply evidence for the superiority of the German race in culture and history. In *Aufgang der Menschheit* he talks about the roots of German culture in the ancient civilization of "North Atlantis."

[50] Dugin extensively expounds the theories of Wirth and Ahnenerbe in *Giperboreiskaia teoriia* (1993g). He worked with the Ahnenerbe archives, captured by the Red Army and recently available. In 1993 he spoke several times on the Russian TV program *Mysteries of the Twentieth Century* about Ahnenerbe and German secret societies.

Dugin's claims concerning relations between the benign intellectuals from Ahnenerbe and the mass genocide of the Jews in Nazi Germany cannot stand criticism. Hermann Wirth, the founder of Ahnenerbe, was a notorious racist and one of the major contributors to the Nordic theory. He believed that the Jews were the mystical enemies of the Aryans and was involved in the development of serological theories about Aryan and Jewish blood types. Wirth's ideas and concepts greatly influenced Alfred Rosenberg and were used by this major ideologist of the Third Reich in his *Myth of the Twentieth Century.* In his major work *Palästina-Buch,* Wirth tried to prove that the Jews usurped Aryan knowledge and that the Bible is derived from earlier Nordic texts, in particular the *Ura-Linda Chronicle,* a notorious late nineteenth-century forgery. The only exemplar of the manuscript was said to have been stolen by members of the Jewish intelligence service (Vorobievskii 1993). The members of this "medieval knightly order" were involved in the realization of the most nefarious projects and policies of German Nazism not only theoretically but also practically. Under the aegis of Ahnenerbe, Dr. Sigmund Rascher conducted a number of medical experiments on the inmates of Dachau for his research to discover the best method of reviving pilots who had been shot down in freezing water. Because of these activities Wolfram Sievers, who took over the Ahnenerbe after Wirth, was condemned to death by the Nuremberg tribunal (Webb 1976: 323).

Dugin's historical revelations are closely connected with his own interpretation of the Holocaust. For Dugin, the phenomenon of Auschwitz is not a realization and logical completion of the illuminated "metaphysical" anti-Semitism of Nazi ideologists, but only an excess of National Socialism and an unfortunate digression from the classical doctrine of Conservative Revolution. It is striking that he confers the same status on the Nazi "final solution of the Jewish question" and the Jewish involvement in the Bolshevik Revolution in Russia. The real tragedy of the defeat of the Axis countries was not Auschwitz, but rather their compromising of the doctrines of the Conservative Revolutionaries by Hitler's distortions. The real disaster for him was the Nuremberg tribunal, which condemned and stigmatized the ideology of Conservative Revolution without making any qualifications.

> The ideological map of the world after Yalta included only two poles. . . . Everything even slightly reminiscent of the ideology of the Third Way or Conservative Revolution was extirpated on the plea of total and universal "de-Nazification" on the global level. The Nuremberg tribunal was the first and unique trial in history which condemned not only people, but also ideas and intellectual doctrines. (1994g: 26)

What "good" groups of National Socialists had managed to preserve the ideas of the Conservative Revolution, the liberal regimes ruled out and tabooed the ideals of the Third Way as a legitimate ideological alternative.

It is remarkable that Dugin identifies the contemporary world as a "liberal Auschwitz," where the mondialists "install into the brains of the population of mankind the computer chips of the fictitious multiplication of capital" (1996d: 54). In terms of Dugin's "Tradition," this "liberal Auschwitz" is much more totalitarian and cruel than National Socialism.

Dugin's employment of the image of Auschwitz demonstrates that he does not see the Holocaust as a radical foundational crisis of Western civilization. He claims that Auschwitz is only a liberal myth closely connected with the concept of the end of history. In liberal mythology Auschwitz functions as "the last immolation, the last sacrifice of history" which anticipates the messianic time. The annihilation of the Jews substitutes the second coming of Jesus and marks the end of history and the beginning of the "eternal *Shabbat*" (1996c: 48).

It is characteristic that in Dugin's "grand narrative" we live in the post-Nuremberg rather than in the post-Auschwitz world. He not only disregards the question of the responsibility of German intellectuals for the Holocaust, but tries to whitewash the activities of the Nazis and to stigmatize their victims, charging them with even more serious crimes. Dugin condemns the Nazis only for their insufficient loyalty to the ideas of the Conservative Revolution.

THE MUSLIM WORLD, ISRAEL, AND THE CONSERVATIVE REVOLUTION

Dugin accepts the thesis of American political analyst Samuel Huntington, according to which the major conflicts of the contemporary world are due to the clash of civilizations rather than ethnic (nineteenth century) or ideological (twentieth century) conflicts (Huntington 1993, 1996). Civilizations are defined in terms of their specific historical and cultural traditions and religious foundations. Dugin claims that the Eurasian civilization is shaped by the religious traditions of Orthodoxy and Islam. The Russian-Eurasian civilization is based on the traditional values of these two religions, which are incompatible with the values and standards of mondialism and Atlanticism. This incompatibility is explained by the fact that Russian and Islamic civilizations have their own concept of special mission in world history, alternative to that of European mondialist civilization. The Muslim world in general and especially the most traditional and fundamentalist trends are the natural allies of Russia-Eurasia in the struggle against the "new world order," oceanic civilizations, and mondialism. Orthodox Islam is even closer to the Primordial Tradition than Orthodoxy, which was distorted by Masonic and moralistic ideas in the last two centuries. Orthodoxy and Russian traditionalism could greatly benefit from intensive intellectual and political contacts with the spiritual and political leaders of Islamic cultures. Dugin emphasizes that it is not a coincidence that Guénon and many of his successors converted to Islam. Dugin collaborates with the fundamentalist "Party of Islamic Renaissance" led by his friend and teacher Geidar Jemal. The special column in *Den'*, "Slavonic-Islamic Academy," contributes to the discussion of spiritual and geopolitical connections between Orthodoxy and Islam.

Dugin claims that the mondialists attempt to split the natural unity of Slavic-Russian and Muslim civilizations against the Atlanticist forces. He distinguishes two major groups of mondialists, hawks and doves. The hawks, the right-wing mondialists, insist on the necessity to sustain direct political and economic pressure on Russia. The tactics of the doves presuppose indirect pressure and are more perfidious. The doves are associated primarily with the American Jewish lobby, in particular, Hammer, Kissinger, Brzezinsky, and the Jewish members of Clinton's administration.[51] They purport to transform Eastern Europe rather than defeat it and, ultimately, to involve Russia in the realization of mondialistic objectives and projects. The dream of the left mondialists is to destroy the natural geopolitical and social ties between the Muslim East and Russia. Conflict between Russia and Muslim worlds is also vitally important for Israel. These tactics presuppose Russian involvement in national and religious conflicts.

> From now on, the foreign policy of the U.S. will proceed from the necessity of struggle against anti-Semitism in Europe and Islamic fundamentalism. Clinton's lobby proposes to denounce the tactics of total destruction and elimination of Russia. . . . Big Bill is going to use Russia for the accomplishment of mondialistic policy against the Muslim South. The fundamental strategy of left mondialism towards Russia is based on the idea that Russia is not a "defeated enemy" but rather a "brainless instrument in our hands." . . . The Russian North can be easily involved in the conflict with the Muslim Central Asian South by some deliberate provocation. Sooner or later, Iran and Iraq, the main enemies of Israel, will be also implicated. This will draw blood from both the Russian and Muslim elite, and thus, two major enemies of the world government will start to destroy each other. This will make both Israel and the "civilized world" happy. (Dugin/Okhotin 1993d)

---

[51] Dugin suggests that Jews were overrepresented in Clinton's administration. He mentions Reich, Berger, Altman, Magasiner, Cohen, Mandelbaum, and Sondenberg. Yurii Begunov's list is more extensive. He claimed that 57% of the members of Clinton's administration were Jewish. During the elections 86% of the Jews voted for Clinton. (Begunov 1995). Begunov's article is based on information from the American racist newspaper *Truth at Last*, 365.

The neo-Eurasianism attitude toward Israel is quite ambivalent. On the one hand, the establishment of Israel is an outcome of the strategy of England and Atlanticist civilization to sustain their political and economic influence in the Middle East (Dugin 1993c: 110). In spite of its geographical position, Israel is "the anti-continental formation begotten by Anglo-Saxon spies" and "the outpost of American influence in the region" (Glivakovskii 1993). On the other hand, Israel is the only country in which Conservative Revolution came to fruition of sorts. The West overlooked this development and because of the Holocaust could not even suspect Israel in this transformation.

> Israel is the only country that has successfully realized in practice some aspects of the Conservative Revolution. In spite of striking ideological similarities [between Nazi Germany and Israel] nobody dared to suspect or blame Israel for "fascism" and "Nazism" bearing in mind the great number of Jewish victims during the rule of Conservative Revolutionaries in Europe. The establishment of Israel was accompanied by the ideas of complete revival of the archaic tradition, Judaic religion, ethnic and racial differentiation, socialist ideas in economy (in particular, of the system of kibbutzes) and the restoration of castes. (1994b)

Vladimir Zeev Jabotinsky, founder of the movement of Zionism-revisionism, is characterized by Dugin as one of the most prominent theoreticians and activists of the Conservative Revolution (1994b: 15). Although the Israeli Conservative Revolution is opposed to the mondialistic principles of the global "melting pot," this does not turn Israeli Jews into allies of the Eurasian cause, since their revived tradition is incompatible and hostile to the Indo-European tradition. Whereas the project of the mondialists is identified with anti-Tradition, the Jewish "Conservative Revolution," probably, can be described as Counter-Tradition. The Jewish Conservative Revolutionaries are better than mondialists only as partners in the "metaphysical" dialogue. However, their ideas are perfectly compatible with the fundamental Atlanticist orientation of Israel. Dugin is trying to say that Israeli "Nazism" was privileged by the mondialists over all other nationalisms. In addition Dugin seems to praise the ideology of Naturei karta, the religious sect of orthodox Jews, which does not acknowledge the establishment of Israel and lambasts Zionism. He seems to identify the doctrines of Naturei karta with the most traditional Judaism.[52] Thus, his ideas about Jewish traditionalism are quite ambivalent.

Neo-Eurasians accept the cliche of Islamic and Arab anti-Zionism and Judophobia. The Palestinian-Israeli conflict is described as a geopolitical conflict where Palestinians fight on the side of the continental forces. Israel is, of course, an aggressive state involved in the genocide of the Palestinian

---

[52] See the interviews with rabbis translated and prefaced by Dugin in *Den'* 18 (1992).

population. Neo-Eurasians give moral support to the intifada and coun-tenance the terroristic activities of the Palestinians and the radical reli-gious fanaticism of the leaders of Islamic fundamentalist organizations, like "Hamas" and the "Muslim Brotherhood." The editorial staff of *Den'* has several times given Shaaban Khafez Shaaban, Chairman of the "Palestinian government in exile," the opportunity to express his extreme "anti-Zionist" position in interviews and publications ("Palestinskoe sopro-tivlenie": 1992). Shaaban is the editor-in-chief of the ultra-anti-Semitic newspaper *Al-Quods* (Arabic for Jerusalem), which is edited and published in Moscow where the headquarters of this Palestinian government are located. *Al-Quods* is preoccupied with topics of the occupation of Palestine by Israel, the Jewish-Masonic conspiracy, the enormous influence of the Jews in politics and media, and the heroic resistance of the Palestinians to the sinister powers of Zionism. Shaaban does not recognize Israel and insists that full-fledged independence of the Palestinians can be reached only by the destruction of the "Zionist state." He is opposed to the peace process in the Middle East and to the government of Yasir Arafat, whom he sees as the puppet of the U.S. and Israel. It is noteworthy that some contributors to *Den'* publish their articles also in *Al-Quods*. During the first Gulf War and Iraqi bombardments of Israel in 1991, Saddam Hussein became a hero for many Russian nationalist groups.

Neo-Eurasians make discriminations between different Muslim coun-tries and different trends in Islam. Shii is better than Sunni, since it combines conservative values with a revolutionary political strategy. The orthodox Shiism of Iran and the ideas of Khomeini are especially con-genial to the ideology of Conservative Revolution, since they presuppose both the commitment to the grand Muslim tradition and the revolu-tionary resistance to modernity and mondialism. The "continental Islam" of Iran is opposed to "ritualism and almost secularized ethics" of Saudi Arabia and Atlanticist and nationalist Turkey, which are akin to Western Protestantism (1993h: 24–25; 1993i). Turkey is regarded as a champion of mondialism in the region and the ideas of Turanism and pan-Turkism are considered a great danger for Russia.

Dugin believes that the presence of the national myth is the only cri-terion by which to decide whether or not a nation has a historical mis-sion. The "esthetization of the political," to use the expression of Walter Benjamin, is one of the dangers of the new political consciousness prop-agated by Dugin. His valorization of the Russian psyche, and his cult of the unconscious and irrational, are quite conducive to physical vio-lence. Dugin does not even try to conceal the violent implications of his political romanticism. For him any activity of the Russian people is beyond good and evil:

> We are the God-bearing people. That is why all our manifestations—high and vile, benevolent and terrifying—are sanctified by their other-worldly meanings, by the rays of the other City. . . . In the abundance of national grace, good and evil turn from one into another. . . . We are as incomprehensible as the Absolute. (Dugin 1996e).

Dugin admits that the nationalist myth can sound strange, but he does not think this is a disadvantage. He deliberately appeals to the irrational driving forces of the psyche and the mythical level of consciousness. His slogans are devised to invigorate the political unconscious. Dugin believes he has a special mission as an intellectual: "The true national elite does not have a right to leave its people without any ideology. This ideology should express not only what the people think and feel but rather what they do not think and feel, but what they have worshipped for centuries surreptitiously even from themselves" (1992b: 135). It is evident from this passage that Dugin believes he is uniquely qualified to interpret the unconscious of the Russian people.

One should acknowledge that Dugin was quite successful in introducing his concepts and images into the nationalistic discourse. Many discussions, both nationalist and liberal, are informed by his account of the geopolitical clash of civilizations and his abstruse visions of the "Jewish question." This valorization of irrational impulses, national unconscious, spontaneity and bellicose instincts, along with the disparagement of moral standards as irrelevant and superficial means for evaluating the nation, makes Dugin's discourse especially dangerous, especially given the widespread dissatisfaction with the political and economic reforms.

I suggest a special name for the type of anti-Semitism advocated by Aleksandr Dugin and his fellow Eurasians: geopolitical anti-Semitism. Their account suggests that the Jews are prone to identify themselves with the Atlanticist geopolitical centers and that they play an important role among the Atlanticist forces. Their account also suggests that within the confines of Eurasia the Jews should be treated as the enemies and potential "geopolitical traitors" of the grand Eurasian community. It is also important to observe that the Jews are not simply the provisional allies of Atlanticism. They are described as eternal and metaphysical enemies of Eurasia.

BIBLIOGRAPHY

Abrahams, Israel. 1932. *Jewish Life in the Middle Ages*. London.
Amler, J. F. 1993. *Cristopher Columbus' Jewish Roots*. Northvale, N.J.
Anninskii, L. 1993. "Prostivaiuschii sled Agosfera." *Zerkalo* 105.
Antonov, Y. and K. Shaaban. 1993. "Ne toropites v Izrail." *Al-Quods* 11.
Artamonov, Mikhail. 1962. *The History of Khazars*. Leningrad.
———. "Khazari i Rus'." In *Mir L'va Gumileva: Arabeski istorii*. Moscow. 334–36.
Attali, Jacques. 1991. *Millennium: Winners and Losers in the Coming World Order*. New York.

Bauman, Zygmunt. 1988. "Exit Visas and Entry Tickets: Paradoxes of Jewish Assimilation," *Telos* 77.

Begunov, Yurii. 1995. "Evrei v pravitelstve Klintona." *Russkoe delo* 8.

Blavatskaiia, Elena. 1937. *Tainaiia doktrina.* Riga.

Breuer, Stefan. 1993. *Anatomie der Konservativen Revolution.* Darmstadt.

Brod, Max. 1947. *Franz Kafka: A Biography.* New York.

Bromberg, Yakov. 1929. "O neobkhodimom peresmotre evreiskogo voprosa." *Evrasiiskii Sbornik* 6.

———. 1931. "Evreiskoe vostochnichestvo v proshlom i buduschem." In *Mir Rossii— Evraziia,* ed. L. Novikova and I. Sizemskaiia. Moscow, 1995.

Buber, Martin. 1911. "Der Geist des Orients und das Judentum." In *Vom Geist des Judentum.* Leipzig. 9–48.

Bulichev, Y. 1993. "V poiskakh gosudarstvennoi idei (razmishleniia nad raziskaniiami 'novikh pravikh)." *Moskva* 5.

Dahl, Göran. 1996. "Will the Other God Fail Again? On the Possible Return of the Conservative Revolution." *Theory, Culture and Society* 13, 1.

Danilevskii, Nikolai. 1871. *Rossiia i Evropa.* St. Petersburg.

David, Robert. 1989. "Veschii Oleg i velikaiia step'." *Vestnik evreiskoi sovetskoi kulturi* 13.

Debord, Guy. 1979. *Society of the Spectacle.* London.

Deutscher, Isaac. 1968. *The Non-Jewish Jew and Other Essays.* New York.

Dreizin, Felix. 1990. *The Russian Soul and the Jew: Essays in Literary Ethnocriticism.* Ed. David Guaspari. Lanham, Md.

Dugin, Aleksandr. 1990. "Probuzhdenie stikhii." *Elementi* 1.

———. 1991a. *Kontinent Rossiia.* Moscow.

———. 1991b. "Prorok zolotogo veka." In René Guénon, *Krisis sovremennogo mira.* Moscow.

———. 1991c. "Velikaiia metafizicheskaiia problema i Traditsiia." *Milii Angel* 1.

———. 1991d. "Metafizicheskie korni politicheskikh ideologii." *Milii Angel* 1.

———. 1992a. "Velikaiia voina kontinentov." *Den'* 4–7.

———. 1992b. "Carl Schmitt: piat' urokov dlia Rossii." *Nash sovremennik* 8.

———. 1993a. "Apologiia natsionalizma." *Den'* 38.

———. 1993b. "Sumerki geroev. Pominalnoe slovo o Jean Thiriart." *Den'* 2.

———. 1993c. *Konspirologiia.* Moscow.

———. (Okhotin). 1993d. "Chego boitsia Bolshoi Bill." *Den'* 9.

———. 1993e. "Ot sakralnoi geografii k geopolitike." *Elementi* 4.

———. 1993f. "Khaos." *Den'* 26.

———. 1993g. *Giperboreiskaia teoriia.* Moscow.

———. 1993h. "Geopoliticheskie problemi blizhnego zarubezhiia." *Elementi* 3.

———. 1993i. "Zaveschanie' Ayatolli Khomeini." *Elementi* 4.

———. 1994a. "Carl Schmitt: 5 urokov dlia Rossii." In *Konservativnaiia revolutsiia.* Moscow.

———. 1994b. "Apologiia natsionalizma." In *Konservativnaiia revolutsiia.*

———. 1994c. "Poniat znachit pobedit." In *Konservativnaiia revolutsiia.*

———. 1994d. "Metafizika natsii v kabbale." In *Konservativnaiia revolutsiia.*

———. 1994e. "Golem i evreiskaiia metafizika." In *Konservativnaiia revolutsiia.*

———. 1994f. "Erotism i imperiia." In *Konservativnaiia revolutsiia.*

———. 1994g. "Konservativnaiia revolutsiia: Tipologiia politicheskikh dvizhenii Tretego Puti." In *Konservativnaiia revolutsiia.*

———. 1995a. *Tseli i zadachi nashei revolutsii.* Moscow.

———. 1995b. "Demokratiia protiv sistemi." *Elementi* 5.

———. (Okhotin) 1995c. "Elevsinskie topi freidisma." *Elementi* 6.

———. 1995c. "Ad Marginem: Sacher-Masoch" (rev.). *Elementi* 6.

———. 1996a. "Begemot protiv Leviafana." *Elementi* 7.

———. 1996b. "The Rest Against the West." *Elementi* 7.

———. 1996c. *Misterii Evrasii.* Moscow.

———. 1996d. "Revolutsiia nevozmozhnaiia, neizbezhnaiia." *Elementi* 7.

———. 1996e. "Imia moe—topor: Dostoevskii i metafisika Peterburga." *Nezavisimaiia gazeta,* June 26.

———. 1997a. "Apokalipsis stikhii." *Elementi* 8.

———. 1997b. *Osnovi geopolitiki.* Moscow.

Dunlop, D. M. 1954. *History of the Jewish Khazars.* Princeton.

"Etika etnogenetiki." 1992. (Collection of articles). *Neva* 4: 223–46.

Evola, Giulio. 1958. *Metafisico del sesso.* New York.

Friedman, Michael Jay. 1954. *Facts Are Facts: The Truth About Khazars.* Boston.

Garkavi, Avraam. 1869. *O iazike evreev, zhivshikh v drevnee vremia na Rusi i o slavianskikh slovakh, vstrechaiuschikhsia u evreiskikh pisatelei.* St. Petersburg.

Gilman, Sander L. 1986. *Jewish Self-Hatred: Anti-Semitism and the Hidden Language of the Jews.*

Glivakovskii, Anatolii. 1993. "Szenarii 'Atlantistov'." *Den'* 12.

Goldstein, David I. 1981. *Dostoevsky and the Jews.* Austin.

Golovin, K. 1992. "Den' smeniaet noch." *Otechestvo* 8.

Guénon, René. 1924. *Orient et occident.* Paris.

———. 1927. *La crise du monde moderne.* Paris.

———. 1945. *La regne de la quantité et les signes des temps.* Paris.

———. 1991. "Mesto atlanticheskoi traditsii v Manvantare." *Milii Angel* 1.

Gumilev, Lev. 1966. *Otkritie Khazarii: Istoriko-etnograficheskii etuid.*

———. 1967. "New Data on the History of the Khazars." *Acta Archaeologica Academiae Scientiarum Hungaricae* 19.

———. 1974a. "Khazaria i Kaspii." *Vestnik LGU* 6.

———. 1974b. "Khazaria i Terek," *Vestnik LGU* 24.

———. 1974c. "Skazanie o khazarskoi dani." *Russkaya literatura* 3.

———. 1989a. *Etnogenez i biosfera Zemli.* Leningrad; *Ethnogenesis and the Biosphere.* Moscow, 1990.

———. 1989b. *Drevniaia Rus' i Velikaya Step'.* Moscow.

———. 1991. "Menia nazivaiiut evraziitsem." *Nash sovremennik* 1.

———. 1993a. "Zapiski poslednego evraziitsa." *Ritmi Evrazii* Moscow. 33–66.

———. 1993b. *Tisiacheletie vokrug Kaspiia.* Moscow.

———. 1994. *Chernaia legenda: Druziia i nedrugi Velikoi Stepi.* Moscow, 1994.

Gumplovich, Ludwig. 1903. *The Origins of Jewish Beliefs in Poland.* Warsaw.

Habel, Norman. 1985. *The Book of Job: A Commentary.* Philadelphia.

Hackethorn, C. 1897. *The Secret Societies of All Ages and Countries,* vol. 2. London.

Huntington, Samuel P. 1993. "The Clash of Civilizations?" *Foreign Affairs* 72 (summer): 22–49.

———. 1996. *The Clash of Civilization and the Remaking of World Order.* New York.

Ioann, Mitropolit. 1993. "Torzhestvo pravoslaviia." *Nash sovremennik* 4: 11–12.

Isaev, I. 1992. *Puti Evrasii: Russkaiia intelligentsiia i sudbi Rossii.* Moscow.

———. 1993. "Geopoliticheskie korni avtoritarnogo mishleniia." *Druzhba narodov* 11.

Karsavin, Lev. 1928. "Rossiia i evreistvo." in *Taina Israilia.* St. Petersburg, 1993.

Kazintsev, Aleksandr. 1993. "Samoubiistvo pod kontrolem." *Nash sovremennik* 3.

Khanin, D. Forthcoming. *A Modernist Conservative: Vasilii Rosanov's Aesthetics and Polemics.*

Klemperer, K. von. 1968. *Germany's New Conservatism: Its History and Dilemma in Twentieth Century.* Princeton, 1968.

Koestler, Arthur. 1976. *The Thirteenth Tribe: The Khazar Empire and Its Heritage.* London.

Kosarenko, S. 1993. "Antisistema." *Den'* 8–10.

Kozhinov, V. 1992. "Istoriia Rusi i russkogo slova." *Nash sovremennik* 10–12.

———. 1993. "Vot uzh deistvitel'no khazarskie strasti." *Molodaiia gvardiia* 11–12.

Kurginian, Sergei. 1993. "Esli khotim zhit." *Den'* 1.

Kutchera, Hugo von. 1909. *Die Chazaren.* Vienna.

Kuzmin, A. "Khazarskie stradaniia." *Molodaiia gvardiia* 5–6: 235, 245–50.

Laqueur, W. 1991. *Russia and Germany: Hitler's Mentors.* Washington, D.C.

Levalois, C. 1991. "Sochti chislo Zveria." *Elementi* 2.

Luks, L. 1986. "Die Ideologie der Eurasier im zeitgeschichtlichen Zuzammenhang." *Jahrbucher fur Geschichte Osteneuropas.*

———. 1993. "Evraziistvo." *Voprosi filosofii* 6.

———. 1996. "Evraziistvo i konservativnaiia revolutsiia: Soblasn antizapadnichestva v Rossii i Germanii." *Voprosi filosofii* 3.

Evrasiia: Istoricheskie vsgliadi russkikh emigrantov (Moscow, 1992); *Rossiia mezhdu evropoi i Asiei: evrasiiskii soblasn* (Moscow, 1993); *Mir Rossii—Evrasiia* (Moscow, 1995).

Mirovich, I. 1991. "Lev Gumilev i drugie." *Strana i mi* 2.

Mohler, Armin. 1989. *Die Konservative Revolution in Deutchland 1918–1932: Ein Handbuch.* 3rd ed. Darmstadt.

Oberlechter, Reinhold. 1995. "The Farmers and the Nomads. The Anti-Neolithic Counter-Revolution as a Law of Modernity." *Ataka* 72: 14–17.

"Palestinskoe soprotivlenie." 1992. Interview of Shamil Sultanov with Shaaban, *Den'* 31.

Pflüger, Friedbert. 1994. *Deutschland driftet: Der Konservative Revolution entdeckt ihre Kinder.* Düsseldorf.

Pletneva, Svetlana. 1986. *Khazari.* Moscow.

Preuss, A. 1924. *A Dictionary of Secret and Other Societies.* London.

Prussakov, V. 1994. "Preodolet' Ameriku." *Zavtra* 16.

Putilov, S. 1993. "Taini 'Novoi Atlantidi' Becona." *Nash sovremennik* 2.

Renan, Ernst. 1883. *Le Judaisme comme Race et comme Religion.* Paris.

Rosenberg, Alfred. 1922. *Plague in Russia.*

Schmitt, Carl. 1950. *Des Nomos der Erde.* Kρln.

———. 1976. *The Concept of the Political.* New Brunswick.

Sedych-Bondarenko, Y. 1993. "Vidali, kto prishel." *Den'* 27.

Sontheimer, Kurt. 1962. *Antidemocratisches Denken in der Weimarer Republik. Die politischen Ideen des deutschen Nationalismus zwischen 1918 und 1933.* Munich, 1962.

Stevens, Anthony. 1994. *Jung.* New York, 1994.

Sviatopolk-Mirsky, D. 1929. "Natzionalnosti SSSR Evrei." *Evraziia* 26.

Thiriart, Jean. 1992a. "Evropa do Vladivostoka." *Den'* 34.

———. 1992b. "Evropa do Vladivostoka." *Russkii vestnik* 30–31.

Thiriart, Jean. and Y. Ligacheov. 1992. "Poka est voini voina ne proigrana." *Den'* 37.

Toporov, Vladimir. 1991. "'Spor' ili 'druzhba'?" In *Aequinox: Sbornik pamiati otza Alexandra Menia.* Moscow, 91–162.

Trubetskoi, Nikolai. 1935. "O rasisme." *Neva* 7 (1994).

Vigotskii, Lev. 1996. "Lermontov." In *Nachalo Puti,* ed. Joseph Feigenberg. Jerusalem.

Vorobievskii, Y. 1993. "Zvezda i svastika." *Novoe russkoe slovo,* December 17.

Wahrmund, Adolf. 1887. *Das Gesetz des Nomadentums und die Heutige Judenherrshaft.* Korisruhe.

Webb, James. 1976. *The Occult Establishment.* Chicago.

Yanov, A. "Uchenie L'va Gumileva." *Svobodnaiia misl* 17.

Zakharov, V. 1992. "Izvraschenie velikorusskoi istorii." *Molodaiia gvardiia* 9.

Zhdanov, Sergei. 1993. "Shto takoe sionist v deisvii." *Russkii puls* 42.

Conclusion

Dmitry Shlapentokh

In post-Soviet Russia, the importance of identitary thought tying the country to Asia, along with the renewal of geopolitical fashions (geoculturalism and "civilizationism"), invites us to reexamine older intellectual traditions about Russian imperial expansion since the second half of the nineteenth century. Ever since the conquest of the Caucasus, Russia has been indissociably binding its imaginary onto the Orient in order to constitute a geopolitics that could legitimate the Empire. This orientalistic geopolitical imaginary has been largely unknown in the West, but it is one of the major stakes of the rediscovery of a memory of an Orient anchored in Russia and of different epistemological traditions from Western ones. The survey in this volume permits us to replace Russian intellectual life in the setting of Western intellectual life of the time. It also explains in original ways the traditional debates on Russian identity. "The Orient" is only mirror image of "the West," and the appeal for Asia and discourses on the "yellow peril" reveal Russian intellectuals' affirmation of a specificity of their country in front of Europe. Russian orientalism is then just one fashion of thinking about the national identity and is a culturalist cover supposed to legitimize such political orientations as imperialism or authoritarianism.

A better knowledge of the heterogeneous Russian imaginary on the Orient, which preceded the foundation of the Eurasianist movement, gives a currently missing historical and theoretical depth to contemporary Russian political questioning, to nostalgia for the Empire, to the new "Eurasianist" legitimations of some Post-Soviet states, and to the reappropriation of Eurasianist ideas by some Turco-Muslim elites in Tatarstan and Central Asia.

The study of the genesis of the Eurasianist ideology in the half-century that preceded its creation permits us to avoid clichés and to question ourselves about the intellectual evolution of the Russian world. Eurasianism belongs to currents of thinking which took their roots in nineteenth-century Russia: the ambiguousness of relation to the Byzantine empire, conservative pan-Slavism, the "yellow peril" myth at the time of progression toward the Far East, literary pan-Mongolism and Asiatism at the beginning of the century, movements of the Conservative Revolution in the 1920s, etc. Eurasianism rephrases in its own point of view, often in ways disconcerting to Western thought, the Russian intellectuals' questioning of the foundations of the identity of their country and of their own identity. The resurgence of this movement with the downfall of the Soviet Union fits into the European renewal of conservative thought that started in the United States and the rest of the West at the beginning of the 1980s.

BIBLIOGRAPHY

Bennigsen, Alexandre and Chantal Lemercier-Quelquejay. 1986. *Sultan Galiev: Le père de la révolution tiers-mondiste.* Paris.

Boss, Otto. 1961. *Die Lehre der Eurasier: Ein Beitrag zur russischen Ideengeschichte des 20. Jahrhunderts.* Wiesbaden.

"Buria nad Aziei." 1932. *Svij put'* 2. April.

Chaadaev, Petr Y. 1829. *Lettres philosophiques adressées à une dame.* Paris, 1970.

Dimtrieva, Katia and Michel Espagne. 1996. *Transferts culturels triangulaires France-Allemagne-Russie.* Philologiques V. Paris.

Evraziistvo. 1926. *Opyt sistematicheskogo izlozheniia.* Paris.

Evrazijskie tetradi. 1935. 5: 13–14.

Guénon, René. 1921. *Le théosophisme: Histoire d'une pseudo-religion.* Paris.

Hauner, Milan. 1992. *What Is Asia for Us? Russia's Asian Hearthland Yesterday and Today.* London.

Ivanov, Vsevolod N. 1926. *My. Kul'turno-istoricheskie osnovi rossiiskoi gosudarstvennosti.* Kharbin/

Laruelle, Marlène. 1999. *L'idéologie eurasiste russe ou comment penser l'empire.* Paris.

Layton, Susan. 1994. *Russian Literature and Empire: Conquest of the Caucasus from Pushkin to Tolstoy.* Cambridge.

Nikitin, V. P. 1928. "My i Vostok." *Evraziia*1, 24 November.

Niqueux, Michel. 1999. "Les différents Orients de la Russie." *Slavica occitania.*

Nivat, Georges. 1966. "Du panmongolisme au mouvement eurasien. Histoire d'un thème millénaire." *Cahiers du monde russe et soviétique.*

Piotrovitch, Michael B. 1966. *The Emergence of Russian Panslavism, 1850–70.* New York.

Savelli, Dany. 1996. "Le péril jaune et le péril nègre: éléments pour une représentation de la France et de l'Allemagne chez V. Soloviev et A.Biély." In *Transferts culturels triangulaires France-Allemagne-Russie,* ed. Katia Dimtrieva and Michel Espagne. Philologiques 5. Paris. 257–72.

Savitskii, Petr N. 1921. Povorot k Vostoku." In *Iskhod k Vostoku: Predchustvija i svershenie.* Sofia.

———. 1993. "Step' i osedlost'." In *Rossiia mezhdu Evropoi i Aziei.* Moscow.

Trubetskoi, Nikita Sergeevich. 1996. Trans. Patrick Sériot, *L'Europe et l'humanité.* Liège.

Vernadsky, G. V. 1914. "Protiv solnca. Rasprostranenie russkogo gosudarstva k Vostoku." *Russkaja mysl'* 1.

Index